CONSTITUTIONALISM IN ASIA

CONSTITUTIONALISM
IN ASIA

EDITED BY

R. N. SPANN

ASIA PUBLISHING HOUSE
LONDON

PRINTED IN INDIA

BY PYARELAL SAH AT THE TIMES OF INDIA PRESS,
BOMBAY, AND PUBLISHED BY P. S. JAYASINGHE,
ASIA PUBLISHING HOUSE, 447, STRAND, LONDON
W.C. 2

CONTRIBUTORS

RT. HON. SIR JOHN LATHAM, G.C.M.G.: *Chief Justice of Australia, 1935-52; First Australian Minister to Japan, 1940-41; and a former Deputy Prime Minister. President, Australian Association for Cultural Freedom.*

MR. VIVIAN BOSE: *Judge of the Supreme Court of India, 1951-56, later an ad hoc judge of the Supreme Court. President, International Commission of Jurists since 1959.*

PROFESSOR R. N. SPANN: *Professor of Government, University of Sydney.*

MR. V. K. T. CHARI: *Advocate General of Madras State since 1951; Senior Advocate, Supreme Court of India; Member, Indian Law Commission, 1955-58.*

DR. RALPH H. RETZLAFF: *Assistant Professor of Political Science, University of California (Berkeley); studied in India, 1955-56, and in 1959-60 on a Ford Foundation grant.*

PROFESSOR W. H. MORRIS-JONES: *Professor of Political Theory and Institutions, University of Durham; Adviser on Lord Mountbatten's staff, 1947; Author of* PARLIAMENT IN INDIA, 1957.

MR. HUGO WOLFSOHN: *Senior Lecturer in Political Science, University of Melbourne; studied in India, 1959.*

DR. MAUNG MAUNG: *Barrister-at-law; Lecturer in Constitutional Law, University of Rangoon; Visiting lecturer, Yale University, 1961; Author of* BURMA'S CONSTITUTION, 1959.

DR. JAVID IQBAL: *Advocate, High Court of Pakistan, lectures at University Law College, Lahore; Member of Pakistan U.N. Delegation, 1960; Author of* THE IDEOLOGY OF PAKISTAN AND ITS IMPLEMENTATION, 1959.

MR. DONALD HINDLEY: *Research Student, Australian National University; at present engaged on research into Indonesian political parties.*

MR. J. A. C. MACKIE: *Senior Lecturer-in-Charge, Department of Indonesian and Malayan Studies, University of Melbourne, author of many articles on modern Indonesia.*

PROFESSOR J. D. LEGGE: *Professor of History, Monash University, Victoria, Author of* AUSTRALIAN COLONIAL POLICY, 1956.

MR. BRIAN BEDDIE: *Senior Lecturer in Political Science, Australian National University.*

PARTICIPANTS AT THE SEMINAR DISCUSSIONS INCLUDED

MRS. R. BRISSENDEN, *Australian National University.*

MR. A. L. BURNS, *Australian National University.*

DR. D. C. CORBETT, *Australian National University.*

PROFESSOR ZELMAN COWEN, *University of Melbourne.*

PROFESSOR L. F. CRISP, *Australian National University.*

MR. JUSTICE R. ELSE-MITCHELL, *Supreme Court of New South Wales.*

PROFESSOR C. P. FITZGERALD, *Australian National University.*

DR. C. JAYAWARDENA, *University of Sydney.*

DR. A. H. JOHNS, *Australian National University.*

MR. H. R. KRYGIER, *Australian Association for Cultural Freedom.*

DR. D. A. LOW, *Australian National University.*

PROFESSOR W. H. MACMAHON BALL, *University of Melbourne.*

MR. H. MAYER, *University of Sydney.*

PROFESSOR V. K. N. MENON, *Director, Indian Institute of Public Administration.*

MR. R. G. NEALE, *University of Queensland.*

MR. IAN NISH, *University of Sydney.*

PROFESSOR P. H. PARTRIDGE, *Australian National University.*

PROFESSOR GEOFFREY SAWER, *Australian National University.*

MR. PHIROZE J. SHROFF, *Barrister-at-law.*

MR. T. O. SIMOS, *Barrister-at-law.*

MR. D. K. SINGH, *Australian National University.*

PROFESSOR JULIUS STONE, *University of Sydney.*

PROFESSOR L. C. WEBB, *Australian National University.*

PREFACE

THIS BOOK reprints the papers and discussions of the Seminar on Constitutionalism in Asia, held in August 1960 at the Australian National University. The Seminar was organised by the Australian Association for Cultural Freedom, and was also sponsored by the International Commission of Jurists. There were thirty-eight participants, including eight visitors from overseas, mainly political scientists and lawyers, with one or two historians and social anthropologists. The papers were not read, but their writers spoke to them as members of the small panels who led the discussions.

The aim of the seminar was to consider how constitutional government was faring in some Asian countries which had achieved independence under Western-type constitutions since the war. On the face of it, it might have been supposed that constitutional government was not faring too well. Of the countries we were mainly concerned with, Pakistan and Indonesia had abandoned parliamentary government; and Burma had just returned to it, but after a period of military rule. Even in countries where parliamentary democracy had survived, as in India and Ceylon, there was often some scepticism about its long-term prospects.

The outstanding impression I gained from the Seminar was that some of this pessimism was unjustified. The Asian participants, at least, exhibited some sober optimism. Some others showed impatience with what they took to be complacency; which led Professor Morris-Jones to remark that they "seemed to have a terror lest they be caught napping by the next military coup d'état".

The reasons for some of this qualified optimism come out clearly in the discussion reprinted below. In part it was the belief that the ideals of constitutional democracy were still often upheld by the ruling elites, even in some countries where parliamentary institutions had been suspended. For example, in Pakistan and Burma, military regimes were felt to be of an 'interim' character, even by the people who operated them. I don't think anyone who heard Dr. Javid Iqbal's sympathetic account of the Ayub Khan government doubted that he spoke in some important sense as a constitutionalist and a democrat; and the same is true of Dr. Maung Maung's perceptive analysis of the period of military rule in Burma.

The effort to work a constitutional system of government itself has effects on the people who work it, and on the political aims they pursue within it. Several of the Indian members of the Seminar described how in India the procedures associated with free elections, parliamentary debate, and independent courts were now well-established, and would not be lightly abandoned. Some of the very deeply engrained and widely shared 'anti-government' attitudes in Asian countries, often regarded (with some justice) as hindering social progress, also encourage popular attachment to constitutional procedures.

All this produced some interesting reflections on the nature of constitutional government itself. As Mr. Beddie says in his summing-up, many of us began the Seminar "with the notion that constitutionalism was a specific kind of thing, something that might fairly accurately be said to be either present or absent in a particular society". We ended by thinking of it much more as a 'tendency', and one with various ingredients, some of which might be present when others were not. Thus the Rule of Law, as described to us by Mr. Vivian Bose (the President of the International Commission of Jurists), did not wax and wane precisely with other elements of a constitutional state, such as a free parliament.

Again, it became clear that a constitution is always, in Europe and Australia as in Asia, to some extent mythological, and gives a very imperfect account of political reality. Sometimes the gap between myth and reality may look uncomfortably wide. But, even when the actual way a political system works differs a good deal from how it is supposed to, we cannot conclude that the constitution is simply a fraud (or at any rate it may be a useful fraud).

There was a good deal of stress on the part the courts have played in protecting the liberties of individuals and minorities; they are among the best-established of the institutions of a constitutional state, and have at times maintained their position better than others. We reprint here the address by Mr. Vivian Bose, President of the International Commission of Jurists, and the paper by Mr. V. K. T. Chari, with its interesting account of trends in Indian legislation and constitutional adjudication. There were however some telling criticisms, by Professor Julius Stone and others, of systems of legal education, of procedural delays; and, basic to all other criticisms, the fear expressed that judicial systems might prove too inflexible, and the judges and lawyers lacking in 'legal statesmanship'.

Another Western inheritance, the political party system, has worked more uncertainly in Asia. Professor V. K. N. Menon, the Director of the Indian Institute of Public Administration, said that some close study was needed of the functioning of political parties in Asia, and how it might be improved. The alternative has often seemed to be either 'one-party dominance', which need not imply the absence of organised opposition, or a fairly large number of competing parties, with the danger that it will be hard to find *any* majority.

One of the problems that occupied us greatly in the later stages of the seminar was consideration of the alleged 'gap' that existed in Asian societies between 'modern' processes of government at one level and the traditional political processes at other levels—village politics, caste politics, religious politics and so on. The papers by Professor Morris-Jones, by Dr. Retzlaff of the University of California, and by Mr. Wolfsohn all raise this issue in relation to India; so do Mr. Mackie's and Professor Legge's papers on Indonesia; and Dr. Iqbal's paper on the Islamic State in Pakistan. How far could these two—Western politics and traditional politics—interact and modify one another in a fruitful way? Or were there some basic incompatibilities that rendered their meeting mutually destructive? One thing we learned is that there is no need to become panic-stricken at the mere contemplation of 'gaps' and incompatibilities in societies. They are not so necessarily fatal in social life as in logical argument.

I would like to thank Miss Shirley Winter and Mr. Ian Nish for their assistance in preparing the manuscript for publication.

R. N. SPANN

CONTENTS

CONSTITUTIONALISM IN ASIA

Sir John Latham

CONSTITUTIONS AND FREEDOM

THIS SEMINAR has been arranged by the Australian Association for Cultural Freedom, which is affiliated to the Congress for Cultural Freedom in Paris. The Association is indebted for financial assistance to the International Seminar Planning Committee of the Congress and for the help of the National University here at Canberra in providing us with accommodation. We are also greatly indebted to Professor R. N. Spann for his work in organising the Seminar.

We welcome our visitors, not only Australians but particularly those who have come from Asia and most especially Mr. Justice Bose, President of the International Commission of Jurists.

The Congress has recently sponsored Seminars at Milan, Tokyo, Ibadan, Rhodes and Hamburg which all dealt with some aspect of freedom or of the conditions of freedom. We are to consider Asian Constitutionalism.

There is a direct relation between a Constitution and the freedom of the citizen. Freedom is not complete liberty to everyone to do as he pleases. We envisage freedom in a society—my freedom must be consistent with your like freedom. This cannot be achieved without some authority which binds both you and me—some recognised and enforced rule of conduct—some law.

A Constitution defines government authority, it specifies the agencies which in the relevant society can make law, administer law, interpret law. Therefore in all Constitutions there is provision for a legislature, an executive and a judiciary and sometimes other governmental agencies such as the Examination Yuan and the Control Yuan which were features of Chinese government.

Constitutions may and do vary with systems of government. Government may be by despotism of a man or committee, an oligarchy, a constitutional monarchy, a presidential system, a democracy as understood in Great Britain, a totalitarian dictatorship.

I hope that all our visitors will understand that Australia is a completely independent country subject to no external control of any description. Australia belongs to the British Commonwealth but there is no Commonwealth organisation which controls anything in Australia.

We understand democracy as dependent upon, firstly, representative government, that is, a legislature chosen by the people, and secondly, responsible government—the ministers in charge of administration being members of the legislature and responsible to it. In America the essence of democracy is regarded as dependent upon the separation of governmental powers and the protection given in the constitution to certain rights of the people.

More constitutions have been framed in the last twenty years than in the preceding century. Constitutions are still being drafted in many countries. New constitutions have recently been adopted or are under consideration in Ghana, Nigeria, Kenya, Tanganyika, Uganda, the Caribbean, Somaliland, Rhodesia and Nyasaland, and in the French African colonies. In recent years new constitutions have been adopted in Egypt, Turkey, Iraq, Pakistan, India, Burma, Singapore, Malaya, China and Japan.

Many of these have embodied, the principle of a parliamentary democracy, but not all have succeeded. In some cases democracy as generally understood has definitely failed, at least for the time being, and to avoid anarchy and chaos the army has taken over. This has happened at different times in Egypt, Turkey, Iraq, Pakistan and Burma.

Democracy in a political sense is not merely the rule of a majority. A democratic system of government cannot succeed and maintain itself as a true democracy unless there is respect for the views and opinions of the minority. The tyranny of a majority is as much a tyranny as the rule of an individual tyrant. The necessity of paying regard to the views of a minority explains why democracy is not suited to all peoples in their present stage of development. Democracy as developed in Great Britain is the result of long centuries of trial and adjustment and error and provisional and tentative success.

For democracy to succeed there must be some understanding among the people as a whole of the system of government and a tradition of obedience to law together with an exercise of political rights. It took many centuries of development in Great Britain before it was established that "Anyone may oppose the Government but everyone must obey the Law". When the people of a country who have had no share in making their laws are told that they have become the lawmakers difficulties naturally arise. They cannot understand submission to law together with political criticism of the government.

A federal system of government can provide guarantees of freedom. A constitution which binds the legislature and the executive and which provides for an independent judiciary may contain restrictions upon the exercise of governmental authority which the courts will enforce. Many recent constitutions have provided something like the Bill of Rights in the United States. There are some such provisions in the Australian Constitution, for example preventing governmental establishment of any religion. The important thing is not merely whether these protective provisions are to be found in a constitution but whether they are enforced.

The present constitution of China contains the following provisions: "Citizens enjoy freedom of residence and freedom to change residence" and "Freedom of the persons of citizens is inviolable". It would be interesting to know how far these provisions provide any real protection to the people of China against arbitrary government edicts.

In this Seminar we have scholars with experience of many peoples and of many constitutions who doubtless have a contribution to make to us in Australia, and I hope also that you will be able to derive some profit from your participation in our Seminar.

On behalf of the Australian Association for Cultural Freedom I welcome you and wish you well in your deliberations.

Vivian Bose

THE ROLE OF THE COURTS IN CONSTITUTIONAL GOVERNMENT

ON BEHALF of the overseas visitors to this Seminar, I would like to thank the Australian Association for Cultural Freedom and its President, Sir John Latham, for inviting us to participate in the discussion of this important topic. I have chosen as the subject of my address, "The Role of the Courts in Constitutional Government". I do not want to give a list of the functions of the courts, most of which are well known, but will concentrate on a few points that raise deeper issues, especially for those who are now making new Constitutions or are in the process of re-forming existing ones.

The first is whether courts should be given the power (*a*) to interpret legislative enactments and (*b*) to declare them invalid. England says the courts may interpret legislation but cannot question the constitutional competency of an Act of Parliament. This is because the British Constitution regards Parliament as supreme. In any case, the British Constitution is not a federal one, so the question does not arise with quite the same cogency as in the case of federal countries. I am told the Swiss courts cannot question the competency of federal laws though they have a certain limited jurisdiction to examine the competency of Canton laws. In the Civil Law countries, broadly speaking, the ordinary courts cannot question the competency of legislation. But in some countries with written constitutions that place limitations on the powers of the legislature the courts have been expressly invested with those powers.

The viewpoint of those who are against investing the courts with these powers can be expressed in the words of Mr. Justice Felix Frankfurter of the United States Supreme Court. "The power of judicial review is not only undemocratic (because it gives a few judges the power of vetoing legislation enacted by the representatives of the nation) but also throws an unfair burden on the judiciary." India has chosen the American practice whereby the

6

courts can review the legislative competence of laws passed by legislatures subordinate to the Constitution. I will merely say that I think that is the better view for our purposes in India and will leave it at that.

The next point on which I will touch is that the courts play an important part in protecting individual rights not only by seeing that legislatures do not overstep their powers but also by seeing that the executive and their officials don't do so. This is enforced, in the main, by the writ jurisdictions of the courts. They also play an important role in maintaining generally the Rule of Law in a country. The writ jurisdictions enable the courts to keep a close control and check on all tribunals and even on officials who exercise quasi-judicial functions. This does have a very healthy effect on arbitrary official action.

There is another very important role that the courts play and that is moulding the laws in such a way that they profoundly affect the habits, lives and customs of the people. The most striking example of this is the way in which the courts in India have moulded the Hindu law; until now it is entirely judge-made law, aside from a few Acts of the Legislature passed in recent years. In the early days of the British rule in India the courts were manned by English judges who did not know the Hindu law. The policy of the British was to administer the personal laws of the peoples of India according to the customs they found there. Thus the Hindu laws of inheritance, marriage, divorce and property were applied in the case of Hindus. As the English judges did not know the Hindu law they posed questions to the *pundits*, or scholars. Now scholars are often pedantic and sometimes ride hobby horses of their own; therefore, the customs of the people were ascertained, not from the people themselves but from academic scholars. So the first step in the process was that the academic and pedantic views of a handful of scholarly pundits were reflected in the answers.

The next step was that these views had to be translated into English so the judges were presented with what the translators thought the *pundits* meant. Next it had to be processed in the minds of judges who, reared in the traditions of the English laws, had an unconscious bias towards those traditions and methods of interpretation. The last stage was that the case would go to an even more remote tribunal, the Privy Council in London, and the law would be crystallised there. Modern research shows that the Hindu law that was thus developed and which now governs the lives and customs of millions of people is very different from the law that would have been applied by the ancient Hindu law givers.

But there are more modern instances where the courts have kept abreast with the times as more human ideas and traditions developed and society became more humane and the courts humanised the laws accordingly.

Not so very long ago men were hanged in England for stealing property worth more than a shilling. This revolted juries so much that time after time they valued property worth several pounds at less than a shilling. This was in flat defiance of their oaths; and often the judges themselves directed the jury to return such a verdict. Then again there was a time when a man who mortgaged his house would lose it unless he paid up to the last farthing on the appointed hour. Equity stepped in and modified the harshness of that law and gave him another chance. This sort of liberalising attitude was also applied to other kinds of forfeiture clauses in contracts. Then the courts invented the doctrine of 'public policy' and refused in the public interest to enforce contracts that were against public policy.

Then judges have another great role to play. On many issues it is reasonably possible for a reasonable judicial mind to reach either one of two conclusions, one on technical grounds, the other on broader, deeper and more human considerations. The technically minded judge will decide the narrow way, but a judge with a broader vision and a wider experience of life will decide the other way. The Privy Council was remarkable for its breadth of vision and it was extraordinary how in case after case they brushed aside the whole cobweb of technicalities and reached a broadbased, commonsense decision much more in accord with the common man's view of justice and right.

Two illustrations will suffice. One is the decision of the Supreme Court of the United States on the segregation issue and the other, a similar decision reached by the Supreme Court of India almost at the same time, about the educational issue in Bombay.

And that brings me to something even deeper. The courts cannot enforce their own decrees. They have no armies and police forces at their disposal. A powerful government with a large majority could ignore their decisions. Why then do they accept them even when they do not like them? The reason was given by Lord Denning at the Delhi Congress in 1959. "The ultimate sanction of the Rule of Law is the force of public opinion, and the Rule of Law does not and cannot rely on armed might for its enforcement. It does not and cannot rely on judges and officers of the court for they are but its instruments. The Rule of Law depends in the last resort on the determination of the people to see that it is obeyed."

And that is the answer. It is the will of the people that says to governments and legislatures and judges and courts: this is our way of life, this is what we have chosen for ourselves. No man shall tamper with it save at his own peril.

R. N. Spann

NOTES ON SOME ASIAN CONSTITUTIONS

I

THESE NOTES result from a short comparative look at the constitutions (in some cases ex-constitutions) of some Asian countries, in particular, Burma, India, Indonesia, Malaya, Pakistan.[1] They aim at raising a few issues of general interest. They are not systematic and the reflections are those of an outsider, whose personal acquaintance with Asia is extremely limited.

The countries and constitutions have certain similarities that may justify a comparative look. The countries are ex-colonial, the constitutions are 'Western-type democratic' (in spite of an occasional indigenous element, for example, an established religion) and were adopted when the countries became independent states after the war. Not all of them are still being run as democracies. In Pakistan and Indonesia parliamentary government has been suspended. Burma has recently returned to a parliamentary system after a period of military rule.

Some people have regarded it as a mark of uninventiveness that so many Asian countries have adopted Western-type constitutions, and drawn so many sections from British practice or from the written constitutions of America, Ireland, the Netherlands, France, even Australia and Japan.[2] There seems to be an implied criticism of this kind in Sir Ivor Jennings' remark that: "It is unlikely that for some time to come any of the Asian countries of the Commonwealth will evolve new political forms. Though their potential may be great their present capacity for innovation in any field of culture is small."[3]

[1] There are also one or two side-glances at Ceylon and some other Asian countries.
[2] The Japanese Constitution of 1946 seems to have decisively influenced the wording of the 'life and personal liberty' clause of the Indian Bill of Rights. cf. M. V. Pylee, *Constitutional Government in India*, 1960, 237.
[3] Jennings, *The Commonwealth in Asia*, 57.

10

One should at least add that most Western countries have not shown any great capacity for formal constitutional innovation, being mainly content to ring the changes between Cabinet and Presidential forms, both in many ways inheritances of British constitutional experience; with occasional odd amalgamations of the two as in de Gaulle's France. American-type federalism seems to have been a real innovation, but that was nearly two hundred years ago. It is true that a few basic forms have in practice been varied in many subtle ways. But that has also been true in Asian countries—except that where Asian countries modify the conventions, we are more inclined to note it as an illegitimate deviation from some rigidly conceived norm, forgetting just how varied Western constitutional *practice* has been.[4]

There are other reasons why the constitutions are Western-type, some of which Jennings himself explained. In many cases the constitution-makers were Western-educated. Again, it is not in the nature of a nationalist or revolutionary movement to do much precise constitutional thinking; it will at most contribute some slogans of broad principle, such as have slipped into some of the sections of new constitutions on 'fundamental rights' and 'directive principles of state policy'. The more sober individuals, who were good at legal drafting, tended to be those who (through serving in the judiciary or the public service) had particularly close connections with Western-type ways of doing things—and even where foreign rule had been autocratic, law and administration operated on many of the assumptions of Western democracy. Some of the countries concerned already had partly self-governing institutions of a Western type, such as those embodied in the 1935 Government of India Act.

---

[4] For example, there have been periods of prolonged one-party dominance in the West (the British Conservatives are almost becoming rivals of the Indian Congress Party), and sometimes intra-party conflicts have become institutionalised and respectable. Professor Morris-Jones has argued that in India the absence of a strong Opposition has been partly compensated for, at least at the Union level, "by the development of an alert and vigorous parliamentary committee system and by the growth of instruments of internal discussion and criticism within the main party". (*Parliament in India*, 330). Some political scientists now think that the two-party system is the product of very special circumstances, and that the true alternative is often one-party dominance (which need not imply absence of organised opposition) or a number of competing parties, with the danger that it will be hard to find any 'majority'.

There was also often a considerable admiration for Western achievements, and a desire to imitate them. It was a tiresome Western habit to say that its institutions were not suited to Asia, to sociologise about it, to point to the peculiar character of Asian societies, or to take the conservative line of, for example, the Simon Commission; though it is true there were also Muslim and Gandhian doubts and dreams.[5] It is mainly since independence that disillusionment has come, where it has. So we have, for example, President Soekarno's wish (not wholly different from, though more influential than, similar pipe dreams in the West) for a form of government that attracts a wider participation from diverse groups than does a Western-type party system.

There may be a more profound reason for the 'Western' character of written constitutions. In many ways the whole modern notion of a constitution as a document which defines the structure and powers which 'the people' allow to 'the government', and which thereby limits the latter, is a Western notion. If one thinks in these terms at all, of political and administrative actions that can be to some degree independently judged and declared illegal or unconstitutional with reference to some antecedent and reasonably explicit body of law, it is hard to escape from the tested ways in which this has been achieved in the West. If one accepts the notion of having a written constitution at all (other than a mainly bogus one), one has already conceded much of the ground.

It is true that there is an older conception of a constitution, as the *ethos* of a people, embodying a scheme of life which tends to bring those living under it into harmony with that scheme.[6] This is the Greek *politeia*, one notion behind which Leo Strauss describes as follows: "Life is activity which is directed towards some goal; . . . but in order to pursue a specific goal, as its comprehensive goal, society must be organized, induced, constructed, constituted in a manner which is in accordance with that goal."[7]

This view has been reflected in some Asian constitutional thinking. One form of it is well-illustrated in Dr. Legge's account of what he calls a distinctively Indonesian (or Javanese) determination to argue that particular forms express a general principle, and "feel-

[5] cf. W. H. Morris-Jones, *Parliament in India*, 77, 80–3.
[6] cf. C. H. McIlwain, *Constitutionalism: Ancient and Modern*, 1947, Ch. II.
[7] *What is Political Philosophy?* 1959, 34.

ing that if the concept is right the machinery will be effective". It seems to be a notion behind the search for an 'Islamic' State in Pakistan. The aspiration is present in other constitutions. "In one sense, the Indian constitution is more than a set of rules guiding behaviour; it is a kind of charter for her westernized leadership, a set of goals and expectations."[8] The difficulty is always to effect the translation of such ideas into concrete constitutional proposals, especially in circumstances where widespread consensus about political and social aims is devoutly believed in and wished for, but not apparent to the outside observer.

II

In this section we shall look at some of the ways in which the constitutions have embodied basic conceptions of Western democracy and at some attempts at innovation.

Cabinet and Presidential Government

The normal pattern in the countries with which we are concerned has been Cabinet, not Presidential Government.[9] The Head of State is given the position of a constitutional monarch, and normally acts on the advice of Ministers responsible to Parliament; in the republics he is usually elected by Parliament, with state parliaments sometimes assisting in federations. In Malaya the State Rulers elect one of their numbers as Chief of State of the Federation. The attempt has sometimes been made to write down a relationship approximating to the British conventions. However, in all cases, the role of the Head of State remains in many significant ways a matter of convention.

Even in the Indian Constitution, which, as has been said, "might give one the impression that provision has been made . . . to settle

[8] M. Weiner, in R. L. Park and I. Tinker, *Leadership and Political Institutions in India*, 29.

[9] Some countries in or adjacent to Asia, e.g. S. Vietnam, the Philippines, and (until recently) S. Korea, have had the Presidential system. In S. Vietnam the President has considerably wider formal powers than his American equivalent, and somewhat greater powers in the Philippines. Under the 1945 Indonesian Constitution (now once again in operation) the President's executive powers are almost unlimited.

every imaginable problem of government",[10] the place of the President must still to a considerable degree be defined by convention. The executive power is vested in him, the Prime Minister and his Council of Ministers 'aid and advise'. There is no reference to the President's discretion, but neither is there a specific declaration that he must act on the advice of his Cabinet (though he must appoint other Ministers on the advice of the Prime Minister). Some other constitutions have explicitly provided for a sphere of discretion, and some have tried to deny it. For example, the Pakistan Constitution of 1956 said that the President shall 'in his discretion' appoint the Prime Minister, the Burmese Constitution says that the Prime Minister is nominated by the Chamber of Deputies. Both rules leave scope for argument as to the proper role of the Head of State, in a situation where there is no clear majority with a well-recognized leader. A similar problem may occur in relation to the right to refuse a dissolution, important in Burma at the time of the AFPFL split. In several of the constitutions, the President's right of dissolution is unqualified. He may also be given considerable 'emergency powers', as in India.

The Indonesian Constitution of 1950 and to a lesser extent the Pakistan Constitution of 1956 (both now abrogated) seem to have allowed a somewhat different role for the President from that of a mere constitutional head of state.[11] In Indonesia, though his Ministers were said to be responsible 'for the entire policy of the Government', the right to dissolve was vested in the President and Soekarno claimed (and exercised) a personal veto over legislation and the right to overrule the Minister of Defence in making military appointments. In Pakistan the President had one or two powers associated with American Presidents, for example, a veto which it required a two-thirds majority of the National Assembly to override. It is true that this seems to have been designed mainly as a protection for a Cabinet faced with an unruly legislature, and as a matter on which the President was expected to act on Cabinet advice.

However, past history suggested that in Pakistan the Head of State would play an important role. The country had operated since

[10] M. V. Pylee, reviewing C. H. Alexandrowicz, *Constitutional Developments in India* (1957), in *Indian Journal of Public Administration*, Jan.–March 1958, 121.

[11] The Malayan Chief of State also has the task of upholding special Malay rights and of maintaining Islam as the State religion.

independence under the 1935 Government of India Act (as modified), and the normal conventions of cabinet government did not establish themselves. The first Governor-General was Dr. Jinnah, certainly no constitutional monarch; his successors used their powers extensively in the political crises of those years, chose and dismissed Prime Ministers, even dismissed the Constituent Assembly in 1954 (an action upheld by the federal court); and so took the steps which finally led to the assumption of power by General Ayub Khan. There was a committee recommendation during the period of constitution-making that a strong President would be in accordance with Islamic traditions, but this view was not accepted by the Basic Principles Committee.[12] The Constitutional Commission now sitting may have different ideas.

It is clear that, especially in multi-party situations, his place in forming governments and dealing with governmental hiatuses is bound to make the Head of State at times an important figure; even in India Dr. Rajendra Prasad has resisted the notion that he is a mere rubber-stamp. In Ceylon, the Governor-General, though in principle a constitutional monarch, was the effective centre of government during the 1958 political crisis, a situation which could recur. There is no clear answer to the more general question of the merits of Presidential Government as a better constitutional solution to the problems of some Asian countries. In countries plagued by sectional rivalries, it seems to be a tempting answer. (For example, the President of Burma recently proposed to the Constitution Revision Committee a change-over to the Presidential system.) But it is a superficial answer. A President's personal charisma does not seem to help much more than a Prime Minister's unless he has an organised and disciplined group of supporters who can permeate government at many levels; and such a state of affairs cannot be brought about merely by adopting the Presidential form, unless it is accompanied by many other changes, as foreshadowed in Pakistan.

Federalism

Of the constitutions we have been considering, those of India, Malaya and Pakistan (1956) are federal, while the Burmese Constitution has a federal element. Indonesia had a federal constitution

[12] K. Callard, *Pakistan: A Political Study*, 1957, 95–6.

briefly, but is now a unitary state. Art. 131 of the 1950 Constitution provided for 'regions', which were promised 'the greatest possible degree of autonomy', but this has not happened.[13]

In India the federal division of powers was based on the 1935 Government of India Act. This set the division out in great detail, and so does the constitution. But there are some important centralist additions to the list of concurrent powers, 'economic and social planning', 'commercial and industrial monopolies, companies and trusts' and 'employment and unemployment'. In Malaya the central government also has a broad power to implement national development plans, and trade, commerce, industry, labour and social security are federal powers.

In Malaya the federal government has also an exclusive power to tax, though the States have certain assigned revenues. In India, taxes have been allocated or assigned, so that the States get, for example, taxes on agricultural incomes and property, some sales taxes, the liquor excise; and there are elaborate arrangements for securing to them a share of other taxes, including income tax on non-agricultural incomes. In practice, the central government of India predominates financially. It monopolises overseas borrowing, and virtually controls the terms and timing of internal borrowing; the tax 'shares' are not fixed permanently and in their determination an important part is played by a Finance Commission appointed by the President. Finally, the Union can make grants at its discretion and conditional and specific grants have become very important.[14]

The Indian Constitution also leaves great discretionary and emergency powers in central government hands, as was recently instanced in the Kerala dispute. With Congress Ministries in power in most States, it has also been fairly easy to make major changes, such as the reorganisation of State boundaries on a linguistic basis.

Morris-Jones has called Articles 256 and 257(1) a 'remarkable testimony to the constitutional unity of India'.[15] "The executive power of each State shall be so exercised as to ensure compliance with the laws made by Parliament and . . . (so) as not to impede or prejudice the exercise of the executive power of the Union, and the

[13] For the unsuccessful attempt to implement this, see J. D. Legge, "Experiment in Local Government, 1950–59", *Australian Outlook*, Dec. 1959.

[14] cf. W. Prest, "Federal-State Financial Relations in India", *Economic Record*, April, 1960.

[15] *Parliament in India*, 4.

executive power of the Union shall extend to the giving of such directions to a State as may appear to the Government of India to be necessary for that purpose." When we add to this the fact that the Indian Administrative Service still staffs the more important State posts, it is clearly only in a very qualified sense that India can be said to be a "federal" State.

Pakistan is a somewhat different case. By the 1956 Constitution its two widely-separated Provinces were given wider powers, including residuary powers. But the concurrent list, like India's, included such items as 'economic and social planning'; and, as in India, the centre was financially predominant.[16] There were also provisions for the extension of central power into the provincial field to meet emergencies. Now the federal system has all but gone, and the country seems to be run in unitary fashion.

Burma is an odd case, basically unitary, but with some special provisions for regional minorities, including the right in some cases for their M.P.s to sit in separate State Councils for certain purposes —rather like some schemes for devolution to Scotland and Wales. Burma 'proper' is a unitary State, and it has been said that the "federal structure is more nominal than real",[17] a sop to minorities.

We might too easily assume that federalism has been of small account in Asia. It would be useful to know more about how it works in practice in India and Malaya. Certainly, federal 'forms' do make some practical difference. For example, the fact that a federal government has the power (say, through grants) to subvert federalism, still leaves the fact that the institutions of federalism exist, and having to get round them may still present some serious obstacles to unitary action. However, it is made clear in the chapters that follow that the political obstacles to unity have been much more important than constitutional provisions.

'Fundamental Rights' and Judicial Review

The constitutions pay some attention to the rights of the individual,[18] variously described as 'Fundamental Rights' (Burma, India,

---

[16] The Pakistan arrangements were not very different from the Indian (both drew partly on the 1935 Government of India Act); but in Pakistan the Finance Commission represented the Provinces. See A. Gledhill, "The Pakistan Constitution", *Public Law*, Winter 1956.

[17] Silverstein, in Kahin, *Governments and Politics of S.E. Asia*, 111.

[18] A minor point is how far rights extend to all 'persons', how far to

Pakistan), 'Fundamental Liberties' (Malaya), 'Fundamental Human Rights and Freedoms' (Indonesia).

However, in many cases the desire for an American-style Bill of Rights has been qualified by the desire to protect parliamentary supremacy, and to limit judicial enforcement where there might be a conflict with what the elected legislature conceives to be the needs of society. In India (and in the 1956 Pakistan Constitution), for example, a number of rights are not unconditionally guaranteed and may be subjected to 'reasonable' restrictions.[19] This imposes some limitations on judicial review, limitations which the Indian Supreme Court has by and large accepted. It also largely upheld the provisions of the 1950 Preventive Detention Act, a statute described by M. V. Pylee as 'an unseemly blot on the fair face of democracy in India'.[20] However, in India some rights, especially non-discrimination on grounds of religion, race, caste, etc. are unconditionally guaranteed; as though American experience taught that one could easily go too far with freedom, and not far enough with non-discrimination. Pakistan only forbade discrimination in public appointments.

Secondly, in common with some other countries, such as Burma, there has been added a list of 'Directive Principles of State Policy', following the Irish pattern. They are not enforceable in the courts, and cannot override the Fundamental Rights, but appear on

'citizens'. In India and Malaya many rights such as equality before the law, religious freedom, etc. apply to 'persons'. Others (e.g. freedom of speech) apply only to 'citizens'. In Pakistan (1956), equality before the law and religious freedom were restricted to 'citizens', though some rights applied to 'persons', e.g. "No person shall be deprived of life and liberty save in accordance with law" (sec. 5[2]). In Burma, the constitution mainly refers to 'citizens', but all 'persons' are guaranteed religious freedom, and cf. Maung, *Burma's Constitution*, 1959, 94.

[19] In Malaya, there are also qualifications. For example, freedom of speech is subject to laws which Parliament deems necessary or expedient in the interests of security of the Federation or public order and morality, or 'friendly relations with other countries'; and the courts are incompetent to decide whether a law has the characterisation validating such restriction.

[20] *Constitutional Government in India*, 246. In *Gopalan v. State of Madras* (1950), the Supreme Court majority, in "English" fashion, put a strict and literal construction on the latter part of Article 21: "No person shall be deprived of his life and personal liberty except according to procedure established by law", and would have no truck with American notions of due process.

occasion (e.g. land reform) to influence the courts' notion of what are 'reasonable restrictions'.[21]

The Directive Principles relate mainly to matters of social and economic welfare, e.g. free education, social security, adequate means of livelihood, and so on. In the case of Pakistan, they included a duty imposed on the State to promote Islamic principles (e.g. to provide facilities, to make the teaching of the *Quran* compulsory for Muslims). In India, they included provisions regarding the promotion of village *panchayats*, cottage industries, prohibition, and protection against cow-slaughter. The Rights are a fairly familiar list, with some additions: e.g. in India, the right of citizens with a "distinct language, script or culture . . . to conserve the same"; in Burma, the right of women to equal pay "in respect of similar work".

One set of rights that it would be interesting to explore further are property rights. People who are agreed about the other traditional rights often disagree about this—it was one on which opinion in the Indian Constituent Assembly was very much divided. Some constitutions (e.g. India, Malaya, Pakistan) declare that property is protected by law and there can be no expropriation without compensation. In contrast, the Burmese Constitution, while recognising a right to hold property, states (art. 23(4)) that: "Private property may be limited or expropriated if the public interest so requires but only in accordance with law which shall prescribe in which cases and to what extent the owner shall be compensated"; and instructs the State to give preference to organisations not working for private profit.[22] However, although the Indian Constitution appears to protect property and compensation rights, this has since been affected by amendment. Article 31 stated that compensation must be provided for property taken over by the State, and the courts

---

[21] M. V. Pylee, *Constitutional Government in India*, pp. 316–7. Mr. Nehru has held that Directive Principles *should* override Fundamental Rights where they conflict. (*loc. cit.*, 317.)

[22] The Thai and Vietnamese constitutions provide for a kind of 'right to private enterprise'. The Thai constitution instructs the State to encourage private initiative; the Vietnamese (Art. 22) gives every citizen 'the right to set up economic associations, provided the aim . . . is not to establish illegal monopoly in order to engage in speculation and manipulation of the economy' (*cit.* S. Rose, in *Far Eastern Affairs*, St. Antony's Papers No. 7, 31–32). They also speak, not of 'Rights', but of 'Rights and Duties', and in Vietnam there is apparently a duty, as well as a right, to work.

interpreted this to mean a 'just equivalent'. The 4th Amendment overrides this, and makes the basis and amount of compensation the sole business of Parliament.

This raises some questions about the role of the courts. In most countries with written constitutions, the courts have power to interpret the constitution and to declare legislative measures void on the ground that they conflict with its provisions. Some form of judicial review is also found in most Asian countries with written constitutions. However, it may be limited in some respects, as we have seen. In spite of this, in most of the countries discussed, the courts seem to have played a fairly active role in maintaining the rule of law, sometimes to the irritation of governments.

This has been of particular importance in situations where constitutionalism has in other respects been precarious. The Burmese courts, for example, have taken a firm line about preventive arrests, and human rights in general. The Public Order (Preservation) Act made it possible to detain a suspect up to two months or, under certain conditions, indefinitely. Section 9 (1) provided that 'no order made in exercise of any power conferred by or under this Act shall be called into question in any Court'. Finally, the Court acted to strike out the section on the ground that 'no legislative provisions in the Union can validly exclude this Court from enquiring into the legality or the sufficiency of any decisions of the judicial or quasi-judicial body".[23] Dr. Maung Maung, no narrow legalist, has expressed the view that "the ideal of the independence of the Judiciary and the rule of law has been a fixed and shining beacon on the shifting scene in Burma".[24]

On the other hand, there are Asian countries where the courts have played a very minor constitutional role, especially those previously governed by countries where the ordinary courts rarely or never undertook judicial review of the written constitution.[24a]

[23] Silverstein, *op. cit.*, 112. cf. Maung Maung, *Burma's Constitution*, 102–3, 154.

[24] Maung, *op. cit.*, 153.

[24a] France and the Netherlands. Ceylon, with the most English of Constitutions, makes no explicit provision for judicial review and has no Bill of Rights. However, section 29(2) prohibits legal discrimination against communal or religious groups, and provides for freedom of religion. Laws offending against this section " may . . . be declared to be void by any Court in the Island " (Ivor Jennings, *The Constitution of Ceylon*, 2nd Ed., 1951, 64).

This is true of S. Vietnam and Indonesia. In Indonesia, the judiciary has had almost no concern with constitutional questions, though the Chairman of the Supreme Court has in the past been asked to advise the President on the legality of his procedures. A more general advisory jurisdiction is provided for in most of the constitutions discussed below, and the supreme court may give advisory opinions on constitutional questions referred to it by the Head of State. In Pakistan "the advisory judgment of the Federal Court on a reference by the Governor-General successfully brought to an end the constitutional crisis following the dismissal of the first Constituent Assembly".[25]

Church and State

Some of the Asian States we have discussed have an 'established' religion—Islam in Pakistan and Malaya, Buddhism to a limited extent in Burma. The Indian State is secular; the Indonesians have never settled the issue, though the 1950 Constitution declared (Art. 43) that "The State is based on the belief in the Divine Omnipotence". There has been pressure in Pakistan for a State based on Islamic law, and in Burma for the fuller recognition of Buddhism as the State religion.

The 1956 Pakistan Constitution, on paper at least, went farthest in this respect, in providing that laws were to be brought into conformity with the injunctions of Islam. Pakistan was described as an 'Islamic Republic'; and there has been, and is, a great controversy on just what would be a constitution of a truly Islamic character, a point on which agreement seems no nearer.

The problem of Church-State relations seems to arise most acutely :

(1) where there is a widespread belief, not only that social institutions and law have a religious sanction, but that some particular set of institutions and laws is inseparable from some particular religion. (The reply to this may be an attempt wholly to separate Church and State, or, more subtly, to amend the social and political conclusions one draws from the religion);

[25] A. Gledhill, *op. cit.*, 362.

(2) where there is an organised body of church 'office-bearers' able to act as a pressure-group protecting their own status in the political system, or pressing their own views on public policy. Thus Hinduism is said to have been handicapped in comparison with others, in having least organisation in this sense. On the other hand, the very amorphous character of Hinduism makes it harder to cope with in some respects. There is no one with whom a State could "come to terms";

(3) where the religion is widely felt to be an important source of social unity and stability (which depends in part on whether there is some influential minority or minorities not adhering to it).[26]

III

Constitutions and Social Structure

A frequent question is whether Western-type constitutional laws and conventions really 'suit' Asian societies. Sometimes the argument is put in terms of *social structure*, that in such societies politics tends to be based largely on social and communal status, and personal and group relations of various kinds, with little integration among political participants from different elites or on different levels, and little consensus on 'legitimate' political means and ends;[27] so failing to satisfy necessary conditions for Western democratic political systems. Sometimes the problem is set more in terms of *social needs*, and doubt is expressed about whether Western-type institutions will promote the desired degree of social and economic progress.

These kinds of arguments are nowadays developed in a highly sophisticated way; and they clearly have some substance. It is interesting to compare them with the relatively simple 'conditions' for a viable constitutional democracy current in many quarters only a few years ago.

Consider what Sir Ivor Jennings had to say ten years ago about Ceylon. "The task of the Ceylonese is . . . easier than those of the

[26] In some such cases e.g. Ceylon, the government may waver between trying to use the majority religion as a cement for majority rule, and seeking an accommodation between the various groups.

[27] cf. Lucien W. Pye, "The Non-Western Political Process", *Journal of Politics*, August 1958.

Indians and the Pakistanis, and they may possibly show the way towards solution of the problems of all three countries".[28] Jennings believed this for good old-fashioned reasons. Ceylon had been subject to Western influences longest. Her population had a fairly high literacy rate (70 per cent among males in 1946), had had adult franchise since 1931, and possessed an allegedly 'stable right-wing government'. Her independence movement had been peaceful and constitutional. She also had the blessing of a short, simple constitution, drafted by a small established group who wanted a flexible system of government on English lines, and one that would not arouse controversy when it came to be ratified by the legislature. It was to be (and was) put through without fuss. Indian literacy rates and the Indian constitution seemed in unfavourable contrast; the latter, a long and complicated document, fought and quibbled over at length by a Constituent Assembly and full of detailed formulae designed to satisfy particular interests.

Of course, Jennings may still turn out to be right. But India has up to now done better than the pessimists predicted; and Ceylon has certainly disappointed the optimists, including the High Commissioner in London who referred to it at a Guildhall banquet as a 'little bit of England'. The cause of the disappointment is now fairly obvious. The English-speaking leadership which ran the system had no mass following. Below it were vernacular groups with demands very imperfectly taken account of in the political system, who irrupted into it with claims that no one could deal with in an orderly way.

I spoke above of two kinds of deficiency that Western-type governments are said to have in Asia, in terms of social structure and social needs. The late Mr. Bandaranaike's government neatly illustrated both horns of the dilemma. He looked at once like a 'progressive' politician responding to economic demands of a 'progressive' sort; but was backed by groups with demands of a much more traditional kind, rural-based Sinhalese, Buddhist monks, and ayurvedic doctors.[29] The Indian Congress Party was much better

---

[28] *The Commonwealth in Asia*, 1951, x.

[29] For both elements in the Bandaranaike programme, see W. H. Wriggins, *Ceylon, Dilemmas of a New Nation*, 1960, esp. 122–123. An extremer form is presented in Ceylon at the time of writing by K. M. P. Rajaratne, reactionary on racial and religious issues, an uncompromising socialist on economic questions.

trained and organised than Mr. Bandaranaike's United Front to cope with such a complex of contradictory claims.

Now that we have so multiplied and complicated the conditions for a Western-type political system, it looks as though nothing that we would recognise as a constitutional government can live up to them. But there are a few things to be said on the other side, which I have only space to state dogmatically.

(1) It is misleading to put the question as though it is one either of the constitution 'conforming' to the social structure (which in a traditional society, might produce a conservative solution) or of its 'conforming' to some arbitrary assessment of social needs, based on Western standards (which sometimes produces a very radical answer). At least if we are thinking in terms of political stability, the basic desideratum is a political system which *can deal with the actual political demands made on it*, and (if we are forecasting) on the demands that seem to be coming up in the reasonably near future.

(2) If the way a political system works seems to differ a good deal from what its written constitution appears to indicate, we cannot automatically conclude that the constitution is useless, or even that it should be changed. It may still limit behaviour in desirable ways. Even if it does not do so in a direct and obvious fashion, it may still have a " legitimising or prestige-creating " role, which may influence political processes in better rather than worse directions.[30]

(3) There is no necessary connection between social stability and stability of political institutions. It is quite possible (as Raymond Aron has argued) to have considerable social stability and great political instability, as in nineteenth-century France; or considerable social change and very stable politics, as in nineteenth-century England. A set of political institutions that acquires 'legitimacy' can survive considerable social upheaval, partly because individuals and groups will hesitate to impose demands that it cannot meet; possibly also because it is easier for a regime that feels basically secure to make the necessary concessions and adjustments in time.

(4) Hence it behoves us very much to ask : who are the people whose sense of the legitimacy of its political institutions is it most

[30] Mackie, below 191.

important to preserve? It has been argued that democratic parliamentary institutions as they exist in most Asian countries exist 'on the sufferance of a small educated minority which could, if it chose, destroy those institutions'.[31] At least in some under-developed countries, this 'sufferance' appears to reflect fairly deeply-seated feelings. Even where constitutional democracy has been abandoned, articulate people feel guilty about it and protest that it is only a temporary measure.[32] They do not yet share Mao's pleasure at having a clean piece of paper on which to write beautiful new words.

---

[31] Myron Weiner, in R. L. Park and I. Tinker, *op. cit.*
[32] " Politicians talk about it all the time and one day democracy should become a habit with them ", Maung, *op. cit.* 93.

V. K. Thiruvenkata Chari

THE COURTS AND THE CONSTITUTION IN INDIA

The Background

THE PREAMBLE to the Indian Constitution is one which could arouse enthusiasm in the people who had adopted it and excite hopes in observers. In a work embodying decades of study and thought, *Principles of Social and Political Theory* (1951), Sir Ernest Barker printed the Preamble at the outset and said in his Introduction:

> "I ought to explain, as I end, why the preamble to the Constitution of India is printed after the table of contents. It seemed to me, when I read it, to state in a brief and pithy form the argument of much of the book; and it may accordingly serve as a key-note. I am the more moved to quote it because I am proud that the people of India should begin their independent life by subscribing to the principles of a political tradition which we in the west call Western, but which is now something more than Western."

Part IV of the Constitution (Articles 36 to 51) embodies certain provisions not enforceable by the Courts but (Article 37 reads) "the principles therein laid down are nevertheless fundamental in the governance of the country and it shall be the duty of the State to apply these principles in making laws". Jurists have doubted the value of general declarations of rights. Having regard to the framework of the Indian Constitution and the extent to which Article 37 has been observed in practice in Indian legislation, it seems that the 'Directive Principles of State Policy' in Part IV have in fact given a definite policy and orientation to law-making in India. Leaving schools of jurisprudence to contend, the Indian experiment is aimed at preserving a truly democratic Government by the very process of required social and economic change, without which democracy is in danger of being supplanted by one or other of its rivals.

The present writer seeks to evaluate the trends in Indian legislation and constitutional adjudication during the first decade to see if we can draw any conclusions significant for the fostering and survival of constitutional Government. It is realised that this approach is a limited one and any inferences on these lines will require modification and correction by studies from other approaches.

Much of what follows can only be understood in the context of India's social and economic problems. India presents the problem of an under-developed country with a large and growing population, 362 million in 1951 and likely to be about 431 million in 1961. The national income has been estimated as:

Year	Total *(in crores)	Per Capita	Contribution of Industry	Agriculture
	Rs.	Rs.	Rs.	Rs.
1950–51	9,530	265	1,530	4,890
1955–56	9,980	261	1,830	4,520
1956–57	11,310	292	2,000	5,520
1958–59	12,470	313	2,140	6,190

* (Note — Rs 1 crore is roughly equal to £ 750,000)

The small proportion represented by industry should be noted. The thesis on which the policies of the Indian Government has been based in the last decade is that the first step is to have industrialisation centred in heavy industry and side by side to improve agriculture. The investment made for this purpose, limited as it was by available funds, during the First Five Year Plan (1951–56) was Rs. 3,360 crores (public sector Rs. 1,560 crores and private sector Rs. 1,800 crores) and during the Second Five Year Plan (1956–1961) Rs. 6,750 crores (public sector Rs. 3,650 crores and private sector Rs. 3,100 crores). The increase in national income over the 2nd Plan period is expected to be about 20 per cent. Over the first two plan periods (1951–61) the national income (at constant prices) will have increased by 42 per cent, *per capita* income by about 20 per cent and per capita consumption by about 16 per cent. The increase in production will have outstripped the increase in population. The third plan is under preparation.

Social and economic legislation in India has had two main aims :

One, positive changes in social pattern and economic organisation;
two, (in recent years by larger use of powers under existing enactments) restrictions arising from the need to conserve foreign currency and to eliminate wasteful economic practices.

The Constitution (following the pattern of the 1935 Act) has distributed legislative power according to subject matter between Parliament (Union List) and State Legislatures (State List), with a concurrent list of matters on which both can legislate. The concurrent list provides a field in which Parliament can legislate uniformly for the whole country, and yet suitable local variation is possible in any State by local legislation with the President's assent.

Recent Legislation

PERSONAL LAWS : Family and property law of the Hindus and Muslims have been governed by the rules of their religion, that is, by sacred texts of their law-givers. From the earliest days of British rule in India it was the policy not to interfere in the religious affairs of the people and this comprised most of their civil law. The courts were to decide matters of inheritance and succession and contract and dealing between party and party according to the personal law or custom of the parties and in case of parties of different personal law or custom according to those of the defendant. (East India Company Act, 1780.) Hence we have in the Legislative Lists List III Entry 5, "all matters in respect of which parties in judicial proceedings were immediately before the commencement of the Constitution subject to their personal law". The incursions in this field were rare indeed. There was the abolition of *suttee* (1829–30), the Act of 1850 preserving rights to property on conversion or excommunication, the Hindu Widows' Re-marriage Act of 1856, the Child Marriage Restraint Act, 1929 etc. Now Article 44 provides that, "The State shall endeavour to secure for the citizens a uniform civil code throughout the territory of India". The law of contract, transfer of property etc. was already codified in the nineteenth century and the criminal law was uniform under the Penal Code and the Code of Criminal Procedure. Recently Hindu law has been codified in separate Acts relating to succession and inheritance (1956), adoptions and maintenance (1956), marriages (1955) and minority and guardianship (1956). The special features of this legislation are the provisions of shares in property for women, the conversion of women's estate (analogous to life estate) into absolute estates and the provisions for divorce.

The pattern of Hindu society has been the joint Hindu family. The lineal descendants of a Hindu male up to the third generation together form a co-parcenary and the property of the family remains joint. On the death of a male member, his interest passes by survivorship to the remaining members. A man could also acquire and own separate property but on a failure of male heirs, the widow, then the daughter, could inherit. The changes in the last few decades have rendered the joint family system an anachronism. The position of women in Hindu society has been a subordinate one. When she inherited from a male she had a woman's estate—the right to enjoy the income without waste. This has now been radically altered. By the Act of 1937 the widow of a co-parcener could take her husband's share and ask for a partition, but still hold only a woman's estate. By the Act of 1956 every woman possessed of such property has been made an absolute owner. In separate property wife and daughter are now equal sharers with sons and get an absolute estate. It is too early yet to judge the specific effect of this on the joint family system but as a result of land reforms partitions are the mode now. For the first time monogamy has been enjoined for all Hindus and divorce has been introduced. Traditional instinct against divorce still operates and the number of petitions for divorce is small. While improving the position of women, divorce will create new problems in a country in which women are not normally equipped to earn a living and the scope for employment is limited.

LAND LEGISLATION: Until recently the land was largely concentrated in the hands of zamindars. Late in the 18th century the India Government accepted, in large tracts of the country, the intermediaries created by permanent settlement as the persons to pay a fixed sum in permanency to the State, they being free to collect any rent they could from the actual cultivators. Against this, to a limited extent, there were settlements by the Government direct with actual cultivators (ryots)—the ryotwari system, with an assessment revisable every 30 years. One change contemplated is to have a pattern of land ownership of small farmers each with an economic holding.

The first stage was the abolition of zamindaris, effected by a series of Acts a list of which is found in the ninth schedule. The Constitution has guaranteed property rights—the rights of enjoyment by Article 19(1) (g) subject to reasonable restrictions, and compensation on acquisition by Article 31. There was the view that zamindars were mere rent-farmers and we could not now pay them the full market value of the property. The First Amendment of 1951 introduced Article 31–B and the Acts listed in the ninth schedule and provided that none of those enactments could be questioned on the basis of fundamental rights. The lands have been acquired by the States on compensation on a most modest scale and the ryots have. become holders directly under the State on revisable land revenue assessments.

Next, there has been legislation giving security of tenure to tenants, with provisions enabling them to acquire ownership. The third stage is a more serious one and is now under way in most of the States. In the notes on clauses of the Constitution Fourth Amendment Bill (in Parliament) in 1954, the following appeared:

"While the abolition of zamindaries and the numerous intermediaries between the State and the tiller of the soil has been achieved for the most part, our next objectives in land reform are the fixing of limits to the extent of agricultural land that may be owned or occupied by any person, the disposal of any land held in excess of the prescribed maximum and the further modification of the rights of land owners and tenants in agricultural holdings."

The area under cultivation in India is about 320 million acres, with about 60 million families owning or cultivating the land. The Plans envisage a pattern of small owner-farmers cultivating their own land and one ideal is a farm of 5 acres as the norm for personal cultivation. Article 39 (b) and (c) provide for a policy of distribution of material resources and discountenance the concentration of wealth. In the case of other forms of wealth, the high rates of income tax and wealth tax (a modest first step), the gift tax and Estate Duty take care of this. Conspicuous consumption is discouraged by the expenditure tax. In the case of land, there has been legislation in every State during the last decade for fixity of tenure, non-eviction except for non-payment of rent, and fixation of fair rent by Tribunals. The rent fixed in most laws is one fourth to one fifth of produce. The new Acts provide a ceiling on ownership (30 standard acres for a family in the Madras Bill). The surplus now existing is to be acquired by the State on compensation, being a multiple (8 to 12) of the fair rent. The land now acquired will be allotted by the State to cultivators. The far-reaching social effects of these measures cannot be exaggerated. Constitutional questions have been raised and must await determination by the courts. Every citizen has subject to 'reasonable restrictions' a right to acquire, hold and dispose of property (Article 19 [1] [g]). Is it a valid reasonable restriction to fix a ceiling?

CONTROL OF BUSINESS: The controls now exercised are mainly from the point of view of foreign exchange conservation and proper distribution in conditions of scarcity. The laws themselves had been enacted in the first Plan period before foreign exchange difficulties came to be felt. No new industry in a list covering a very large field can be established except under licence from the Central Government under the Industries (Development and Regulation) Act, 1951. The aims were: (i) that all development should be according to plan priorities and (ii) location was to be regulated on the basis of broader social purposes. In the controversy over Article 31(2) in its original form, the Supreme Court referred to this Act in a case relating to land tenure (*Subodh Gopal*, 1954 S.C.R. 587) and refused to pass on its validity. But it will be seen that no one would gain by challenging this enactment. If a licence be granted the undertaking would get the benefit of eminent domain to acquire lands, the necessary licences for foreign exchange etc. To say the Act is void would only mean that no licence under this Act is required for starting the industry but the other necessary facilities cannot be enjoined by the Courts. This Act has been used to distribute the location of factories (for example, fertilisers) geographically in different regions.

The Imports and Exports (Control) Act, 1947 is a short enactment of only 7 sections, vesting all control in the Central

Government by notifications and orders. The Foreign Exchange Regulation Act, 1947 follows the pattern of the English Act. Import control is exercised by licensing under a policy till recently enunciated half-yearly. Distribution is controlled by orders under the Essential Commodities Act.

The other major development is government industry and trading. The Government have declared their policy in the Industrial Policy Resolutions 1948 and 1959. By and large heavy industry is being developed by government factories with foreign government aid and technical assistance. A State Trading Corporation has been set up. Life Insurance has been completely nationalised. In each case separate governmental corporations have been set up. Apart from the economic relationship between the public and the private sector in industry, this raises the question of responsibility to Parliament (a matter which has been anxiously investigated in English experience) and the question of place-men in the legislatures. Are directors and employees of these corporations to be regarded as disqualified for being members of the legislatures as holding offices of profit (Articles 102 and 191) under the Government of India or of a State? In England the common law refused to extend Crown immunity to such incorporated bodies. But after the Crown Proceedings Act, 1946, the extension of Crown responsibility may possibly lead to a reversal of thought. As regards Articles 102 and 191 perhaps the best view would be to hold that any one whose appointment is made by a Minister or is subject to confirmation by him holds an office of profit under the Government. Even this would be too limited from the point of view of legislative independence. The decision in India, however, is that employees of these corporations do not hold an office of profit under the Union or the State Government. This is a matter of some concern in relation to the independence of legislatures in India. It is, however, a problem present in all democracies and not so easy of solution.

Labour legislation in India is highly developed. Probably India is the one country which has implemented many of the recommendations of the I.L.O. The reason is not far to seek. Rapid industrialisation has become the chief tenet of the State. The Industrial Disputes Act, 1947 is modelled on the Australian Commonwealth Acts. The wide definition of 'Industry' has been adopted from the Australian Commonwealth Act and interpreted in the same way as in the

Jumbanna case (6 C.L.R. 309 at 370). Governmental industry is within its scope. So are municipalities, as was decided by the Supreme Court in *Bannerji* vs. *Mukherji* (1953 S.C.R. 302) following the Australian decision in the *Melbourne Corporation case*, (26 C.L.R. 508). The set-up of Tribunals under the Act has varied. At first there were local tribunals and an all-India appellate Tribunal. To reduce delays, the Appellate Tribunal was abolished; there is now a move to revive it. In adjudication on wages, allowances, etc. there has been no uniformity.[1] This is a direct result of the fact that the law itself does not contain any rules, but leaves everything to the Tribunal.

A just summing up would be that this is still in the experimental stage. If a dispute has been referred for adjudication the continuation of any strike or lock-out can be prohibited. Another feature is that pending adjudication the dismissal of workmen must have the approval of the Tribunal, which may order reinstatement of dismissed workmen. There is a Minimum Wages Act under which floor wages are fixed for employment in specified occupations. Recently Employees Provident Funds have been taken under State management and an Employees State Insurance Organisation has been set up for medical benefits. Apart from safety and health provisions in the Factories Act and in the various State enactments for shop assistants, the latter enactments provide against dismissal or termination of service of employees except for misconduct or reasonable cause, with an appeal to a Tribunal. Between reinstatement under the Industrial Disputes Act and Appellate orders under the Shops Acts, the class of employees who are *inops consilii* have some security of tenure in recognition of 'the right to work' mentioned in Article 41.

The credit structure of the country is largely under control by the Reserve Bank of India. Every Bank requires a licence from the Reserve Bank.

The Attitude of the Courts

The attitude of the Courts to these legal developments is significant. As already mentioned, any law made by Parliament or by any

[1] The awards have been reviewed in official papers e.g. Industrial Awards in India (1960), papers on Wage Policy (1957).

State Legislature has to be characterised as being 'with respect to' one matter or other specified in the legislative lists. The pith and substance doctrine of Canada and Australia has been adopted in this connection. Assuming a valid law, it has to run the gamut of the freedoms guaranteed in Article 19(1) and the restrictions on such freedoms have to be justified as 'reasonable restrictions' under the relevant following clauses of Article 19. Access to the Courts to question the validity of laws is easy and, by and large, fairly cheap. The aggrieved person can petition the Supreme Court direct under Article 32 for enforcement of fundamental rights or move the High Court for a writ for a larger variety of purposes. If he raised the question in the lower Courts, the matter would be referred to the High Court under provisions of the Procedure Codes. On constitutional questions, appeals lie from the High Court to the Supreme Court as of right.

FREEDOM OF EXPRESSION: In the region of freedom of expression, the newspapers enjoy practically unrestricted freedom. There are however a few State laws under which publication of certain types of matter can be prohibited, a power used when there is communal tension. Similarly the various Police Acts confer power on the Police Commissioner to make orders requiring a licence for meetings. Drama was under control under the Dramatic Performance Act, 1876. We had to concede it was void after the Constitution as under it any Magistrate could prohibit any drama. Since then in Madras we have a Dramatic Performance Act, 1956 in which the grounds of prohibition are laid down and the party could have the order tested in the High Court.

Cinema films are censored under the Cinematograph Act. Various excisions and alterations (puritanical in the main) are insisted on by the Board: these are published in the official gazette. A periodical recently published one such notification under the heading 'What the Indians can't see'. What does not come before the Courts at all is the work of the novelists, poets, painters, and sculptors; our artists and writers work in an atmosphere of the greatest freedom.

FREEDOM OF MOVEMENT: Article 19 guarantees to citizens the right to move freely throughout the territory of India. The Courts have, however, upheld as reasonable restrictions orders passed under State enactments for the maintenance of public order prohibiting particular persons from entering the State for a specified period.

Such orders are generally made during periods of local turmoil. A less acceptable development is the order of externment from an area. In *Hari Kamu,* (1956 S.C.R. 506) the appellant, who had been convicted of certain offences and was considered likely to engage in commission of similar offences, was ordered to leave Greater Bombay and this was upheld by the Supreme Court (with one dissent).

Freedom to travel outside the country is not recognised. Somewhere in the Holmes-Laski letters, Holmes asked what right an American citizen who had left the country had to return! The Supreme Court has recently held (*Abdul Rahim,* 1960 S.C.J. 50) that the provision of the Passport Act, 1920 which requires even an Indian citizen to produce a passport before he can be allowed to enter India may be regarded as a proper restriction. The grant of passports to Indian citizens to travel outside India is entirely discretionary. In *V. G. Rao* (I.L.R. 1954 Madras 399) the Madras High Court held that the issue of a passport is a matter entirely within the discretion of the State Department and being purely an exercise of a political function is not subject to judicial review. There seems to be no chance of liberalization in this regard.

FREEDOM OF ASSOCIATION: This is perhaps a field in which India is too broadminded. Every political party has its full freedom. There are too many Trade Unions—with more than one Union (of different political complexion) in the same industry the employer is buffeted between them. Moves are on foot to provide for 'one industry, one union'.

India is (as far as the present writer is aware) the only country which has enshrined security of tenure and safeguards against termination of service for Government servants in the Constitution (Article 311). The statutory provision for this began in 1935 with section 240 of the Government of India Act, and was owing to the distrust of Indian politicians by the British Government. The writer's view is that this has been overdone, as almost every dismissed government servant now brings an action or a writ on 'reasonable opportunity' to defend himself and pursues it through appellate Courts upto the Supreme Court, often leading to reinstatement with back pay on technical grounds. In many countries some provision for security of tenure is felt to be essential but perhaps no one will go so far as India.

PROPERTY: Article 19 gives the right to acquire, hold and dispose of property, and Article 31(1) provides that no person shall be deprived of his property save by authority of law. Article 31(2) provided that property could be acquired only for a public purpose and on compensation. It is in this Article that two developments have taken place which constitutionalists may well question. Firstly the various zamindari abolition Acts came under fire in the courts. If zamindars were owners, the compensation was inadequate; if they were rent-farmers, it was more than adequate considering the excess income they had enjoyed for one and a half centuries. In this context the First Amendment introduced Articles 31–A and 31–B, placing these enactments beyond the protection of the fundamental rights guaranteed by the Constitution and review by the courts. The inspiration for this device was De Valera's Public Safety Measure.

Secondly, there was a decision by the Supreme Court in 1954 S.C.R. 674 relating to Government taking over management of a textile mill. An attack on it had failed in 1950 S.C.R. 869 on the ground that a shareholder could not complain. When does the right to enjoy property (Article 19) end and the right to take it under Article 31 begin? The Australian decision in *Dalziel* 68 C.L.R. 26 was pressed into use and though it was management only which was taken over, it was held to be void as offending Article 31. This was the precursor to the Fourth Amendment which altered clause 2 and introduced clause 2–A. Under these clauses, if title or right to possession is not transferred to the State it is not to be regarded as acquisition or requisition. As to acquisition or requisition the law must fix compensation or specify the principles for determining it but 'no such law shall be called in question in any Court on the ground that the compensation provided by that law is not adequate'. No such law however shall have effect unless the President has assented to it. The net result of this is that the compensation has to be approved by the Government of India, on whose advice the President acts in giving his assent. On zamindari abolition over Rs. 500 crores was fixed as compensation, payable sometimes in cash but largely in negotiable bonds payable over 30 to 40 years.

Whatever the justification for this provision in the present stage of Indian development, as a legal provision it is not in line with concepts of rule of law. It is true there are democracies where Parliament is supreme and legislation cannot be questioned in the courts. But the Indian Constitution is of a different type. It can be said that the President will secure provision for fair compensation. Still, to provide that there shall be compensation but that it is not justiciable perhaps involves a contradiction in terms of the legal order in which the provision appears.

BUSINESS RESTRICTIONS : Under this head we may examine the criteria which the Indian Courts apply in determining whether any enactment is valid or void, and compare the American method, which seems to depend on the current social philosophy of the judge. The United States Supreme Court has really applied its views as to whether the legislature ought to make a law for the purpose. It invented the doctrine of 'business affected with a public interest' which the legislatures could regulate, and common occupations which they could not. The change of attitude came with *Nebbia* vs. *New York* (1934) till it was openly confessed in *Lincoln Federal Labour Union* vs. *North Western Iron & Metal Co.* (1949) 335 U.S. 525. The Court began by saying "The Allgeyer-Lochner Adair-Coppage Constitutional Doctrine was for some years followed by this Court". The cases referred to were decisions of 1897, 1905, 1907 and 1914 striking down labour legislation; and the doctrine was also used to strike down laws fixing minimum wages, laws fixing prices and laws regulating business activities. The Court then said,

"This Court beginning at least as early as 1934, when the *Nebbia* case was decided, has steadily rejected the due process philosophy enunciated in the Adair-Coppage line of cases. In doing so it has consciously returned closer and closer to the earlier constitutional principle that states have power to legislate against what are found to be injurious practices in their internal commercial and business affairs, so long as their laws do not run afoul of some specific federal constitutional prohibition, or of some valid federal law. See *Nebbia* vs. *New York* and *West Coast Hotel Co.* vs. *Parrish*, and cases cited. Under this constitutional doctrine the due process clause is no longer to be so broadly construed that the Congress and State legislatures are put in a strait jacket when they attempt to suppress business and industrial conditions which they regard as offensive to the public welfare."

The approach of the Supreme Court of India has been entirely different. The question asked is: Is there a valid law (one within legislative competence under the legislative lists) and what is the object of the law? The restrictions imposed by the law conflict with fundamental rights. If the restrictions are reasonably connected with the object, then they are 'reasonable restrictions', and the law is valid. Let us take a few examples:

(1) A law was enacted in 1948 in the Central Provinces (Madhya Pradesh) under which a District Officer could make an order prohibiting manufacture of bidis during the agricultural season. After the Constitution came into operation, this was questioned by direct petition in the Supreme Court to enforce fundamental rights (Article 32). The challenge was of actual orders of 1950 forbidding all persons residing in named villages from engaging in making bidis. Article 19(1) (g) gives the right to a citizen to carry on any trade, occupation or business; under clause (6) the State may impose reasonable restrictions in the public interest. In its decision, *Chintaman Rao* vs. *State of Madhya Pradesh* 1950 S.C.R. 759, the Court first says: "The object of the statute is to provide measures for the supply of adequate labour for agricultural purposes in bidi manufacturing areas in the State". It proceeds to say that this could be done by prohibiting the employment of agricultural labour for bidi making during the agricultural season. But the total prohibition is bad, for "the effect of the provisions of the Act, however, has no reasonable relation to the object in view but is so drastic in scope that it goes much in excess of that object". Again, "such a prohibition on the face of it is of an arbitrary nature inasmuch as it has no relation whatever to the object which the legislation seeks to achieve and as such cannot be said to be a reasonable restriction on the exercise of the right". The Act was declared wholly void.

(2) Under the Essential Supplies (Temporary Powers) Act, 1946 an order was made, the Cotton Textiles (Control of Movement) Order, providing that no person could transport cloth yarn or apparel except under general permit notified by the Textile Commissioner or a special permit granted by him. In *Harishankar Bagla* vs. *State of Madhya Pradesh*, 1955–1 S.C.R. 380 the Supreme Court overruled the objections to this order. First, it held that the object of the Act is to ensure the supply of essential commodities to the public and if transport was left uncontrolled, supply to the public

would be seriously hampered. In this context the requirement of a licence is a reasonable restriction. Secondly, the policy of the order was to regulate the transport of cotton textiles so as to ensure an even distribution of the commodity throughout the country and make it available at fair prices to all. Hence the Commissioner had to exercise his discretion in granting or refusing permits in such a way as to effectuate this policy. So the delegation was valid.

(3) The Minimum Wages Act 1948 empowering the State Governments to fix minimum wages in specified occupations was questioned in the Supreme Court by a petition under Article 32. The Court upheld the law in *Bijay Cotton Mills Ltd.* vs. *State of Ajmer* 1955–1 S.C.R. 752. The Court says: "it can scarcely be disputed that securing of living wages to labourers which ensure not only bare physical subsistence but also the maintenance of health and decency is conducive to the general interest of the public. This is one of the directive principles of state policy embodied in Article 43 of the Constitution. If the labourers are to be secured in the enjoyment of minimum wages and they are to be protected against exploitation by their employers, it is absolutely necessary that restraints should be imposed upon their freedom of contract and such restrictions cannot in any sense be said to be unreasonable."

(4) Marketing legislation is of special importance in India. For example, the wholesale marketing of coffee has been placed in the hands of a Marketing Board. In view of the nature of this Board, we reviewed the Australian cases. But the major development has taken the form of regulated markets where the agriculturist could take his produce and obtain the best price, eliminating middlemen. The Commercial Crops Markets Acts of Bombay and Madras States have been upheld by the Supreme Court in *Arunachala* vs. *State* (1959 SCJ 297).

(5) In a Madras Judgment (*Guruviah*, I.L.R. 1958 Madras 35) it has been held that a statute itself may create a 'public interest' in its enforcement.

One may conclude that on the question of restrictions on the right to carry on business, the Courts are prepared to hold any restriction reasonable which is calculated to effectuate any of the objectives of legislation laid down in the chapter on Directive Principles of State Policy. The 'justice, social, economic and political' of the Preamble may be achieved by legislation by democratic legislatures. We can take heart from the words of S. R. Das J. (as he then was—later Chief Justice of India) in *West Bengal* v. *Subodh* 1954 S.C.R. 558 at 655:

"It is futile to cling to our notions of absolute sanctity of individual liberty or private property and to wishfully think that our Constitution-makers have enshrined in our Constitution the notions of individual liberty and private property that prevailed in the 16th century when Hugo Grotius flourished or in the 18th century when Blackstone wrote his Commentaries and when the Federal Constitution of the United States of America was framed. We must reconcile ourselves to the plain truth that emphasis has now unmistakably shifted from the individual to the community. We cannot overlook that the avowed purpose of our Constitution is to set up a welfare State by subordinating the social interest in individual liberty or property to the larger social interest in the rights of the community. As already observed, the police power of the State is "the most essential of powers, at times most insistent, and always one of the least limitable powers of the Government". Social interests are ever expanding and are too numerous to enumerate or even to anticipate and, therefore it is not possible to circumscribe the limits of social control to be exercised by the State or adopt a construction which will confine it within the narrow limits of Article 31(5)(*b*)(*ii*). It must be left to the State to decide when and how and to what extent it should exercise this social control. Our Constitution has not thought fit to leave the responsibility of depriving a person of his property, whether it be in the exercise of the power of eminent domain or of the police power, to the will or caprice of the executive but has left it to that of the legislature. In the matter of deprivation of property otherwise than by the taking of possession or by the acquisition if within the meaning of Article 31(2) our Constitution has trusted our legislature and has not thought fit to impose any limitation on the legislature's exercise of the State's police power over private property. Our protection against legislative tyranny, if any, lies, in ultimate analysis, in a free and intelligent public opinion which must eventually assert itself".

RELIGIOUS FREEDOM: This is guaranteed by Articles 25 to 28 and the leading decisions thereon strike a reasonable mean between

freedom of religious practices and the duty of legislatures to control
the proper management and application of property and money
dedicated by the public for religious purposes.

MINORITIES: Article 29 and 30 are directed to conserve the
distinct language script and culture of minorities. This is perhaps a
sphere in which we shall fail, having regard to the recent linguistic
reorganisation of States in India. If education in State schools and
aided schools is in the regional language, how are the Telugu-
speaking or Gujerati-speaking children (and there are many such in
Madras) to get proper education in a Tamil State? In a country in
which Government service is the main avenue of employment, the
discussions have been largely centred on giving them some posts in
State services on terms of their learning the local language. It must
not be forgotten that Article 29 contemplates conservation of their
culture in the place where they are in a minority and not their
gradual absorption.

ELECTIONS: Elections to Parliament and to the State Legislatures are under the control of an Election Commission. Article 326
provides for adult suffrage. There were serious doubts whether adult
suffrage would work in a country of the size of India with low
literacy. The two general elections of 1952 and 1957 have been so
efficiently conducted that all criticism is at rest. The delimitation of
constituencies is done by an independent Commission, set up by an
Act of Parliament. The electoral rolls in 1952 contained 96 per cent
of the adult population and those in 1957 98·8 per cent. Actual
votes polled were 51·59 per cent in 1952 and 47·54 per cent in
1957 of those enrolled. The Representation of the People Act, 1951
follows largely the pattern of the English law. In 1952 when there
were elections in 3,316 constituencies, there were 338 election
petitions. In the 1957 elections an appeal was provided to the High
Court against decisions of tribunals. The number of constituencies
was 2,921, and there were 472 election petitions, of which 54 were
successful and 282 appeals were filed. The amended law provided
for the disposal of an election petition within six months and of
appeals within three months. The magnitude of the task may be
gauged from the fact that 220,500 polling stations were set up and
Rs. 60 million was spent in the five years 1952–57 to prepare and
revise electoral rolls. The conduct of elections on such a large scale
with such efficiency has excited admiration from all observers.

DELEGATION: Two other aspects of law and judicial adjudication should be mentioned briefly. One is the vexed question of delegation of legislative power. This was discussed at great length by the Supreme Court, each Judge delivering a separate judgment, in *In re* the Delhi Laws Act, 1951 S.C.R. 747, the report running into 379 pages. Australian decisions (e.g. *Victorian Stevedoring*, 1931-46 C.L.R. 73) were among those considered. A good summary of the decisions stated as propositions was given by Vivian Bose J. in *Rajnarain Singh* (1954 S.C.R. 290). Many of our Acts of everyday impact on citizens involve a high degree of delegation. The courts have upheld the validity of the laws themselves but held that the individual order issued thereunder could be tested in the courts. Thus the Essential Supplies Act is valid, but particular orders issued under its authority have been held void.

The second aspect is the scrutiny of the court by way of mandamus, certiorari and prohibition of orders of Governmental authorities and quasi-judicial proceedings. In Madras High Court alone the number of Writ Petitions is about 1,200 a year. The effect of this in inculcating in officials and authorities an attitude of acting according to law is a major development after 1950, in contrast with official absolutism of the past. This aspect of free resort to Courts in which the public has confidence cannot be overstressed. As Sankey L.J. (as he then was) said in another context,

> "It is not admissible to do a great right by doing a little wrong. The inequalities of life are not so dangerous in a State whose subjects know that in a Court of law at any rate they are sure to get justice, and it is not sufficient to do justice by obtaining a proper result by irregular or improper means." (1929–2 K.B. 1 @ 53.)

In the control of authorities we face a problem of jurisdiction. If an order of an authority in Madras is affirmed upset or altered by a higher authority in Delhi, is there merger? For example, if the import controller or customs collector makes an order forfeiting goods as contrary to the permit, the Madras High Court can review it on certiorari. If the party appeals to higher officials in Delhi, it is said the Madras order is merged in the Delhi order. If so, the Madras party must approach the Punjab High Court, a difficult matter.

Problems of inter-State freedom (Article 301) await solution, notwithstanding Nicholas's belief that "the draftsmen (of the Indian Constitution) would appear to have studied the decisions of the Australian Courts and of the Privy Council and to have sought to avoid Australian controversies while applying the section (section 92) to Indian conditions".[2]

To sum up, by examining Indian legislation, we get a picture of a nation which is trying to achieve a degree of industrialisation and improvement of economic conditions under a plan with specific targets. This is conceived as the minimum advance which will create the conditions for further advance. This process is sought to be achieved by expenditure on a scale hitherto undreamt of, heavy taxation, foreign aid and strict controls. From the point of view of the privileged classes (rentiers, businessmen, professional men with large incomes) it is a period of irksome restrictions. From the point of view of the masses, the improvement contemplated is small enough in material terms but perhaps large enough in terms of hope. Barbara Ward's summing up is accurate :

"However we have to remember that, one way or another, the nations of Asia are determined to achieve modernisation and the Russian model at least shows how it can be done, at whatever cost. If there is no alternative, then Asia will no doubt follow the Communists and try to bludgeon its way through. The hope for more liberal methods lies therefore in the success of the Indian attempt to transform their system by basically democratic means."[3]

The Prospect

If one has claimed that, notwithstanding adverse factors, we in India have a 'charted freedom', there are disquieting factors which could retard development. The success of the democratic experiment depends on the people being informed about and taking an intelligent interest in what we are working for.

(1) *Illiteracy* is the main problem. Article 45 enjoins that the State should endeavour to provide within ten years for free and compulsory education for all children till age 14. The progress in

[2] *The Australian Constitution*, 2nd ed., 283–284.
[3] *The Interplay of East and West*, 49.

this respect is not up to expectations both because of limited finance and more so because of dearth of trained teachers. In the primary stage (6–11 age group) 43 per cent were at school in 1950–51, 60 per cent in 1960–61 and the target for the third plan is 80 per cent. In the middle stage (11–14 age group) the figures are 12·9 per cent for 1950–51, 22·6 per cent for 1960–61 and the target for third plan is 30 per cent. The 1951 census showed a percentage literacy of 16·61 per cent (males 24·88 per cent and females 7.87 per cent). According to the pre-tests of the 1961 census literacy has risen to 40·7 per cent (males 51·7 per cent, females 28.8 per cent).

(2) *Caste.* The Preamble speaks of equality of status and opportunity and Article 46 specially refers to promotion of educational and economic interests of the weaker sections of the people, and in particular of the scheduled castes and the scheduled tribes. The State is to protect them from social injustice and all forms of exploitation. Article 17 provides that 'untouchability' is abolished and its practice in any form is forbidden. Article 340 provided the appointment by the President of a Commission to investigate the conditions of socially and educationally backward classes and to make recommendations. The Report of the Backward Classes Commission (1956) is in the writer's opinion a major blow to the growth of democracy in India. The caste system has been the bane of Indian politics and untouchability the final disgrace. The election law makes it a corrupt practice to make systematic appeals to vote or refrain from voting on grounds of caste, race, community or religion. But adult suffrage has by itself exaggerated the influence of caste, as political parties with an eye on success at the polls tend to choose candidates belonging to the predominant caste or sub-caste in the particular electorate. The Constitution exempts from the equality of Article 14 'any special provision for the advancement of any socially and educationally backward classes of citizens'. The result has been a race for each sub-caste among the Hindus to claim that it is a backward class. It has been estimated that in the list compiled by the Commission, scheduled castes and scheduled tribes number 7 crores; other backward castes form a list of 2,399 communities, out of which 913 alone account for a population of about 11·51 crores. Such a report points to the general backwardness of the whole country, but also by its lists creates privilege lobbies based on religious sub-castes.

(3) *Administrative problems and problems of public order* remain. The incidence of so-called 'corruption' is probably exaggerated. We get good service from the large body of Government officials considering the new types of work which they are entrusted with. Political complaints there are and there will be as ministers work 'in that fierce light which beats upon a throne and blackens every blot'. Breakdowns of law and order (dacoity in U.P., Bihar, Madhya Pradesh and Rajasthan) and student indiscipline on a large scale present special problems. Add to this the surviving demands by one State against another of territory on a linguistic basis.

(4) Perhaps *white-collar crime* does not call forth the social opprobrium which could help in measures to put it down. As a result of traditional social attitudes, men with large wealth, however amassed, still have too much prestige and influence.

All these problems (except caste) are discussed at various appropriate levels in a free atmosphere and in public. As is only natural, there are differences of opinion both as to the causes of the evils and the remedies. So far as the caste problem is concerned there are repeated general exhortations at high level, but many factors (in the writer's opinion) tend to accentuate it.

PROF. V. K. N. MENON : No person can hope to have an intimate knowledge of all Asian constitutions. Since the experience of one Asian country may have a bearing on others, I shall speak mainly of the problems of India as I see them.

In many Asian countries which have recently attained independence, there has been no evidence of a lessening of the values of democracy. In some European countries in difficulty, in Nazi Germany and Fascist Italy, democracy was wholly rejected. But this has not been the experience of many Asian countries. There may be 'basic democracy' or 'guided democracy'; but constitutions have not generally been suspended; and, even when they have, the ideals of constitutional democracy have not been forgotten.

India enjoyed certain advantages in adopting a democratic system. She underwent a long period of political training, in which a competent administration and army developed, and in which the concepts of parliamentary democracy became familiar. Education was widespread at the top levels. The ideals and conventions of democracy were cultivated in the Congress Party. The Gandhian renunciation of violence became part of its creed. In contrast with some other Asian countries, the political standing of the army was low.

The main danger is that throughout Asia there is a distrust of parties and parliaments. The aim of Asian countries should be to improve some of the political institutions of democracy: the electoral process, parties and legislatures. It is here that study is necessary. It is too often said that the fault is not in the working of the system, but in the individuals who work it. In my view there are some important faults in the working of the institutions, which could be remedied by careful study. We might look, for instance, at the United States' experience of the legal control of parties. Asian countries must have a second look at democratic institutions and undertake a revision of some of their assumptions about how these should operate.

PROF. G. SAWER: In the broadest sense, a constitution is any system under which a country is governed. In a narrow sense, it is a written document. But if we are looking for some test of 'constitutionalism', we might do so in terms of what is acceptable to the lawyer. That is, the best test of the existence of a constitutional system in a country might be: can you meaningfully ask a lawyer what the constitution is?

In this sense India, Malaya, Burma, and Ceylon are all 'constitutional' states; the first two federal, the third having some federal elements, and Ceylon closest to the United Kingdom pattern. On the other hand, Pakistan and Indonesia can best be thought of as still being in a 'revolutionary' or 'pre-constitutional' situation, in the sense that the shape of the constitution to come is still not settled. In Pakistan, the lawyers seem to have bowed themselves out. In Indonesia, President Soekarno has said there will be a return to the 1945 Constitution, but this amounts to a fresh declaration that a 'revolutionary' situation exists.

Inventiveness in constitution-making has not been spectacular at any stage in human history, and it cannot be expected that Asian constitutions would show anything fundamentally new, but they do show some inventiveness in detail. I am most attracted by some of the responses to the problem of federalism, from which Australia has something to learn. For example, there is the Indian Administrative Service, which mans important posts at both the federal and the State level and so helps to maintain uniformity of administrative standards. There is Malaya's decision to accept the principle that taxation must be centralised, but with guarantees built into the constitution that the States will get a fair share. There is also in Malaya the interesting device of the rotating Head of State, drawn from the old hereditary rulers of the different parts of the federation.

MR. P. J. SHROFF: Professor Spann mentioned the place of the President in the Indian Constitution. The Constituent Assembly made it clear that he would normally exercise the same powers as a British Monarch. All the same, he is clothed with certain powers not available to the British Crown.

He is elected by a special electoral college consisting of the members of both central and State Parliaments, so (although the central government has enormous powers) the President is constitutionally the Head of the entire Union. He is the formal head of the executive; and though he normally acts on the advice of his

Ministers, he can exercise certain functions in his own right. He takes an oath similar to that taken by the U.S. President, to "preserve, protect and defend the Constitution and the law" (Art. 60). If he honestly concludes that advice given him is subversive of the constitution, he would be justified (as Jennings argues the English Monarch would be in certain circumstances) in rejecting it. The constitution also enjoins him to safeguard the legitimate interests of the States, of the scheduled castes, and so on. Article 111 provides that he can return Bills other than Money Bills to the Houses for reconsideration; this suspensive veto can hardly be supposed to require advice, as his Ministers could have done the needful already in the Legislature if they had wanted to, before the bill got to the President.

In India there is not parliamentary sovereignty in the same sense as in England, as the constitution is supreme, and can only be amended by a special process, which sometimes involves the State Parliaments. It is unfortunately true that Parliament has amended some of the Fundamental Rights with as much ease and despatch as if they were tramway by-laws about smoking in the back seats. Our quasi-federal form of government in India also requires that the President shall hold the scales even between the Union and the States, especially when the two are controlled by different parties.

This position of the President is important in view of the power now exercised by Mr. Nehru. The Indian Prime Minister is like a great banyan tree under which we can all take shelter but under which nothing grows. Some people ask: who can succeed a man with such powers? The President has worked with extreme propriety. He has sent letters to the Prime Minister with views on certain subjects. Nehru, asked about them, declined to reveal their contents on grounds of public interest. The President will continue to be an important influence provided he remains an elder statesman like Rajendra Prasad.

PROF. W. H. MORRIS-JONES: A word on the role of the President. There is evidence that on some issues his letters to the Prime Minister have expressed strong views contrary to Nehru's. It may even be that he has spoken for men in the Cabinet who have found it difficult to argue openly against the P.M. Also, it seems clear that not all the President's public statements are first seen by Nehru:

the latter recently made this clear with reference to Prasad's Madras speech.

One of the leading influences on Centre-State relations in India is certainly the Planning Commission—in spite of its being unknown to the constitution. It is generally thought to enhance the power of the centre, for the states are expected to operate on the lines of the Plans. But it may not be so simple. For there is perhaps some truth in the view that the Commission is subject to pressures from the states governments on whom, after all, the Plans largely depend for implementation.

Professor Sawer spoke of the Indian Administrative Service. This has obviously been a great unifying force, but it is perhaps becoming less so with the switch to linguistic states. The idea is still there of an all-India service, with Bengalees in the Punjab cadre. But the growing importance of regional languages and the preferences of at least some strong States ministers may pull in the opposite direction.

Professor Spann asked if I had changed my views on one-party rule in India. When writing *Parliament in India*, I had been impressed by the extent to which one-party dominance was modified by the work of vigorous parliamentary committees, internal party pressures and press criticism. I admit that this is less evident in state politics than at the centre. More generally, I remain convinced of the blessing of strong government which Congress has given India and I think that the great social changes are made manageable by the continued coherence of this 'umbrella' party. At the same time, I have indicated in my paper here that the disadvantages are increasing.

PROF. MENON: The wording of the constitution on the position of the Indian President is obscure. But there is no doubt about the intention of the framers of the constitution, which was that the President's role should conform to that of the British monarch. It is true that Ambedkar used some rash words.

DR. J. IQBAL: I object to Prof. Sawer's assessment of Pakistan as a 'revolutionary' state. The Ayub Khan regime is not 'revolutionary' in the sense that it is in the position of a usurper of power, or plans to erase the past and to start with a programme based on some new and radical ideology. There was a feeling among the people that a strong man should take over. I would say that the regime aims at reviving the fundamental principles on which Pakistan was originally founded. Therefore, the regime is 'revivalistic' rather than 'revolutionary'. We had a bad experience of some politicians and worst side of democracy under a multi-party system. We had the divisive effect of East and West Pakistan being so far apart; the real unifying factor is religion. In non-contiguous countries the multi-party system is inadequate.

I also object to Prof. Sawer saying that the lawyers bowed themselves out. The courts continue and work roughly the same as, in many cases better than, before.

If parliamentary democracy is unsuitable and my country is likely to be overrun by the Communists, then I do not want parliamentary democracy but strong rule. How can Australians speak of such a situation which they have not even remotely experienced? This is the trouble with comparative study of constitutions—it tends to make one feel that his institutions are better than the other man's.

MR. J. A. C. MACKIE: On the position of Presidents, I doubt whether it was the intention of the 1950 Indonesian Constitution to give the President a very special role. The role of the President was not described very differently from that of the Queen of the Netherlands in the Dutch Constitution.

The minor constitutional role of judges in Indonesia is partly because (as Furnivall shows in his book) Dutch colonial rule tended to minimise litigiousness. It is important for us to ask whether the place of judges and lawyers is of primary importance, or whether it is rather their job to fit into and make verbally precise those governmental modes of operation which have become standardised.

MRS. R. BRISSENDEN: I have found much of our discussion today unrealistic. Is not the truth that many of these countries are governed by rootless elites, who simply know how to manipulate Western institutions? And that there is a great gap between government and people? That is what we should be talking about.

PROF. L. F. CRISP: What we hope especially to hear from our Asian guests is an account of the informal factors which are the real supports of constitutionalism in Asia today.

MR. V. K. T. CHARI: Some of the criticism of constitutional democracy as inappropriate to countries in a backward state is misleading. Take the case of adult suffrage. At the time the Indian Constitution was framed, there were differences of opinion about this. Of course it is true that many voters do not understand what they are doing. India was like a person starting a school, and having no buildings and no teachers and no money. But you still want to make a beginning, and hope that in time you will be able to get some of these other things, and that the people will come to understand more and more. So far the results have been encouraging. The mass of the people are aware of the constitution and of the goal of social and economic development.

In most countries it has been argued that law lags behind social change. In India, on the contrary, it is often true that law is in advance of social change. We are inclined to look at other countries and say: "That is a good law. Let us pass that." But it sometimes takes a long period for the law to have any real impact. An example would be the Hindu Divorce Bill. Cases are few, but the principle has been established.

PROF. Z. COWEN: I visited India early in 1959 for the meeting of the International Commission of Jurists at New Delhi. My experience there leads me to some reflections on attitudes *to* lawyers and on the attitudes *of* lawyers to various issues. At the opening session of the meeting Mr. Nehru made a speech which suggested not very obscurely some impatience with Indian lawyers and their attitudes to the problems with which government was faced. Then at the working session of the conference, it seemed to me that our Indian lawyer colleagues were among the strongest supporters of resolutions restrictive of the powers of government.

This has led me to reflect on the proper attitude of lawyers and courts to the problems of government, if I may so describe them, in a society faced with the problems of rapid development with which India is faced. It seems to me that it is the duty of courts to look with critical scrutiny at governmental actions which threaten to undermine the basic liberal values of society. At the same time I think that it is important to distinguish between measures of economic regulation and measures which threaten basic individual liberties, and the approach of the courts to them. There is relevance in the history of judicial interpretation by the Supreme Court of the United States over the last half century.

But there can be little doubt that courts in Asia have a very important role in safeguarding individual rights. In a world where pressures lead to guided democracy and to despotism they, the

courts, have an historic role in pointing to dangers and in safeguarding individuals from inquisitorial processes and from arbitrary governmental acts.

Lawyers also have to think out the tough problems of adaptation of the law to the conditions of the particular society. In developed Western societies the notion of bail, to take one example, is important and significant. It gives an accused his liberty pending trial. But it presupposes the possession or availability of property to furnish bail. In Western countries this makes sense, generally speaking, but in such a country as India it makes no sense at all for millions and millions of people. If the notion of bail in this sense is to be part of Indian law it may well mean that many many people have no prospect of liberty while awaiting trial. The point I make by example is this: in providing safeguards for individual liberty can we appropriately transfer traditional concepts of English law or do we have to think anew about the structure and character of the particular society? The answer to that question seems to me pretty obvious.

DR. D. C. CORBETT: I would like to ask the question: Are Indian lawyers and judges held in respect in their society? Do they enjoy public confidence? Is this prop of constitutionalism sound?

PROF. MENON: I think that Bar and Bench in India both still have prestige and a reputation for competence. But I have observed two tendencies which might prove dangerous to the independence and impartiality of judges. First, there has been a regrettable reduction in the income of judges as compared with formerly. Secondly, judges are frequently sent on diplomatic appointments or appointed to semi-judicial commissions of enquiry.

DR. MAUNG: In Burma judges have also often been used on special commissions, and this can sometimes lead to difficulties. In one case I remember, the judge reluctantly accepted a role which might have involved political complications. However, he delayed and was saved by a change in government.

At one time there were great delays in trials in Burma. There were only a small number of Burmese lawyers in the aftermath of the war. When they appeared in suits, they flitted from court to court seeking adjournments, sometimes on the ground that their mother was dead.

MR. I. NISH: Having been sued in a number of Indian courts in various capacities, I may perhaps be permitted to venture an opinion

on the quality of the courts, the Bench and the lawyers. Indian judges in the important courts seem to be of high quality; but in the lower courts such as industrial tribunals, they give the impression of being less competent and their awards are sometimes obscure though this may be due to the difficulty of writing the judgments in English.

Much the same applies to the legal profession. Indian barristers are in my experience as good as those anywhere in the world and a client can be sure of being well represented in the higher courts. At the lower level of the police courts, the standard leaves something to be desired. The position in India is certainly unlike that in Burma as described by Dr. Maung: there is a glut of lawyers, not a shortage, and more people try to get into the profession than it can absorb.

PROF. JULIUS STONE: How deep do the roots of the common law go in India? Obviously they do not go down to the villages. Then in what sense is Indian law and constitutional law as a part of it an emanation of Indian consciousness? It has been pointed out that the stability of a legal order often depends on much smaller groups than the whole people. It would be fruitful to study this relation of the common law to Indian society.

We should realise the 'limits of lawyering'. By putting constitution-making in the hands of lawyers, you put it into the hands of those whose skill in operation normally *pre-requires* a common consciousness of the community concerning the problems of social life.

I may perhaps also say something of the problems of legal education, which was one part of my concern on my recent mission to India for the Ford Foundation. The British legacy to India is seen by Indians today as of great value in many respects, but it has also left some heavy burdens: one of them touches this matter of 'lawyermanship' now under discussion. Historically, Indian law schools were designed to train law clerks rather than judges and legislators or 'legal statesmen', that India so vitally needs since independence. A complete overhaul of the law schools and of legal education should, therefore, have had the highest priority in national planning. But these things were not attended to, with the result that generations of legal leadership have been lost. Until this overhaul has taken place, there will be substance in Mr. Nehru's impatience with the alleged delays and resistances in social policy matters resulting from the activities of lawyers and judges. Yet part of the responsibility for this must be placed on Mr. Nehru's own studied neglect of these national problems, not to speak of his little concealed contempt and hostility towards lawyer-manship generally.

Ralph H. Retzlaff

THE PROBLEM OF COMMUNAL
MINORITIES IN THE DRAFTING
OF THE INDIAN CONSTITUTION

ONE OF the principal tasks of any constitution-making body is the need to secure consensus among its members on the nature of the polity to be established and then to articulate that consensus as precisely as possible in the constitutional document. In a relatively homogeneous society, this task is considerably less difficult than in societies where marked cleavages are to be found. An almost uniform characteristic of the newly emerging States in the former colonial areas of Asia has been the existence of substantial minority communities, based on religious, linguistic, ethnic and socio-economic considerations. The task confronting the constitution makers in these States has been to secure agreement on a constitutional arrangement which on the one hand gives a feeling of confidence to the members of the minorities that they will not be discriminated against by the majority, and that they will be allowed to retain and develop those characteristics which have set them apart from the majority; while still meeting the equally genuine fears of the majority community that continued acquiescence in what are seen as 'minority extremist demands' does not lead to the fragmentation of the nation and the generation of separatist demands. At the heart of the matter lies the question of how far the minority communities must be assimilated into the majority in order to insure their allegiance to the nation and the development of a sense of national consciousness devoid of extra-territorial loyalties or separatist notions.

Such a consensus cannot be brought about within the span of a year or two, during which a Constituent Assembly may sit. Rather, it must be the product of generations of education and interaction between the majority and minority communities, during which time a sense of mutual dependence, respect and trust are bred. At best, a

Constituent Assembly may embody in a constitutional document the institutions, forms and procedures which, under the particular circumstances, would be most conducive to its development.

In few of the newly emerging States was the question of the position of minorities more exacerbated than in India. Confronted with the prospect of a partition which would still leave substantial minorities within her borders, and an aroused majority community, segments of which were becoming increasingly intolerant of minority demands, the members of the Constituent Assembly of India were obliged to secure consensus where virtually all facets of past behaviour, history and tradition, which might have contributed toward such a condition, were in the process of being shattered on the rocks of partition.

I

India contains numerous minorities, which vary greatly in size as well as in the extent of their distribution throughout the subcontinent. The principal minority groups which were involved in the constitutional debates on safeguards for the communal minorities were the Muslims, the Scheduled Castes, the Sikhs, the Indian Christians, the Anglo-Indians, and the Parsees.[1] In the century preceding the transfer of power in 1947, the problem of constitutional safeguards for these minorities developed from a non-existent issue into one which brought about the partition of the subcontinent, and one of the greatest mass migrations in world history. The reasons underlying the origins of the problem are still a matter of controversy. To some it was entirely a British creation resulting

[1] The percentage of the total population, for both British India and the Indian States, represented by each of the communal minorities according to the Census of India, 1941, was as follows: Muslims, 24·3 per cent; Scheduled Castes, 12·5 per cent; Sikhs, 1·5 per cent; Indian Christians, 0·8 per cent; Anglo-Indians, 0·04 per cent; Parsees, 0·04 per cent. The majority Hindu community comprised 53·0 per cent of the population. The Tribals, the other significant minority group, not discussed in this paper, comprised 6·5 per cent of the population. It should be noted that there had been a long-standing controversy as to whether the Scheduled Castes should be considered as a separate minority, or as a depressed segment of the total Hindu community. While this disagreement continued, it did not alter the fact that the Scheduled Castes were treated as a distinct entity and that certain safeguards specifically applicable to them were ultimately adopted.

from the introduction of separate communal electorates; to others it was largely the result of a fundamental antagonism between the Hindu and Muslim cultures. One of its principal manifestations was the Muslim demand for Pakistan. Among its major components were fear and insecurity, intensified by economic and political considerations. In the decades preceding the transfer of power, the British held the minorities problem to be the principal stumbling block to a constitutional settlement in India. To the Muslim League it was the *raison d'etre*. To the Indian National Congress it was an insincere issue put forward by anti-national elements.[2] The last decade before partition witnessed a growing inability on the part of each of the three parties to the controversy to communicate effectively with the other two. This was due, in no small measure, to the inability of each to perceive that the considerations put forward by the other parties were, from their own standpoint, genuine, though certainly hedged in by bargaining considerations. The ill-fated Gandhi-Jinnah talks in 1944 are an excellent example of this.[3]

In the early part of the present century the debate on communal safeguards centered primarily around the method of selecting Indian representatives to the legislative bodies which were gradually being developed. In any system of representation based upon direct election, to the extent that political action was an expression of religious or ethnic group consciousness, the minorities were destined to remain in a subordinate position to the Hindu majority. As the Independence movement gained strength, Muslim spokesmen, in particular, voiced increasing concern over this situation. British attempts to secure communal accord resulted in the gradual introduction of a series of safeguards in the constitutional system, which included separate communal electorates, weightage (i.e., granting minorities seats in the legislatures in excess of the number they would merit on a direct population basis), reservation of posts in the

[2] For a discussion of the minorities problem and its origin *see*, B. R. Ambedkar, *Pakistan or Partition of India*, 2nd ed., Bombay: Thacker and Co., 1945; K. B. Krishna, *The Problem of Minorities in India or Communal Representation in India*, London: George Allen and Unwin Ltd. 1939; Asoka Mehta and Achyut Patwardhan, *The Communal Triangle in India*, 2nd ed., rev., Allahabad: Kitabistan, 1942; and Dhirendranath Sen, *The Problem of Minorities*, Calcutta: Univ. of Calcutta, 1940.

[3] See Pyarelal, *Mahatma Gandhi, The Last Phase*, Vol. I, Ahmedabad: Navajivan Publishing House, 1956, 87–100, for an interesting insight into Gandhi's response to Jinnah during these talks.

public services for the minorities, and the convention of assuring minority representation in the cabinets formed in the Provinces.[4]

While spokesmen for all the minority groups participated in the numerous conferences held by the British to try to solve the minorities problem, the main disputants were the Muslim League which claimed to be the sole spokesman for the Muslims of India, and the Indian National Congress, which claimed to be the sole spokesman for the nationalist movement representing Indians of all creeds and communities. As the possibility of British withdrawal from India grew, the differences of approach between the Congress and the League became more pronounced and uncompromising.

During the last decade before Independence the settlement of the communal minorities problem was inextricably linked to the proposals for the creation of a constitution-making body, which in turn depended upon a verdict on the Muslim League's demand for Pakistan. After prolonged discussions with representatives of all parties and groups, the British Government's Cabinet Mission, which came to India in the Spring of 1946, issued a statement known as the Statement of May 16th, containing its recommendations on three matters—the demand for partition, the basic form of the future constitution, and the machinery for constitution making. The Statement rejected the partition demand. Its proposals were based upon a united India, with a weak centre, a considerable degree of provincial autonomy, and the inclusion of safeguards for the minorities. The specific nature of these safeguards was to be a matter for the Constituent Assembly to decide. In accordance with the terms of this Statement elections to the Constituent Assembly were held in the Summer of 1946, and the Assembly was finally convened on December 9, 1946.[5]

The problem of the demand for safeguards for communal minorities was not finally resolved by the Constituent Assembly until it had virtually completed the drafting of the entire constitution in November 1949. In attempting to secure the consent of the minorities, while still satisfying the majority, the Congress Party was confronted with a dilemma. It was clear that if detailed safeguards

    [4] The most detailed discussion of these safeguards is contained in Ambedkar, *op. cit.*, *passim*.
    [5] The best discussion of the events leading up to the convening of the Constituent Assembly of India is in V. P. Menon, *The Transfer of Power in India*, Calcutta: Orient Longmans Ltd., 1957.

were included in the Constitution, to secure the agreement of the minorities, they would also serve to perpetuate the separate consciousness of the minorities and work against the basic desire of the Congress to strengthen Indian national unity. Yet a complete refusal to grant these demands would have left the Congress open to the charge of having disregarded minority rights and interests, and thereby justify the charges of the Muslim League. As Sir Ivor Jennings has commented:

> To compromise with communal claims may be the height of statesmanship because it enables the majority to secure the support of the minorities. To recognize communal claims, on the other hand, is to strengthen communalism.[6]

II

The initial phase through which the communal minorities problem passed may be said to have lasted for the seven months immediately following the convening of the Constituent Assembly. The first important step taken by the Assembly in this connection was the formation of the Advisory Committee on the rights of citizens, minorities, and tribal and excluded areas. Under the terms of the Cabinet Mission Statement of May 16, the Advisory Committee was to be the principal instrument for securing the just consideration of the minorities problem. The Congress Party took considerable care in forming the Committee, to ensure that its entire strength was fixed in accordance with the wishes of the minorities,[7] so that no charges of unfairness or discrimination could be levelled against it.

The Advisory Committee, under the Chairmanship of Sardar Patel, met and divided itself into four sub-committees; one on fundamental rights, a second on minority rights, and the remaining two on the tribal and excluded areas.[8] The two sub-committees, one

[6] Sir Ivor Jennings, *Some Characteristics of the Indian Constitution*, London: Oxford University Press, 1953, 64.

[7] Speech of Pandit G. B. Pant, Constituent Assembly Debates, II, 4, 331. *See* also *Hindustan Times*, January 23, 1947, 4, which indicates that the members of the Advisory Committee were chosen at a meeting of the Congress Party on January 22.

[8] The problem of Constitutional safeguards relating to tribal and excluded areas was dealt with separately from that relating to the communal minorities, and will not be discussed in this paper.

on Fundamental Rights, the other on Minority Rights, typified the approaches to the minorities problem held by the Congress and the minorities respectively. Ever since the adoption of a resolution on fundamental rights at its Karachi Session in 1931, the Congress had held that the sole method of solving the minorities problem, which would be compatible with the demands of nationalism, was to include in the Constitution a detailed list of fundamental rights applicable to all citizens, majority and minority alike. These would protect all citizens against discrimination, regardless of the communal affiliation. The minorities for their part regarded this as insufficient, and demanded additional constitutional safeguards, as well as other special arrangements in such things as employment in the public services.

It was in the deliberations of these two sub-committees, as well as in those of the main Advisory Committee, that the settlement of the minorities problem was gradually arrived at. During this phase of the Assembly's operation the Fundamental Rights sub-committee met and drafted a report which came before the Assembly in its third session, from 28 April to 2nd May, 1947. The Assembly, after consideration and debate, approved virtually all of the articles recommended by the sub-committee in its report, and these, with some later minor modification, constitute the fundamental rights embodied in Part III of the Constitution of India. The articles adopted stipulated that untouchability was to be abolished; discrimination in access to public places on the basis of religion, race, caste or sex was to be prohibited; and in virtually all matters to which the authority of the State extended in regard to the activities of its citizens, the minorities were guaranteed that, constitutionally, they would stand on a par with the majority community. Thus, at the very outset of the Assembly's deliberations, the approach of the Congress to the minorities problem had been implemented. It soon became evident, however, that the principal minority communities still had not budged from their demands for special constitutional safeguards, which implied a recognition of the existence of communal minorities *per se* in the Constitution.

III

A fundamental shift in the political situation began during this period. The Muslim League, which until this time had refused to allow its members to enter the Constituent Assembly, adopted a resolution on January 31, 1947, contending that the actions taken by the Constituent Assembly up to that time were *ultra vires* and demanding that the Assembly be dissolved forthwith. This shattered completely the hopes that the League might reconsider its previous decisions and allow its members to participate in the constitution-making process. On February 29, 1947, His Majesty's Government issued a statement declaring that power should be transferred to Indian hands no later than June 1948. The wording indicated that power might be transferred to more than one successor government, thus acknowledging the possibility of partition.

The statement had a catalytic effect. The Muslim League began an agitation in the Punjab, seeking to bring about the downfall of the non-League government in that pivotal province, and communal rioting broke out in several parts of India, particularly in the Punjab. As a result, the Hindus of Bengal and the Hindus and Sikhs of the Punjab began to demand the partition of their provinces in the event that the partition of India was granted. Much of this took place during the Assembly's third session, when it had before it the report on fundamental rights, mentioned above.

By the beginning of the Assembly's fourth session on July 14, the entire character of the Indian political scene had been altered. The Statement of June 3rd, providing for the partition of India into two separate sovereign nations of India and Pakistan, had been issued by His Majesty's Government. The representatives of the Muslim League, from the provinces which remained in India after partition, entered the Assembly and began to participate in the deliberations of its committees, in particular the Advisory Committee and the Minority Rights Sub-committee. Psychologically, as well as strategically, the situation had been materially altered. Whereas earlier the Congress had been forced to tread extremely lightly for fear of taking an action which the Muslim League might be able to seize upon as a 'pretext' for refusing to join the Constituent Assembly, thus strengthening its argument for partition, now the die had been cast. India was to be divided, and there was no further need to be extremely cautious in order to conciliate the League.[9] The pressure

---

[9] An indication of how this shift in conditions affected other aspects of the constitutional deliberations may be seen in a comparison of the first and second reports of the Union Powers Committee, dated April 17, 1947 and July 5, 1947

on the Congress leadership for an alteration in its minority policies began to mount, as those who argued for a change could point toward the partition as an indication of the failure of the previous policy of conciliation and compromise. The Muslim League leaders who entered the Assembly at this time refused to adopt a penitent attitude, but rather continued to press for the same constitutional safeguards which the League had sought in undivided India. Intransigence bred suspicion and distrust.

As the assembly reconvened in its fourth session it had before it the reports of the Union and Provincial Constitution Committees. The minorities problem arose during the debates on these reports, in connection with the use of the system of proportional representation. It is interesting to note that the first suggestions placed before the Assembly for the adoption of proportional representation came not from the Muslim League or any of the other minority representatives, but from the Congress, and, in fact, this move was opposed by several of the Muslim League representatives.[10]

In none of the instances in which the Congress suggested it be employed was proportional representation to involve the general electorate. In three of the four instances it was to be used in the election of a single individual, a point which was sharply criticised by the Muslim League representatives. In electing a single officer, in the event voting took place along communal lines and several candidates divided the vote of the majority community, it might be possible that a minority community candidate could be elected by a plurality. Using the system of proportional representation with the single transferable ballot, it could be assured that the successful

respectively, in Constituent Assembly of India, *Reports of Committees, First Series*, Delhi: Manager of Publications, Government of India, 1948, 1–5; 70–80.

[10] The Report of the Provincial Constitution Committees called for the use of proportional representation in two instances—first, when and if the Provincial Legislature was called upon to fill a casual vacancy in the office of the Governor; second, when a provincial legislature was to have an upper house, one-third of the membership of that house was to be elected by the lower house by proportional representation. The report of the Union Constitution Committee called for the use of proportional representation in the election of the President and Vice-President of the Union. The method of selection of both houses of Parliament, as well as of the lower house in the Provincial Legislatures, was left unspecified at this stage.

candidate would have to receive the support of at least a part of the majority community.[11]

Equally interesting was the manner in which the Muslim League representatives sought to introduce proportional representation. They proposed that it be used in the selection of the Council of Ministers in the Union Parliament and in the Provincial Legislatures, a move aimed at securing minority group representation without a dependence upon the majority party. This was bitterly opposed by Sardar Patel, who contended that:

> Election by proportional representation of ministers is a system which is contrary to the whole framework of this constitution. It cuts at the very root of democracy and therefore does not fit in here.[12]

A case where the issue of proportional representation might have been expected to arise was in the composition of the lower houses of the Legislatures in the Provinces and the Union Parliament; however, all recommendations (and therefore debate) on these matters were withheld pending the receipt of the recommendations of the Minority Rights sub-committee. It seemed clear, from the indications in the debates, that the representatives of the Muslim League were still united in support of separate electorates as a means of electing representatives to the Legislatures, and that they did not place too much reliance on the possible effect of the Instrument of Instructions to be included in the constitution, which would direct the Provincial Governors to take steps to include minority representation in the Provincial Cabinets.

Further action on these matters depended upon the recommendations of the Minority Rights sub-committee on the subject of political safeguards. The problem addressed by the sub-committee covered the following points:

(i) representation in legislatures; joint *versus* separate electorates and weightage;

---

[11] This point was made unmistakably clear by Dr. K. M. Munshi, C.A.D. IV, 3, 611–12. Munshi was a leading spokesman for the Congress Party and later became a member of the Drafting Committee of the Constituent Assembly.

[12] C.A.D., IV, 4, 646.

(*ii*) reservation of seats for minorities in Cabinets;
(*iii*) reservation for minorities in the Public Services;
(*iv*) administrative machinery to ensure protection of minority rights.

When its report came before the Assembly it contained the following recommendations:

(1) Separate electorates and weightage should be rejected. The Assembly should adopt joint electorates with seats reserved for the minorities on a population basis.
(2) The demand that seats be reserved for the minorities in the Cabinets should be rejected.
(3) The demand for reservation of posts for the minorities in the public services on a population basis should be accepted.
(4) Special officers should be appointed to safeguard the interests of the minorities and report on infringements of their rights.

In addition, in a supplementary report the Advisory Committee recommended extending certain special safeguards to the Anglo-Indian community in connection with the educational system and the position of Anglo-Indians in certain public services. The recommendations contained in the report of the Minority Rights sub-committee represent the high watermark in Congress concessions to the minorities, and it is significant to note that these were made several months after the partition, when the need for conciliating the minorities, particularly the Muslims, had greatly diminished.

It is important to note that they were made to meet the almost universal demand for them by the minority representatives in the sub-committee. Only the Indian Christians and the Parsees, two of the smallest and, comparatively speaking, more advanced minorities, had not sought special consideration. The three most important minority communities, the Muslims, the Scheduled Castes and the Sikhs, had refused to yield on their demands. The Congress, while rejecting separate electorates, weightage and reservation of seats in the Cabinets, had nonetheless made significant concessions by offering to all minorities reserved seats in the legislatures and posts in the public services on a population basis. Both of these represented very considerable movements from the Congress's previous position of supporting only the adoption of a list of fundamental rights applicable to all citizens. The outstretched hand of the Congress leadership was not, however, readily accepted by the minorities and, in particular, by the Muslim League leaders.

During the debate on the minority rights report, while it was clear that there was a substantial consensus on the concessions made by the Congress with respect to the public services and the appointment of special officers to safeguard the interests of minorities, it was equally apparent that consensus was lacking on the nature of the electoral system.[13] The Muslim representatives in particular were still unwilling to yield on their demand for separate electorates. The Congress, which had agreed to the principle of reservation, bitterly opposed the demand for separate electorates, and its spokesman reiterated the Party's view that separate electorates had been a major factor in the creation of Pakistan. Sardar Patel in particular requested the representatives of the Muslim League to withdraw their demand for separate electorates, but the League persisted, and a noticeable stiffening of attitude on the part of the Congress towards the League representatives took place from that time forward.

It was necessary for the Congress leadership to win the confidence of the minorities by submitting to some of their demands, but as an editorial in the *Eastern Economist*, written in mid-August 1947, pointed out:

There are appreciable sections of Hindus in the Indian Union, sections which are progressively becoming more extensive and voluble, which have genuine fears that the present national leadership may not prove to be the proper guardians of the just rights and status of the premier community in the new state. The spectre of continuing appeasement of intransigent minorities haunts them and they are unable therefore to pledge whole hearted support to the policies of the new state.[14]

Pressure for the withdrawal of the political safeguards, motivated by a variety of reasons, continued to mount and finally brought about a considerable change in the status of the minorities. But it is

[13] See speech of Sardar Patel, C.A.D., V, 8, 198.
[14] *Eastern Economist*, August 15, 1947, 245.

important to note that (1) had the initial timetable which called for the completion of the drafting of the Constitution by the Fall of 1947 been adhered to; and (2) had the minorities, especially the Muslims, adopted a conciliatory attitude, it is clear that the Constitution would have included specific political safeguards for the minorities.

IV

The Assembly adjourned and did not sit again in its constitution-making capacity until November 1948. From the Fall of 1947 until February 1948 the Drafting Committee of the Constituent Assembly worked on the preparation of a draft constitution, and from February until November the draft was circulated for public comment and consideration. During this time the various forces which went into the making of the minorities problem—social, psychological and political—underwent substantial changes.

As an immediate consequence of the violence of partition the position of Hindu communal groups in India tended to be strengthened considerably; however, the assassination of Gandhi on January 30, 1948 by a right-wing Hindu fanatic created a feeling of revulsion toward all aspects of communal agitation; either of the majority or the minority. As a result, when the Constituent Assembly convened in its legislative capacity in April 1948, the Prime Minister, Pandit Nehru, supported the adoption of a resolution declaring that no communal organisation be permitted to engage in any activities other than those essential for the *bona fide* religious, cultural, social and educational needs of the community, and recommended legislative and administrative steps to prevent such activities. In the course of the debate on the resolution, Nehru noted that in the draft constitution, which was then being circulated, there were 'certain definite communal elements'. He added, "What the final decision will be about that I cannot say. I hope personally that the less reservation there is the better."[15] Nehru's statement typified the growing mood of all sections of Congressmen against the inclusion in the Constitution of political safeguards for the communal minorities, which they held would only serve to perpetuate, rather than resolve, communalism.

15 *Hindustan Times*, April 4, 1948, 4.

A second major change during this period was that taking place in the political party system. During February and March of 1948 the Muslim League leaders held repeated meetings, and the majority of them finally decided to disband the Muslim League within the Constituent Assembly, as well as within the majority of the Provinces. The League members from some Provinces, such as Madras, refused to go along with this decision. What resulted was the break-up not only of the Muslim League as a political party, but further, the fragmentation of the previously united Muslim group within the Constituent Assembly. As a result, from this point forward, when the debates on the issue of safeguards took place, the Muslims were no longer able to speak with one voice, and a considerable segment of them were gradually won over to the nationalist point of view.[16] In the same month the Akali Dal decided to disband the Sikh Panthic Party, both in the East Punjab Assembly and in the Constituent Assembly. Members of the Panthic Party were advised to sign the Congress pledge and to unconditionally join the Congress Party in the Central and Provincial Legislatures.[17] As a result, the Sikhs also split into several groups, one of which, led by Master Tara Singh, strongly supported maintaining the separate identity of the Sikh community for political purposes.

There appeared no notice in the press to the effect that the Scheduled Caste Federation, the principal non-Congress organisation claiming to represent the untouchables, had considered the possibility of its dissolution as a distinct political organisation. However, it should be noted that its President, Dr. B. R. Ambedkar, was Chairman of the Drafting Committee of the Constituent Assembly, and had raised no criticism of the handling of the minorities problem up to that time, or of the apparent changing mood within the Congress.

The three remaining communal minority groups—the Anglo-Indians, the Indian Christians and the Parsees—did not undergo any appreciable shift in attitude during this period. The Parsees had raised no demands whatever for safeguards, and the demands of the

---

[16] The events surrounding the break-up of the Muslim League in India are summarised in *The Indian and Pakistan Yearbook and Who's Who*, 1949, I. S. Jehu, ed., Bombay: Bennett, Coleman and Co., Ltd., 1950, 507–12.

[17] *Hindustan Times*, March 19, 1948, 1.

Indian Christians and the Anglo-Indians had both already been met
to their satisfaction.

The fragmentation of the political organisations of two of the
main minority groups, the Muslim League and the Sikh Panthic
Party, was of major importance in enabling the Assembly to move
forward in its attempts to solve the minorities problem. During the
period from February to November 1948, as the draft constitution
was debated in the various Provincial Legislatures, an increasing
number of spokesmen of the minority communities, particularly
those of the Muslim League, came forward to request that
reservation of seats be deleted from the Constitution.[18]

V

As the Constituent Assembly began its seventh session in November, 1948, considering the clauses of the draft constitution, the
debate on the minorities problem proceeded at two levels—one
within the Assembly itself, and the other within the Advisory
Committee.

The debate within the Constituent Assembly centred largely on
the method of selection of the executives and the legislatures in the
Union and the Provincial Governments. The main feature of this
debate was the continued attempt by some of the minority representatives, in particular those of the Muslim League, to secure the
adoption of proportional representation. The arguments put forward
and the general character of the debates were the same as those
which took place on similar provisions of the reports of the Union
and Provincial Constitution Committees, with the exception that at
this time the method of composing the lower house of the Union
and the Provincial Legislatures was also discussed. One marked
difference from the earlier debate was the effect of the break-up of
the Muslim League as an official party within the Assembly. The
Muslim members supporting proportional representation were even
unable to agree among themselves as to which of the many systems

[18] See, for example, the speech of Janab Abdul Hasen, West Bengal Legislative Assembly, *Extracts from the Assembly Proceedings, official report ... Debate
on the Draft Constitution. Part I: General Discussion on the Draft Constitution
... Part II: Motions on the Draft Constitution*, Alipore: Supt., Govt. Printing,
1948, 174.

should be used in selecting the lower house of the Union Legislature. At this time some of the Sikhs joined the Muslims in demanding proportional representation. Sardar Hukam Singh, a Sikh representative, pointed out that it was evident that separate electorates would never be adopted, and that it seemed increasingly apparent that the system of reservation of seats was considered objectionable. In these circumstances he stressed that it was only through the adoption of proportional representation that the rights of the minorities could be safeguarded.[19] As with the Muslims, the Sikhs were also split. Thus Giani Gurmukh Singh Musafir opposed the continuation of the reservation of seats, contending that they would be of no benefit to the Sikhs.

The Congress vigorously opposed the adoption of proportional representation, both as a means of selecting the executives as well as the legislatures. It was evident that the Congress believed that proportional representation would have served only to perpetuate the separate existence of communal political parties, and would have had much the same effect as separate communal electorates.

While the debate on the floor of the Assembly, during the Fall of 1948 and the Spring of 1949, demonstrated the differing points of view and attitudes on the communal problem, steps to arrive at a solution were being taken in the Advisory Committee and its sub-committees. These concerned two matters. First was the special problem created by the award of the Boundary Commission regarding the partition of the Provinces of Punjab and Bengal and the effects of the population migration after partition. Decisions in this respect affected the safeguards to be awarded to the Sikh community. Second, and much broader in its implications, was the question of revising the decision adopting reservation of seats in the legislatures taken by the Assembly when it had considered the report of the Minority Rights sub-committee.

Dissatisfaction within the Sikh community had been limited largely to the group supporting Master Tara Singh; however, when a special sub-committee[20] recommended that no additional safeguards

---

[19] C.A.D., VII, 32, 1250.

[20] The special sub-committee consisted of Sardar Patel, Chairman, Pandit Nehru, Rajendra Prasad, B. R. Ambedkar and K. M. Munshi. *See:* Government of India, Parliament Secretariat, *Reports of Committees of the Constituent Assembly of India* (Third Series), Delhi: Manager of Publications, 1950, 243–5.

be given to the Sikhs beyond those given to other communities, many other Sikhs joined in criticism of the Advisory Committee. Since at that time a move was developing to eliminate reservation of seats entirely, those Sikhs who had not adopted the nationalist view, but had nevertheless remained relatively quiet, became increasingly vocal and critical of the Congress.

The meeting of the Advisory Committee on December 30, 1948, represented the beginning of a concerted effort to secure the consent of the minorities to the abolition of the principle of reservation of seats in the legislatures. It took the form of placing before the Committee a series of resolutions for this purpose. The principal resolution was put forward by Dr. H. C. Mookerjee, Vice-President of the Constituent Assembly and leader of the Indian Christian community. Dr. Mookerjee's position was also supported by Mr. Tajamul Husain, a Muslim representative from Bihar. It was evident that there was considerable opposition on the part of sections of the various minority communities to the attempt to withdraw the principle of reservation of seats.

In commenting on the specific motions given notice of by Mookerjee and Husain, seeking to do away with reservation of seats, Sardar Patel suggested that the movers confine their proposals to their own communities, as in the absence of a general agreement it would not be proper to force a minority to give up its right of separate representation. He suggested that if the Muslims by general agreement among themselves felt that they did not want any reservation, their view should be accepted; but the proposal should come from them and not from a member of any other community. He concluded that unless there was general agreement the conclusion already arrived at should not be disturbed. It was suggested that the members of each minority community meet and decide what their position was with regard to reservation. The Committee then adjourned until May 1949.

During the intervening period attempts were made to convene meetings of the various minority communities represented in the Constituent Assembly, with a view to determining their position on the matter of safeguards, and, in particular, on the question of reservation. In the case of the Muslims and the Sikhs these attempts were unsuccessful. When the Advisory Committee met again on May 11, 1949, it had before it the resolutions of Dr. Mookerjee and

Tajamul Husain, and an amendment to Mookerjee's resolution by V. I. Muniswamy Pillai, seeking to exempt the Scheduled Castes from the effect of Mookerjee's resolution. The effect of the fragmentation within the Muslim and Sikh communities played a decisive role in enabling the committee to adopt the resolution calling for the abolition of reservation.

At this point the Committee took the following decisions: First, it adopted the resolution put forward by Dr. H. C. Mookerjee, calling for the abolition of reservation, as amended by Muniswamy Pillai's proposal exempting the Scheduled Castes. The Committee then considered the report of the special sub-committee concerning the position of the Sikhs in East Punjab. One of the Sikh representatives, Sardar Ujjal Singh, moved a resolution which was unanimously adopted by the Committee, accepting the recommendations of the special sub-committee as modified by Mookerjee's resolution, with the additional proviso that there be included in the list of Scheduled Castes in the Punjab four groups within the Sikh community. It was clear from the minutes of the Committee that most of the Sikhs had agreed to this arrangement. Having taken these decisions, the Advisory Committee was then dissolved and its report forwarded to the Assembly. The position of the various minority communities at this point was: (1) The Scheduled Castes had been granted reserved seats, as well as the right to vote in the elections for general seats. (2) The Indian Christians and the Parsees had neither demanded nor received special consideration. (3) The earlier decision of the sub-committee on minorities regarding special consideration for the Anglo-Indian community still stood. (4) In the two remaining communities, the Sikh and the Muslim, a portion of their representatives had been won over the nationalist point of view and supported the abolition of reservation, in the case of the Sikhs, in return for special concession in regard to Sikh Scheduled Caste recognition, while a substantial segment of each of these communities, typified by the Akalis within the Sikhs and the Madras group within the Muslim League, still demanded a wide range of special considerations and safeguards. But even within these two intransigent segments there was an evident inability to agree on a joint set of demands, and thus their ability to oppose any change was rendered ineffective.

VI

It will be remembered that in addition to the question of reservation of seats in the legislatures, the problem of political safeguards for minorities had encompassed three other factors: (1) reservation of posts in the services; (2) reservation of posts in the Cabinets; and (3) the creation of administrative machinery to insure the adequate supervision and protection of minority rights. Provisions concerning reservation of seats in the legislatures embodied in article 292 of the Draft Constitution had been amended by the Assembly in May 1949, in accordance with the recommendations of the Advisory Committee, as we have just noted. Provisions concerning the three other aspects of political safeguards still remained in the Draft Constitution and were applicable to members of all minority communities in accordance with the decisions taken in the Fall of 1947. Article 296 set forth the provisions concerning special consideration for appointment of the minorities in the public services; article 299 set forth the provision concerning the creation of a commission to safeguard minority rights; and Schedules 3(a) and 4 contained the Instruments of Instructions to the President and Provincial Governors respectively, concerning representation of minorities in the Cabinets. (This had been modelled on similar provision in the Act of 1935.) The Assembly, with virtually no debate, on October 11, 1949 voted to delete Schedules 3(a) and 4 from the Draft Constitution. Surprisingly there was no opposition from the minorities at this point.

However, heated opposition arose when several days later Dr. Ambedkar introduced an amendment to make the provisions of articles 296 and 299 applicable only to the Scheduled Castes. In particular, Sardar Hukam Singh, a representative of the Sikhs, made a most bitter speech charging the Congress with having gone back on its previous promise. In reply, Sardar Patel denied that the majority community had broken its promise to the minorities. He argued that the representatives of the Sikh community had given in writing an agreement to the Advisory Committee that subsequent to the agreement to include the four Scheduled Caste Sikh groups, "no other question hereinafter is to be raised".[21] He went on to maintain that the decision taken in the Advisory Committee regarding

[21] C.A.D., X, 7, 247.

reservation was clearly understood by all communities as an attempt to remove completely from the Constitution all semblances of communal reservation, and held that this obviously included the provisions contained in articles 296 and 299. A bitter debate followed, and it was clear that while many of the Sikhs concurred in the removal of all provisions pertaining to communal reservation, there still remained a group within the Sikh community which demanded the retention of safeguards.

The Assembly adopted Dr. Ambedkar's amendment to draft articles 296 and 299, restricting the effect of these two provisions to the Scheduled Castes. But the inability of the Constituent Assembly to carry with it substantial segments of the Sikh and Muslim representatives was clearly a set back to those whose hopes encompassed an agreement on the minorities problem which would foster a sense of national unity to the satisfaction of both the majority and minority communities.

VII

Ideally, in the decade which has passed since the adoption of the Constitution, considerable progress should have been made toward allaying the fears held by members of these two communities, both real and imaginary, that their status as distinct minorities would in some way be jeopardised by the actions of the majority. The years 1960 and 1961 have witnessed intensified agitation by segments of the Sikh community under Master Tara Singh for a separate Sikh communal State, as well as the more recent resurgence of Muslim communalism on the political level with the reorganisation of units of the Muslim League Party in Central and Northern India. The dilemma propounded by Ivor Jennings still remains. While special constitutional safeguards seem out of the question, some steps will have to be taken to allay the increasing feelings of discontent which certain political leaders within these communities have not hesitated to exploit for personal political purposes. The most effective solution to the problem, as noted at the outset, must be the product of generations of education and interaction between the majority and minority communities directed toward developing a sense of mutual dependence, respect and trust, and a complete acceptance of the constitutional settlement, which embodied the largest possible measure of consensus at the time of its adoption.

W. H. Morris-Jones

BEHAVIOUR AND IDEAS
IN POLITICAL INDIA*

I

The study of the politics of a society undergoing transformation is important, exciting and difficult. All three qualities are enhanced when the transformation is being effected not by an outside power (as in India under British rule or Tibet today) nor by a single coherent political force (as in China) but by a variety of internal pressures and pulls. The best introduction to an analysis of Indian politics can be an examination of the nature of the difficulty.

One very general way of putting the difficulty is by pointing out that the student of Indian political institutions soon forms the impression that the main thing he has to learn is that nothing is ever quite what it seems or what it presents itself as being. At first he may put this down to his own faulty vision, to his unavoidable tendency to try to fit new things into categories which he has brought with him. But later he realises that the matter is not so simple; there are different categories operative within the Indian context itself.

It is worth emphasising that this is—at the very least, in its degree—as unusual as it is baffling. The idiom in which political activity is conducted certainly varies from country to country. The Britisher who seeks to understand American politics knows that he must master a new idiom—one which is dictated by the size of the country, the peculiar character of the nation-building process which has taken place there, the separation of powers, and so on. But at least it is, by and large, just one idiom. The regional variations are related to the main theme. The conversation of American politics may be 'tapped' at any level and any place and the language will

* A related paper is to be published in *Politics and Society in India*, edited by C. H. Philips (Allen and Unwin).

remain the same. And I should think that the same is true of most countries whose study has figured in the development of political science. It is possible that in Communist countries the matter may be a little more complex. It could be that an idiom derived from Marxism gets mixed in with a primarily national idiom without quite forming a coherent new language. In that case it would be only what we should expect if different political languages are to be heard in such countries, changing according to the level being tapped or the audience being addressed. (By using the terms 'language' and 'idiom' I may be misunderstood as referring merely to the way in which men talk of their political activities. But, of course, I mean the terms to extend to behaviour and activity itself.) The observer of politics in such a state may easily get the impression that things are not what they seem.

Whether or not this is a useful approach with regard to communist politics, it certainly has relevance for Indian politics. (I do not have sufficient knowledge to speak of other 'developing' countries. But I would be wary of assuming that the Indian pattern is general: very few countries have all the important features which seem to give rise to the different languages.) Tentatively I would distinguish three main idioms in Indian politics. I believe that fairly 'pure' manifestations of each are encountered but this is not to say that in important and perhaps crucial areas they are not mixed together.

The first idiom may be termed 'Western'. This is not to identify it with any particular Western nation's idiom but merely to indicate its sources and very general character. This language is important in India (here a difference from some other parts of Asia?) not simply because of the long period of British rule but mainly because of the existence over nearly 100 years of an Indian elite steeped in its grammar and masters of its accents. Members of this elite were not merely the agents of much of the administrative and economic development of the country; they also provided the leadership of some of the more important movements of social reform and of the nationalist movement itself. It is true that an important change came over the nationalist movement with the impact of Gandhi's leadership after 1917, but it would be a mistake to imagine that Gandhi did not employ this 'Western' idiom; he combined it with another, but by no means abandoned it or prevented its continuous development.

This idiom is so widespread in India that it is possible to give a well-nigh comprehensive account of Indian political life without moving outside its terms. It is the language of the Constitution and the courts; of parliamentary debate; of the higher administration; of the upper levels of all the main political parties; of the entire English press and much of the Indian press. It is a language which speaks of policies, programmes and Plans. It expresses itself in argument, deliberation, discussion and decision. Within this idiom there are several important differences of view and political and economic conflicts—but this is only what we would expect, this is indeed the very stuff of politics as we have come to understand it. Thus there is a debate going on (partly within the Congress Party, partly between it and the Swatantra Party on the 'right' and the Socialist and Communist parties on the 'left') about the size of the public sector of the economy and the degree and form of governmental controls. A similar discussion is carried on with regard to land reform measures, especially in relation to agricultural productivity. A different trend of argument—but still conducted in this idiom—is that carried on along the 'federal' front: the relative roles of Centre and States, the impact of the Planning Commission, the Supreme Court's interpretation of the federal aspects of the Constitution, and so on. Similar to this is the whole range of interstate and linguistic disputes: the successful demand to split Bombay State into Maharashtra and Gujarat, the Sikh demand for a separate Punjabi Suba, the violent struggle between the Bengalis and Assamese in Assam, the tussle between Hindi and the regional languages and between both and English, the boundary dispute between Mysore and Maharashtra, and so on. A third type of argument within this idiom is concerned with forms of political organisation and relations between organisations. Into this category might be placed the discussion within the Congress Party on nominated *versus* elected Working Committee and on the proper roles of party bodies (principally Pradesh Congress Committees) and party legislature groups; relations between Ministers and back-benchers and between Ministers and civil servants; relations between Governments and opposition parties; the powers of Municipal Commissioners in relation to elected corporations and district officers in relation to elected boards; the composition and powers of the Planning Commission and of State Corporations, etc.

Evidently this is an important idiom; it seems to cover everything. A good index to a book written in these terms on Indian politics and government would bear comparison with an index to a Jennings on Britain or a Ferguson-McHenry on the U.S.A. or a volume on 'major foreign governments'. Not that there would not be many special items peculiar to India; nor that the items would on closer examination prove to be identical with those belonging to another country; nor that the items would have the same import-ance in the Indian book that acquaintance with British or French books might lead one to suppose. That is to say, the idiom could be 'Western' but still be quite specifically Indian. If this idiom com-prehended the whole of Indian politics, this would in no degree imply that the Indian polity was dependent or undistinctive or anything other than peculiar to India. It would only imply that it could be studied as other political systems with which we are familiar can be studied, that it could take its place in the field of 'comparative government' (with that subject's several approaches and many limitations).

This, however, is not the case. The observer of Indian politics will not look at his subject for long before he gets the feeling that he is missing something. This feeling can perhaps be described only by metaphors. The actors on a stage do not know why the audience should laugh just then, because they have not seen the cat which is playing with the stage curtains. Or, again, the audience may detect an awkward pause but they do not know that the actors are preoccupied because the hero's make-up is coming apart. Such a feeling with regard to Indian politics is perfectly justified; what the observer has so far not taken into account is a play within the play.

A second idiom of Indian politics is what may be styled 'tradi-tional'—though the word is as unsatisfactory as 'Western' used for the first. This is the language which social anthropologists and sociologists in India are busy discovering or re-discovering for us at the present time. In its purest forms it is spoken in rural India. It knows little or nothing of the problems of anything as big as India and its vocabulary scarcely includes policies and Plans. One way of indicating how different it is would be to use the term 'feudal', for this word although in some ways misleading and inexact would at least put us at an appropriate distance from the first idiom. 'Tribal' might also do the trick and would not be without some justification. It is the language of a particular kind of highly developed status society. As a language of politics it has two characteristics of outstanding importance. The first is that its basic structure rests on the unit of caste (or sub-caste or 'community'). This unit embraces all and is all-embracing; every man is born into a particular caste and with it he inherits a place and station from which his whole behaviour and outlook may be said, in idea at least, to be derived: his occupation, the range from which his parents will negotiate for his bride, his fairly precise standing in relation to every other person in terms of privileges and obligations, his attitude towards other men as members of his own or other caste groups. Each group is a natural focus of loyalty but together they constitute a crucially interdependent whole, the village. This whole is resistant to change because change is a threat to the system of status relations; and if changes are forced from outside, then the effort is to restore coherence in terms as little altered as possible.

The second characteristic of the 'traditional' idiom is closely related to the first and concerns the nature of authority. In the modern political idiom authority is something accorded by an exercise of choice and will. In the traditional idiom authority has its natural, substantially hereditary, seats. In most villages in a particular region there will be a certain 'dominant' caste and the natural repositories of village authority will be men of certain families within this caste. (Economic status seems to have some, rather variable, part to play in this and each of the other castes will also have leaders or spokesmen.) They will expect and will be expected to provide leadership—as one, albeit important, status contribution to the system of privileges and obligations. And of course one of the customarily vital expressions of leadership in such a community will be the reconciliation of disputes which threaten the stability of the little society: the foremost role of the village and caste panchayats. The other main call for leadership comes when a response is required to some approach or request or challenge from outside. Leaders must be able to intercede with the outside world and its *raj* or government. It must 'secure favours' in order that it may be able in turn to 'grant favours'. The language of traditional politics has a structure of caste and its tone is authoritarian. It should be added that although it has to do with the 'earthy' calculation of material things this is not to say that it is without great subtleties and fantastic complexities of its own.

The third idiom is to be found 'at the margin' of Indian politics. By this I certainly mean that it is in some quantitative sense relatively unimportant, spoken only by a few and occupying a definitely subsidiary place on the political page. But I would also be content to be taken to mean 'margin' to have something of the importance given to that term in economics: there may be few or none actually at the margin but the location of the point has an effect on all operators as a kind of reference mark. This third language is that of 'saintly' politics. The outstanding figure of nation-wide importance in this idiom is Vinoba Bhave, the 'Saint on the March' who tours India on foot preaching the path of self-sacrifice and love and a polity without power. His effective active followers may not be many but his own activities and pronouncements are reported week by week, almost day by day, in the Press. The direct impact of Bhave is a matter of some uncertainty and dispute. The startling initial success of his call for donations of land for distribution to the landless prompted all political parties to pay tribute to him and accord him respectful recognition. Subsequently, doubts about the motives of land donors and a certain ineffectiveness in the distribution programme have lowered the temperature of enthusiasm. More recently, there has been the experiment of accepting Bhave's help in dealing with the dacoit menace in the region south of Delhi; police action was called off while Bhave went in to talk to the brigand gang leaders; the present impression is that the dacoits were keen to benefit more from the withdrawal of police attention than from the message of Bhave.

But the direct effects of Bhave are less important than the indirect. This language has a widespread appeal to all sections in India. For many people it is identified with the political style of Gandhi. This is a bad over-simplification: for one thing this was only one of Gandhi's styles; for another, this idiom was already present in Indian society before Gandhi undertook its systematic and organised development. I do not know if in European history there are any even remote parallels to this kind of influence: possibly the sort of direction in which one might look would be that of the early Christian Church or some of the monastic orders. Be that as it may, the influence of 'saintly' politics in India cannot be ignored.

Admittedly it affects men's actual behaviour very little; remarkably few men engaged in political activity within the other two idioms are striving to be saintly. Its influence is rather on the standards habitually used by the people at large for judging the performance of politicians. In men's minds there is an idea of disinterested selflessness by contrast with which almost all normal conduct can seem very shabby. I do not imply that such a standard is applied continuously or to the exclusion of other standards. I would argue, however, that it contributes powerfully to several very prevalent attitudes to be found in Indian political life: to a certain withholding of full approval from even the most popular leaders; to a stronger feeling of distrust of and disgust with persons and institutions of authority; finally, to profoundly violent and desperate moods of cynicism and frustration. I repeat that I am not making 'saintly' politics a sole cause of these sentiments; I am only indicating how it can add, as it were, a certain bitterness and 'edge' to them. I would also (much more tentatively, for I do not know what social psychologists would say) suggest that the existence of this standard may if anything affect actually behaviour in a morally adverse manner: if the only really good life is one which seems to belong to a world beyond reach then a man might as well not strain too hard in that direction and indeed might as well be hung for a whole big black market sheep as for a little irregular lamb.

II

The tale of the three idioms is not one simply to be told and repeated; it is intended to be put to work. Does it help us to open up and interpret behaviour and thought in Indian politics? I would suggest that it does so at two different levels: at the level of certain general features of Indian politics and at the level of particular institutions and developments.

Its value at the former level has been hinted at in what has already been said. The very general feature that the way in which things are really done is different from the way in which they seem to be done or are presented as being done—this certainly arises because the idioms 'get crossed'. It is not simply that those people whom a foreigner is likely to question will reply in the 'Western' idiom for his benefit—though this certainly happens. It is also that such people will in any case habitually use that idiom when explaining things to each other. That is to say, Indian political life becomes explicit and self-conscious only through the 'Western' idiom, that is practically the only language in which the activity of description, giving an account of matters, will normally take place. But this does not prevent actual behaviour from following a different path. This situation is of course to be found in many spheres besides the strictly 'political'. 'Applications for scholarships will be considered by the Committee on the basis of recommendations submitted by the Head of the Department', but the natural tendency will be for the aspirant to tackle this problem in terms of 'favours' and 'influences'. Likewise with such matters political as the casting of votes, the selection of candidates and distribution of portfolios, and with such matters of administration as the siting of a new school or the granting of an industrial licence. One must be careful not to exaggerate and careful not to imply that in English local government or in American party organisation everything is as in the textbooks. But I believe there is a substantial difference.

The gap between supposed and real patterns of behaviour is a much wider matter than that of corruption, but it is no accident that the preceding paragraph should have led up to the latter subject; it has a great importance in practical Indian politics. Substantially I would say that much if not most of what is called corruption is no more than behaviour conducted in terms of one idiom being looked at in terms of another. Anyone holding any kind of position of power may be inclined to regard that position in both modern and traditional terms. Even if he is himself peculiarly free from the grip of traditional categories and loyalties, he will be subjected to steady pressures framed in those terms—and it will be very difficult not to give in. Is it not heartless to decline to 'do a kindness'? Of course, the proportions in which modern and traditional are mixed will vary greatly: there may be 100 per cent modernism in the Planning Commission and 90 per cent traditionalism in a Mandal Congress Committee in Madhya Pradesh. But at most levels two mainly antagonistic sets of standards will be in competition for the power to control a man's conduct. Equally important, these two sets will also be employed—frequently by the same persons—for judging his conduct. I do not 'approve' of 'favours' but I may yet 'expect' them and be duly grateful for them.

This type of conflict can be greatly sharpened when the third idiom is present. This will happen more often than one might imagine. This is not simply because of the personal influence of Bhave or the traditional appeal of those ideas or even because of memories of the saintly aspect of Gandhi. It is also on account of the actual experience of many people in the nationalist movement. That movement did bring out of ordinary men and women a remarkable standard of behaviour. From a sense of dedication or merely from sheer excitement and exhilaration men forgot about themselves and thought only of the cause. There is perhaps a tendency today to exaggerate this in retrospective glances at the golden age, but there is a big element of truth in it. There is a natural unwillingness to accept that period as exceptional and therefore a strong inclination to be severely critical about the decline in standards.

Related to this is a further striking feature of Indian political life —and again it is a feature rather of social life which politics shares : a certain caution and distrust in relations between people. In the courts a man in India is innocent until he is proved guilty, but in social and political life the position tends to be reversed. One has noticed the wariness with which people encounter each other and the relative difficulty of establishing friendships except within 'community' groups. In politics this has its equivalent in the extraordinary extent to which the other man's motives are suspect, the difficulty of concerted action and so on. Weiner has already discussed one aspect of this in his *Party Politics* : the resistance to unification on the part of political groups with almost identical policies and the readiness in many groups to split and break-away. He offered the explanation that in many cases party has become a substitute for a community group and that the members demand the snug and reassuring coherence of a unit in which there are no strangers or outsiders. A more general (though not incompatible) explanation would be that even in the sophisticated world of urban party politics men have not wholly shed the traditional attitudes. No one can be regarded as an individual, taken as he stands; he is always to be 'placed' in terms of the group to which he 'belongs'. This makes complete frankness and trust difficult. Shils has put the point very well when speaking of the Indian intellectual. "If Indian intellectuals are 'cut off from the people' . . . it is perhaps attributable to the caste system. . . . That system . . . 'cuts human beings off' from each other .... The alienation of the Indian intellectual from Indian society is probably less pronounced than is the alienation of most Indians from Indian society". It may be less pronounced but it is more agonising for, as Shils goes on to say, the ideal of national unity is more real for the intellectual and the sense of its loss since independence all the more 'poignant'. There is the further problem of accommodating in one organisation (or in one concerted effort) a number of people who desire power and/or expect to have authority. Here again the nearness of traditional politics has to be remembered. Men who have such a status society just behind them might be expected to swing rather violently into the extreme of ruthless competition; it is not easy to learn the rules of the new game when you are busy trying to forget those of the old one. To caution and distrust comes to be added disregard for the other man. Of course such sentiments can be overcome or at least suspended. That is what happened in great measure in the national movement and it has continued to happen, though in smaller measure, in Congress Party and Government under Nehru.

In all this we have again the idiom lines getting crossed. I should emphasise that it is this mixing up of languages which gives Indian politics its distinctive character. The languages have their separate sources or bases but the 'pure' expressions of each are far less significant than their areas of co-habitation. The Western style is no doubt strongest in the towns, certainly in the administrative and political leadership. The traditional style is least disturbed in villages, especially those at a good distance from sizeable towns. But the important and difficult question concerns what happens when they meet. On this divergent views may tend to be taken by observers coming from different disciplines. Indian politics looks like becoming something of a minor battlefield between sociologists and political scientists. The sociologist sets off from a base in caste and kinship groups and finds himself moving into the sphere of political behaviour; the political scientist starts with parliaments and parties and gets carried back into social patterns. But this is all as it should be, for the clear fact is that such movements correspond to changes that are actually taking place in practical, social and political life. The point merits some little elaboration.

The sociologist's discovery is clear and important. Briefly, it is that with the coming of independence (which incidentally made the serious study of caste possible and no longer an unpatriotic betrayal of the nationalist cause!), a wholly Indian administration and parliamentary democracy, caste and community have been able to move out of the villages and penetrate further towards the centre than ever before. The modern elite is no longer protected from the influence of traditional politics by the triple bulwarks of British administrative overseers (who mostly kept out of the caste network), the Indian national movement and a restricted electorate. The Constitution and the national leaders proclaim the goal of a casteless society and hardly a day passes without the vigorous condemnation by Nehru or one of his colleagues of the divisive forces of casteism, linguism and the like. But these are the only terms in which the newly enfranchised masses know how to operate. And so, in the middle and lower reaches of the parties and the administration, realistic men learn that they must also talk that language if they are to be understood and if they are to be effective. What sounds good up in the Delhi Parliament or for the newspaper reading public will cut no ice at the grass roots. Nor should it be imagined that caste has stopped at the city limits. It is true that the long-run effects of urban life may lead to a weakening of its hold, but there appears to be sufficient evidence that in the shorter run caste not only continues to prevail in city life (caste members often settle in the same localities within the city; immigrants from rural areas keep very close economic and social ties with their village bases) but under urban conditions finds it desirable and possible to attain a higher level of organisation than in rural India.

Work already done or in progress indicates clearly enough the pattern of sociological interpretation of Indian politics. Behind the voting figures there is revealed the work of intermediaries who secure the votes of their group for a given candidate. Behind the choice of candidates is discovered careful calculation of caste appeal. The whole shape of Mysore politics, which a political scientist might have been content to describe in terms of relations between parties and between the parliamentary and organisational wings of the major party, is shown to be determined by an age-old rivalry between two powerful castes in that region. Orissa's interesting political history of the last dozen years is likewise explained in terms of shifting caste positions and alignments. The working in practice of much of the movements of 'democratic decentralisation' and community development is shown to be conditioned and/or distorted by traditional politics' powerful grip. (Srinivas, Bailey, Dube are among the pioneers in these studies).

All this is enormously interesting, valuable and convincing. India, however, is too complex even for the sociologists. For although all these things are really happening and it did need sociologists to show them up, it is only one part of a double process. The modern idiom is also moving out from its bases. Unfortunately, political scientists have not yet done as much work as the sociologists and it is therefore more difficult to assess how far this trend has gone. Unfortunately, too, the sociologist often misses this. In his anxiety to expose modern political institutions as the playthings of ancient social forces, he is inclined not to see the institutions in their capacity as modern social forces. If anything is clear it is that both processes are at work in reality and both require to be studied side by side. This can perhaps best be illustrated by choosing a couple of examples.

III

Probably the most important single political institution in India today is the Congress Party. It certainly displays within itself most of the important features of Indian political life, while its present role and future development in great measure determine the course of Indian politics. It has not yet been made the subject of serious systematic study.

In terms of our analysis, the Congress is a crucial meeting ground of the three languages of politics. Within the Party are to be found many men who speak the modern idiom—many of them with skill and polish, some of them even with love. Most of the internal party debate would seem to be conducted in this language : for instance, the arguments between the 'right-wingers' (supposedly, for example, Desai, Pant) and the left (Menon and members of the one or two 'ginger groups') on the size of the public sector, the seriousness with which land reforms are to be tackled, the tone of voice to be adopted when speaking to China and the U.S. When commentators talk of the wide range of opinion held together by Nehru, it is a range within this one language which they have in mind. (The same range is to be found, though more obscurely, in the top administration.) The 'federal' tussles within the party are also for the most part in the modern idiom—the location of new steel mills and the choice of ports for development.

At the other end of the machine, so to speak, there is to be found a very different kind of person engaged in a very different kind of operation: the Mandal and District party leaders. Now I am aware that local party secretaries in England and ward bosses in the U.S. are concerned with rather different issues from those which pre-occupy the parliamentary and senate leaders. The difference to which I refer in India is, however, a profounder one of the very manner and style of behaviour; the difference in social setting imposes quite different techniques and is associated with quite different values and standards. The Congress worker in 'rural' India (I use the quotes since the term has to be taken to include sections of cities too) has to operate in the traditional language but it is not the case that this requires any special effort from him; for he is part and parcel of that traditional society. Most observers would agree that some change has taken place since independence in the character of the men who represent Congress at the lower levels. Any old party worker will explain with scorn how a new type of man has come in now that the party is in power. The motives which impelled a man to join and work for Congress before independence was in sight may have been quite varied; even 'national sentiment' can be of different kinds. The position since independence is not simply that a new motive—that of getting on to the government power wagon—has become powerful. Rather, it is that village India, playing always its own game of politics, adjusts itself to the new regime. The men who for socio-economic reasons count in any area must regard it as their proper function to get placed in positions where they can do what is expected of them by those for whom they intercede for favours. And in the new set-up this means getting in with or into Congress.

This is the crux of Indian politics—the coming together of these two political systems within the body of one political organisation. The journalists and opponents of Congress cry out that Congress is courting and capturing the influential and dominating leaders of 'rural' life. Of course it is. But it is equally true that such leaders have been in their own ways courting and capturing the Congress organisation. Who conquers whom? Whose language prevails? It does not seem to me that any clear answer can be given, partly because so little is known, partly because the issue may indeed be in balance. All I can do here is to indicate that this is the matter demanding investigation and to list some of the specific areas where close observation could yield important evidence. Some of these would be: the procedures by which Congress' internal elections take place; the negotiations leading to the choice of Parliamentary and, even more important, State Legislature candidates; the relations between Pradesh Congress Committees and Congress State Ministries; the character of the agitations and campaigns on linguistic and communal (e.g., reservation of posts for scheduled castes) issues; the extent and character of party pressures on State Congress Governments in relation to land legislation. On each topic there would be at least two main features to examine. First, the extent to which community and caste considerations were present and influential; second, the extent to which the exercise and reception of authority was conducted in modern terms of the institutions and offices or in traditional terms of social status and customary respect. Lest it be thought that all this is in some derogatory sense academic, let me add that it is to me clear that the battles being conducted within the modern idiom as between 'right' and 'left', 'centralist' and 'statist' will be most significantly influenced by the outcome of the underlying conflict between the two languages. The traditional way points to the right and points away from the centre.

As a second example I would briefly take the representative institutions. In this world too, as in the world of party, the two idioms meet (with the third idiom again keeping up, as it were, an influential running commentary on the proceedings). I have already said much elsewhere about the central Parliament. My impression is that it is a powerful instrument of political education for members and public alike. The education it conveys is almost entirely in the modern idiom; this is certainly true of the debates on the floor of the House, in all the parliamentary committees and in some party committees; it is less certainly so in the case of certain other party committees and in regard to general lobby conversation. The members are powerfully influenced by its atmosphere and they are under that influence for by far the greater part of the year. The public that reads papers is also accustomed to watch it closely—so large is the space devoted by the press to its proceedings. The talk is all of issues and problems and programmes and the scale is emphatically all-India. As Asoka Mehta strikingly said recently, Parliament is the great unifier of the nation. This is true; it has taken over that role in large measure from the freedom movement. (I find the parallel with the Tudor Parliament close and instructive. Nehru is like the Queen in Parliament; in no other place does he 'stand so high in his estate royal'; and through Parliament the feudal powers in their country seats are left subdued and in order.)

Much less clear is the character of the State Legislative Assemblies. Students have already pointed out (Morris-Jones, Weiner) that the members of these bodies are drawn from layers much closer to those of traditional politics. Also they are in the assemblies for quite a short part of the year; the rest of the time they will be in their home districts which are, increasingly, their constituencies. No one can visit the lobbies of a State Assembly without realising quite vividly that the M.L.A. is 'in touch with' his constituents; the corridors are full of them, some still bearing the dust of the village tracks if not the earth of the fields themselves. The M.L.A. is thus another critical point in the drama of Indian politics: which language of politics does he speak? He is himself undergoing 'modern' education from his seniors on the front benches, but the 'courses' are shorter and of a fairly 'elementary' nature. Still he learns to think of his State (even if not yet of India) and to talk of power projects (even if the big decisions are taken in Delhi). At the other end there are the pressures from home and in the corridors—to remember that he comes from the Vidarbha part of Maharashtra, or that he is a Mahar or that he must please those who count in his district party. So evidently he becomes 'bilingual'. But we would still like to know in which language he does his thinking and his dreaming. And anyone anxious to secure the victory of the modern language over the traditional would do well to concentrate on the M.L.A. and should presumably try to strengthen the links that join him to circles where the modern idiom is spoken. The M.L.A. is one of the great 'gap-closers' in Indian politics but we do not yet know whether he is achieving this in ways favourable to the modern or to the traditional style.

Finally a word on the really threatening force in Indian political life: the discontent of the educated middle-class. (None of the popularly supposed threats to democracy in India—a failure sufficiently to increase agricultural production, a slower rate of economic growth than China, etc.—has any political significance except in so far as they can operate through the opinions of this section of the population. And these opinions can be affected by many things besides economic statistics.) This discontent is as it were not in the direct line of fire between the modern and traditional idioms, but it is greatly influenced by factors arising out of that conflict.

The present mood of the educated mainly urban middle-class is dictated by those of its less successful members. There are many men (and an increasing number of women) who are in secure and satisfying employment in the services and in industrial and commercial enterprises—as technicians, administrators, educators and entrepreneurs. And it is of course true that they are relatively contented with their own lives. Yet it is striking to note the extent to which even such people will speak of India's political life in terms which seem to belong more appropriately to those of their fellows who are unemployed, mal-employed or insecurely employed. The general attitude is one of deep disgust with those in power and profound scepticism about the effectiveness or suitability of existing political institutions. The fact that much of the criticism is based on very great ignorance of what is actually going on does not lessen its significance. There is a conviction that all holders of political power great and small alike—are abusing their positions for illegitimate ends. These may be personal or family or group. There are no men of 'public spirit' in public life, no disinterested politicians of pure motives. In other words, this influential section of the public is engaged in a continuous complaint against the conduct of 'modern' politics—largely because it is suspected of being 'traditional' politics in disguise; and the attack is bitter because its makers are dominated by notions derived from 'saintly' politics as mediated to them through experience or impressions of the great days of the national movement.

This discontent is able on occasion to find release in agitations which really bear little relation to its own deeper causes. Young students may get involved in Assamese-Bengali killings or the campaign for Maharashtra. There may be an element of direct class interest involved in these cases—a belief that, for instance, the Bengalis are keeping you out of a decent job or the Gujeratis are not giving the others a chance. But mainly it seems that these agitations are irrelevant to their main needs. Perhaps the central problem is that suitable channels for political action seem to be fewer than the demand for them. India's is an under-developed polity from the point of view of the needs of its educated middle class. It is shaped like a narrow pole rather than a solid pyramid. It is not exactly that there are no organisations and associations at a convenient level ('infra-structure'?) but rather that most of these are talking the wrong language. There are plenty of caste organisations but few lively professional bodies or opinion-propagating societies. It may be that the middle-class feeling of wanting to 'participate' is abnormally developed (a hang-over from the national movement where all were excitingly employed, a sign of lack of absorption in their own jobs, a genuine misunderstanding of the meaning of democracy— some of all these things and no doubt more) but there is certainly no room on the narrow pole for all who seem to want a place there.

The structure of 'modern' political institutions is not only frustratingly narrow—limited to legislatures and parties. There is also the difficulty that that structure is itself dominated by one organisation, the Congress Party. And there is very little that the middle-classes can do about this in the short run. They might organise other parties, and indeed have of course done so—P.S.P., Jan Sangh, Swatantra. But how can such parties make any impression on the solid base of the Congress which is located in the world of 'traditional' politics where P.S.P. and even Swatantra alike hardly know how to walk? (The Communists do rather better. They have boldly adjusted themselves to traditional politics and concentrated on specific socio-economic caste blocs—as in Andhra and Kerala.) In any case, in the world of 'traditional' politics, governments are not changed or chosen so much as used or evaded. The circle is a most vicious one: you can't be taken seriously by the local men who matter until you are the government, but you can't be the government until you have been taken seriously. It is interesting to reflect that nothing but adult franchise could have secured Congress rule with such certain stability; a more restricted franchise would have meant the conduct of politics in much more purely 'modern' terms, and that would have permitted a much greater 'openness of texture' and flexibility.

Thus, the vital educated middle-classes are politically quite frustrated. (This is what I meant elsewhere by calling India's polity one of frustration.) They have no liking or trust or confidence in

Congress but they cannot budge it because the levers are not in their hands. So the 'modern' opposition remains puny, the 'traditional' 'opposition' works in other ways, and the student masses (the jargon seems correct in India's case) become a shade more cynical and despairing as each year passes. Of course, a dozen years of stable government in the wake of independence and partition is no mean blessing, as every administrator in India knows. Yet the disadvantages are now beginning to outweigh the advantages. The ice-pack is forming and the ships of state will soon be crushed. The most obvious dynamite available to break the ice and to permit free political navigation is the withdrawal of Nehru. If that were to happen, the Congress could scarcely hold together. (No one else has such wide and varied appeal. No one else is so regularly forgiven. No one else has his ability and dedication. No one else could confuse the issues and blur the distinctions to the degree that Congress leadership demands.) And in that case the struggle could become open and real. There would be dangers and losses but these seem each day to be less terrifying than those of getting frozen up.

Hugo Wolfsohn

ASPECTS OF THE SOCIAL STRUCTURE OF UNDER–DEVELOPED COUNTRIES WITH SPECIAL REFERENCE TO INDIA

THIS PAPER attempts to illustrate the thesis that in countries undergoing processes of modernisation the activities of the government are likely to be dysfunctional to the majority of the population, which almost invariably is dispersed in large agrarian areas. The political processes in non-Westernised societies (including Russia before and after the Revolution) are characterised by a 'gap'[1] between rulers and ruled,[2] between the inarticulate masses of predominantly illiterate peasants and the comparatively narrow area of rationally organised systems of administration and power, usually referred to as the government.

A good deal of attention has been given to this question in recent literature[3] as the gain of independence by large countries previously under imperial control has added the problems of rapid economic and social development to the traditional limitations and difficulties of government in non-Westernised societies. The passionate interest and faith in the regenerative scope of modern political organisation shown by members of the intelligentsia which inherited power and responsibility from their previous colonial rulers as a matter of

---

[1] For a detailed description of the 'gap' and its influence on politics generally, see E. Shils, "Political Development in the New States", *Comparative Studies in Society and History*, Vol. II, No. 3, April 1960. Cf. his article in *World Politics*, Vol. II, April 1960, No. 3, "The Intellectuals in the Political Development of the New States".

[2] The isolation of the Russian intellectuals played a vital part in their activities. Attempts to overcome it ranged from terrorism to the method of 'going to the people'.

[3] See F. W. Riggs, "Agraria and Industria", in W. J. Siffin (ed.) *Toward the Comparative Study of Public Administration*, pp. 23–110; also G. M. Kahin, G. J. Pauker, L. W. Pye, "Comparative Politics in Non-Western Countries", American Political Science Review, Vol. LI, 1955; also L. W. Pye, "The Non-Western Political Process", *Journal of Politics*, Vol. 20, No. 1, February 1958.

course, stand in stark contrast to the continued lethargy and hostility of the villages. In their eagerness to raise the status of their nations in the eyes of the rest of the world, the new leaders operating the Western-inspired political machinery have adopted constitutions, the provisions of which assume without question the existence of a society which may be economically and industrially retarded but which is politically mature enough to form a reliable social base for the sophisticated administrative structure at the invariably urban centre of power.[4] The Indian Constitution, for instance, can be considered a magnificent essay and summary of all that is 'best' and 'progressive' in recent Western political advances. It assumes the existence of an alert electorate of individual voters whose alleged or real attachment to the nation made possible the abandonment of the complicated provisions for 'communal' representation, which was a serious and virtually insoluble issue in the period of British control. The Constitution has laid down the blueprint of a welfare state in which every conceivable social demand has been given precise constitutional expression. In essentials, however, the Indian Constitution is a summary of British ideas and a deliberate codification of British political traditions and arrangements.

In adopting it, the constitution-makers have in their optimism ignored the segmented nature of Indian society. They have superimposed it upon a social structure which has so far been unsuitable for its proper operation. It is the work of men who were either educated in Western countries or who are strongly under the influence of Western cultural and political values.

The Constitution and the administrative and political structure sanctioned by it are, as Jayaprakash Narayan has recently stressed, the expression of 'urban' values in a society where 80 per cent of the people live in the dispersed villages of the agrarian sector of Indian society. Government is to the villagers "something remote, inexplicable, uncontrollable".[5] In his recent book on the Indian Parliament, Professor Morris-Jones referred to the same problem by introducing the helpful concept of 'levels of politics'. He has made the distinction between 'normal' politics and a "manner of political

[4] K. A. Wittfogel: *Oriental Despotism; A Comparative Study of Total Power*, 444.

[5] G. Wint, "Narayan in Oxford", *Encounter*, Vol. XIV, No. 3, March 1960, 62.

thought and behaviour which it is difficult to regard simply as the local modification of some aspect of Western politics ".[6] He argues that Indian politics takes place at "two different levels or in two distinct modes, the one Western and secular, and the other religious and Indian".[7] And he finds it difficult "to see the two levels as alternative ways of politics available to India as a whole".[8] But if the majority of the Indian people practise 'spiritual politics' which cannot be assimilated by the country as a whole, then they are not engaging in the type of politics which the Constitution and administrative apparatus of the country take for granted. The gap between a rational centre of organised procedures distinguished by a high degree of social mobility, a well-developed occupational system, by a class structure based on generalised patterns of occupational achievement and by the prevalence of functionally specific, non-ascriptive associations; and an agrarian society of stable local groups with ascriptive status and deferential social stratification sanctioned by religious ritual[9] can be bridged only by either the one or the other level of political activity becoming totally dominant in the country. If, with Narayan, we opt for the creation of a 'communitarian' system of government, we must do away with political parties and shift "the focus of political life to the village".[10] The mode of political activity will then be 'spiritual'. If, on the other hand, we follow the leaders of newly independent societies, the eventual removal of the 'traditional' sector of their agrarian societies is the *sine qua non* for the successful achievement of their aims. The mode of politics will then be 'normal'.

The emergence of independent Asian countries committed to the policy of rapid modernisation has made the discrepancy between country and city, between 'agraria' and 'industria', more dramatic. The main political task by which the leaders of the new societies are confronted is the extension of Western (or 'normal') political processes into the remainder of society. Shils has defined this task as the process of 'politicising' the social structure of under-developed societies.[11]

[6] W. H. Morris-Jones, *Parliament in India,* 37.
[7] *ibid.*   [8] *ibid.*
[9] F. W. Riggs, in Siffin, *op. cit.,* 29.
[10] G. Wint, *Encounter,* 62.
[11] E. Shils, in *World Politics, op. cit.,* 338.

It appears that the existence side by side of two different types of politics has been the outstanding peculiarity of Asian societies. It lies at the basis of Wittfogel's analysis of Oriental Despotism and it was not without influence during the period of the struggle for independence in India.

Indian nationalists[12] in their understandable eagerness to achieve national independence as rapidly as possible were inclined to play it down or ignore it altogether, but their British opponents used it as a weapon against nationalist demands for self-government. In 1918, for instance, the Government of India declared, "It is on the increased experience to be gained in the administration of local affairs that the country must to a large degree rely for the expansion of its self-independence in the sphere of central government".[13] One of the reasons for the hostility and frequent contemptuous attitudes the British displayed towards the Congress movement was their awareness that the urbanised intelligentsia of the Congress represented, in Lord Curzon's words, only a "microscopic minority of the total population". To Curzon, the people of India were "the voiceless millions who can neither read nor write . . . the people of India are the ryots and the peasants whose life is not one of political aspiration but of mute penury and toil. The plans and policy of the Congress Party in India would leave this vast amorphous residuum absolutely untouched."[14] Had he been able to witness the degree to which Gandhi succeeded in mobilising the Indian peasantry during certain phases of the independence struggle, Lord Curzon might have modified his judgment. But while Gandhi succeeded in acquainting Congress with the urgency of India's agrarian situation, he had no interest in 'secularising' the Indian village to the extent where it would be gladly receptive to the Western political ideas and ambitions of the Congress leadership. The modernisation of India was after all hardly Gandhi's ambition, and the speed with which his vague political and constitutional suggestions disappeared from the scene after 1947 strongly indicates their irrelevance to the

---

[12] For the general attitude of Congress to local government, see H. Tinker, "People and Government in Southern Asia", *Transactions of the Royal Historical Society*, 5th Series, Vol. 9, 153–7.

[13] Quoted by H. Tinker, *op. cit.*, 154.

[14] Quoted by H. Tinker, *op. cit.*, 156–157. In the same debate Sir Richard Temple argued that villagers would look upon Congress politicians as 'semi-foreigners', (157).

new leaders of the government. At the same time, his mystique of village life and his emphasis on the glorious past of self-contained 'village republics' provided in a curious way a basis for the national pride of westernised intellectuals seeking 'affinity' with the greater part of the nation of which they had little experience and from which they were alienated.[15] This alienation, common to intellectuals in under-developed countries,[16] provided a "matrix for the idea of a deeper national culture and, therewith, of a nation which had only to be aroused to self-awareness".[17] The outcome of all this has been the revival of the village as the allegedly ideal entity for self-government[18] when at the same time the policy of westernization seeks ultimately to dissolve village society, the symbol of India's poverty and backwardness. Government's approach to the village is therefore ideologically contradictory and administratively confused.

The search for deeper national traditions led further to the discovery of a political theory which beautifully illustrates the traditional, and we may add, the geographical distance, between government and peasantry. Nationalist historians like the late Dr. R. K. Mookerji argued that "India presents the rare and remarkable phenomenon of the State and society coexisting apart from and in some degree of independence of each other, as distinct and separate units or entities, as independent centres of national, popular and collective life and activity . . . the limits of State interference were accordingly so defined and fixed as not to encroach upon the sphere of the activities of the social organizations . . . there was a well-understood delimitation of the respective boundaries of the political and social organisations, both of which were co-operating agencies for the promotion of the common weal".[18a] The distinction between state and society on which Mookerji based his theory of contractual limitations on the power of the state was, however, geographically conditioned. It was not the outcome of a deliberate political arrangement.[19] Once the democratic theory is ignored, we are left with the existence side by side of two social arrangements, i.e. the autonomous villages (Mookerji's "social

---

[15] E. Shils, *World Politics, op. cit.*, 342–4.
[16] E. Shils, *World Politics, op. cit.*, 343.
[17] E. Shils, *World Politics, op. cit.*, 338–51.
[18] Article 40 of the Constitution promises the establishment of Panchayats.
[18a] Quoted by H. D. Malaviya, *Village Panchayats in India*, 52.
[19] G. S. Ghurye, *Caste and Class in India*, 23.

organisations") and the state confined to a highly concentrated centre of power. The connections between the two are reduced to the 'irreducible minimum', not for contractual reasons, but rather as the result of the state's inability efficiently to extend its control permanently into the countryside.

In this way, the distinction between state and society is useful and can be seen to be closely connected with Wittfogel's theory of Oriental Despotism. Wittfogel came to the conclusion that the autonomy of the agrarian sectors in many Asian societies was due to what he called the effects of the "law of diminishing administrative return".[20] The despotic 'agromanagerial' state successfully prevents the permanent establishment of secondary and intermediary organisations which could challenge the basically unlimited power of the government. Villages may enjoy autonomy and some freedoms which, however, in the absence of firm institutional checks are uncertain and therefore "irrelevant". The Indian nationalist picture of contented self-governing village republics becomes, in Wittfogel's hands, the system of 'beggars democracy'.[21]

Wittfogel's work throws a good deal of light on the functioning and scope of Asian government. What emerges is the existence of a highly concentrated power centre to which are subordinated innumerable autonomous villages subject to oppressive but *intermittent* exploitation. The implication for contemporary Asian societies is clear. As long as they remain 'static', i.e. as long as they do not embark upon wholesale modernisation, the autonomy of their agrarian sectors can go on for long periods of time, accompanied by a good deal of social stability and economic stagnation. But as most contemporary Asian governments are determined to achieve rapid Westernisation, the task of extending the administrative techniques of a modern state into the agrarian sector becomes both urgent and unavoidable. In a country with a democratic constitution such as India, the attempt is being made to permeate the villages gradually with the agreement of the peasants and the deliberate utilisation and encouragement of what local initiative may be available. The process may be facilitated by the growth of trade and industry and by the impact of a modern system of communications, all factors that have started the slow erosion of traditional values inside the villages.

[20] Wittfogel, *op. cit.*, 110.
[21] Wittfogel, *op. cit.*, 108–13.

7

Asian constitutionalism should be viewed in this context. Its ideological basis is radical, left-wing and collectivistic, and its political aim is the total re-structuring of Asian societies. Constitutions are sign posts, promises for the future rather than reliable indications of the political life of those societies at the present time. For the majority of Asian peasants, therefore, any constitution, be it democratic or totalitarian, must have far-reaching dysfunctional implications. This does not mean that it does not matter what sort of constitution has been adopted. This analysis merely emphasises that the distinction between democratic and authoritarian constitutions in the context of Asian problems lies in the methods used to penetrate the agrarian sector of society. Stalin's wholesale attack on the peasantry in 1928 was the first dramatic example of 'normal' politics being imposed upon the peasantry by force, and Mao's China is following the same policy, although with some modifications. Totalitarian control in both Russia and China has deprived us of a good deal of first-hand knowledge of the reactions of the peasants to government policy. India, by contrast, as an open society, is providing evidence of the difficulties following increasing contact between government and villages.

We have already noted the disappearance of Gandhism from the Indian political system, which Paul Appleby numbered among the dozen most advanced governments in the world.[22] During the debates in the Constituent Assembly, the late Dr. Ambedkar, the distinguished spokesman for the untouchables and chairman of the Drafting Committee, sharply attacked right-wing Hindus as reactionary 'champions of the village'.[23] "What is the village", he said, "but a stink of localism and a den of ignorance, narrowmindedness and communalism? I am glad that the Draft Constitution has discarded the village and adopted the individual as a unit."[24]

For this he was widely attacked as betraying Gandhi's dream of a constitution broadly based upon the village. But Ambedkar's views, which were shared by the majority of Congress leadership,

[22] P. A. Appleby, *Public Administration in India, Report of a Survey*, 8. (Published by Cabinet Secretariat, O. and M. Division.)

[23] H. D. Malaviya, *op. cit.*, 258.

[24] H. D. Malaviya, *op. cit.*, 258.

prevailed,[25] even though the government's approach to the villages became somewhat contradictory. On the one hand, panchayats—to be set up under article 40 of the Directive Principles of State Policy —were envisaged as democratically elected organs of village self-government, perpetuating the villages as self-contained social units and acting as instrumentalities for transmitting government-inspired improvement policies to the villagers. On the other hand, the planned development of agriculture and industry runs counter to the efforts to revitalise the villages as autonomous units. What is given with the one hand may be taken away with the other.

By 1954, no less than 98,256 panchayats had been established,[26] but the results were utterly disappointing. Tinker quotes the report of the Balvantray team of investigators to the effect that "possibly not more than 10 per cent of the total number of panchayats are functioning effectively".[27] In many villages hereditary panchayats had been in existence for generations and they were recognised by the villagers as legitimate authorities. In such cases, therefore, the election of the panchayat simply meant the automatic continuation of the hereditary body on a statutory basis. In cases where no panchayats were available at all (probably the majority of the villages),[28] the new statutory bodies were rejected by the villagers, probably because they were intruding on the informal structure of authority in the village. In cases where the membership of the elected and hereditary panchayats differed, the villagers tended to regard the latter as the legitimate authority.

In terms of government influence, the official reports available do not provide a reliable picture from which any definite conclusion could be drawn. In cases where villagers' participation is described as 'good', or even 'enthusiastic', no proper attempt has been made to account for it. The same applies to cases where participation is 'bad' or entirely lacking.[29]

[25] Gandhi never worked out a detailed scheme for constitutional reform. The only constitution rigidly based upon his teaching to my knowledge is that by S. N. Agarwal, *A Gandhian Constitution for Free India* (Kitabistan, 1946). Gandhi approved of it in a foreword.

[26] H. D. Malaviya, *op. cit.*, 270.

[27] H. Tinker, "Authority and Community in Village India", *Pacific Affairs*, Vol. XXXII, No. 4, December 1959, 361.

[28] H. Tinker, *Pacific Affairs, op. cit.*, 359, footnote.

[29] I gained this impression from *Three Years of Community Projects* (Planning Commission, Programme Evaluation Section, August 1956).

From the investigations carried out by Hitchcock[30] in a village of North India, it appears that an outstanding individual of high caste and comparatively great wealth may exercise effective control over the village. Most of his reforms, however, fell into abeyance after his death,[31] and the panchayat established by statute was never properly accepted by the villagers.

In his study of leadership in a Mysore village, Beals came to the discouraging conclusion that "there can be no village-wide leadership"[32] owing to the prevalence of factions which throw up their own leaders whose authority extends only to their own faction. In this case, however, a considerable degree of urban influence appears to have demoralised the village. Again, the statutory panchayat met only on rare occasions and "merely forms a platform for the airing of mutual grievances".[33]

One of the most interesting village surveys, carried out in 1955 by Y. B. Damle,[34] covered seven villages in the vicinity of Poona. The villages were arranged in terms of distance from Poona, the closest being eleven miles and the farthest seventy-two miles removed. What makes Damle's study somewhat unusual was his attempt to test the political knowledge of the villagers. The results were on the whole depressing. The villagers' knowledge of what Damle called "world political structure" was nil in almost all cases. The same applied to international affairs. In six out of the seven villages examined, Damle found almost complete ignorance of "modern ideas on caste and religion". Only in Bopudi, an incorporated suburb of Poona, did he find the villagers well informed on general political matters. But even here there was some opposition to the reform of the caste system. In the remaining villages, the government's policy of social equality was almost totally rejected.[35]

---

[30] J. T. Hitchcock, "Leadership in a North Indian Village", in *Leadership and Political Institutions in India* (eds. R. L. Park and H. Tinker), 399 and ff.

[31] *ibid.*, 405.

[32] A. Beals, "Leadership in a Mysore Village", in *Leadership and Political Institutions in India*.

[33] *ibid.*, 437.

[34] Y. B. Damle, *Communication of Modern Ideas and Knowledge in Indian Villages* (Center for International Studies, M.I.T., 1955). One of the difficulties of Damle's study is that he did not report his questions in detail. Knowledge of 'world political structure' may be a tough proposition even for the inhabitants of farming areas in advanced countries.

[35] In another study of a village close to Bangalore, Mysore State, Beals found considerable hostility in the village to government in general. He gives many

From the investigations quoted, two tentative conclusions may be inferred: (1) the government's policy of revitalising the villages as self-governing units has not been successful. The slow erosion of traditional values due to factors we will discuss later has been proceeding, irrespective of the efforts of local authorities. (2) The authority of local government bodies is growing at the expense of the panchayats. The protagonists of the panchayat as the agent of economic development do not have a clear idea of the realities of the social structure in which administration is conducted. The role of the district officer, and that of his subordinates, is laid in a highly stratified rural society. The evidence of the last few years indicates that the discretionary powers of this officer and his subordinates are likely to be strengthened.

In addition to the activities of local government bodies, the villages have been exposed to 'strains' coming from contacts with modern civilisation. Whilst it is difficult to pinpoint these strains in detail, their effects may be vaguely indicated. Barrington Moore, Jr.[36] distinguishes three of them. One comes from the extension of market relations into the village. The market introduces into the village the need for individual decision-making. The enterprising peasant may use his opportunities and obtain a special position which is incompatible with the village system of rigid ascribed status. The second strain is illustrated by the increase in class differentiation on the basis of new economic activities and functions. These may come into conflict with the rigid status structure of caste society and lead to a rudimentary class struggle in the village. And the third strain consists of the impact made by modern communications, transport and general facilities. The younger men of the village in their search for employment and entertainment are getting acquainted with urban values and show increasing disrespect

examples of tensions, bribery and intimidation. One of his diary entries, which is a good indication of the general attitudes prevailing in the village, may be quoted in full: "We are afraid of government in this village. Therefore, we will never say anything against any government. Almost all villagers have fought for the benefit of their villages. By change, if the government does any good to us, we will accept it as a God-sent". A. Beals, "The Government and the Indian Village", *Economic Development and Cultural Change*, Vol. II, No. 5, June 1954, 394–407.

[36] Barrington Moore, Jr., *The Western Impact upon the Structure of Authority in Indian Society*, M.I.T., Center for International Studies, 1955; paper entitled "Dictatorship and Industrialism", 1–23.

for the traditional values in their villages. Modern village studies illustrate this trend. Dube, for instance, mentions that "as a general rule people observe prohibitions on interdining within the village but ignore them when they eat in the shops or restaurants in the city".[37]

The autonomy of villages affected in this way is bound to decline as the major activities of traditional Indian life can no longer be channelled through the village structure. The bonds that attach the Indian peasant to the traditional order are being gradually undermined by the various influences of modern civilisation. The slow but inevitable rise of class differentiation favours members of higher castes but leaves the landless labourers behind.[38] Whilst the latter are turning into a mass of atomised individuals, the former may succeed in linking themselves meaningfully to the system of modern politics through caste associations taking on the functions of secondary associations and pressure groups outside and inside the Congress government.[39] The process of gradual 'politicisation' favours the wealthy and discriminates against the poor. 'Normal' politics is getting into the villages, but the penetration is spotty and its social effects may be critical in the long run.

To impose panchayats by statute upon villages passing through a critical transition period can neither assist the government nor hold up the processes of internal dissolution. In a sense, it may make it worse. At best, the panchayats may be pushed into a vacuum where

[37] S. C. Dube, *Indian Village*, 224. Dube's village shows a considerable degree of government penetration and Western influence. But its closeness to Hyderabad makes it atypical. Damle, when discussing the village of Muthe, speaks of the "draining of Muthe of its youth and the consequent dissipation of the springs of enthusiasm and activity. Besides, the youths who go out to work come back alienated from the village folks . . . being dissipated physically, mentally, and morally, they cannot in any way become useful to the community". *Op. cit.*, p. 14.

[38] *Leadership and Groups in a South Indian Village* (Planning Commission, Programme Evaluation Organisation, June 1955). This report shows dramatically the degree to which village extension workers are prepared to attach themselves to the wealthier sections of the village. To quote one instance (130): "The village extension worker also generally did not mix with the poorer people because he felt that he was unable to help them. His contacts remained limited to the well-to-do persons who were in a position to follow some of his advice . . ." An experimental training camp for future village leaders consisted entirely of well-to-do people.

[39] L. I. Rudolph and S. H. Rudolph, "The Political Role of India's Caste Associations", *Pacific Affairs*, Vol. XXXIII, No. 1, March 1960.

they do not function at all. At worst, they may be drawn into the faction and incipient class struggles in the villages exposed to the individualising effects of modern market influences. To sentimentalise the importance and functions of panchayats under such circumstances seems to be singularly out of place. When confronted with these difficulties in practice, local government authorities have as a matter of course tended to bypass the panchayats altogether and to co-operate with the more prosperous and energetic elements among the cultivators.[40]

The dangers in this situation are obvious. The atomisation of countless cultivators without land may prove a fertile ground for the rise of fanatical and totalitarian movements in the future.[41] If we could assert with confidence that the 'eroding' influences of modern civilization have made themselves felt in the *average Indian village,* the future political and constitutional stability of Indian society would indeed appear to be in serious danger. In actual fact, however, we do not know with any precision how many of the 500,000 Indian villages have in fact been exposed to the unsettling influences described. If, as I suspect, the unsettling process has reached only a comparatively small number of villages in the vicinity of cities and specially selected industrial development areas, the revolutionary potentialities of the eroding process should not give cause for undue alarm at this stage.[42] On the contrary, it could be considered a blessing in disguise. The resources of the Centre are at present totally inadequate for a full and efficient penetration of the subsistence sector of Indian society. To try and 'politicise' the Indian peasantry under the present circumstances could eventually lead to a premature demand by the peasantry on services which neither the Centre nor the governments of the States could meet satisfactorily. To avoid this contingency, the Centre could gain immensely valuable time by leaving the majority of the peasants in what would be

---

[40] This emerges clearly from the Report of the P.E.O. of the Planning Commission referred to footnote 38 on page 102.

[41] Barrington Moore arrives at this pessimistic conclusion largely because he believes all Indian villages to be passing through stages of social disintegration. *Op. cit.*, chapter 3, "The Threat to the Village".

[42] The meaning of 'eroding processes' is far from clear. We need criteria by which we can determine when 'market forces' do have a seriously unsettling effect. The fact that most Indian villagers wear factory-made shirts may not have the socially critical implications many observers take for granted.

described emotionally as a 'politically primitive condition', as a 'reactionary' policy, and so on. But the gain would be constitutional stability.

Most modern studies deal with villages in various stages of social disintegration. Unfortunately, the authors never ask how representative their villages are of Indian peasant society as a whole. But if we ignore this question, we are still faced with a social situation which is in some ways strikingly similar to the Russian village community, the *Mir*, after the Stolypin reforms. The 'strong and sober' among the Russian peasants 'contracted out' of the community and tied themselves to the developing market outside. It was on those left behind with bad land and increased burdens that the Communists based their power in the early stages of the revolution and laid the basis for the later 'Asian Restoration' under Stalin's leadership.

While it is tempting to derive lessons from Russian developments, the analogy should not be driven too far. There is, for instance, no Indian social unit equivalent to the Russian *Mir*. And there is no Russian equivalent to the Indian caste system and its remarkable effect in stabilising social relations between groups and imposing a spontaneous type of social discipline upon individuals. It is obvious that class and income differences between Indian peasants would be felt less acutely than among the peasants of the *Mir*. The Russian peasantry had already been extensively politicised by local government bodies whose personnel consisted of dedicated liberals bent on drawing the peasants into politics. When Stolypin deliberately introduced the competitive market forces into the *Mir* in order to destroy it he triggered off the ultimate destruction of the Russian political system.

There is, however, still a sense in which one can talk of the possibility of an 'Asian Restoration' in India. Indian nationalists may not be prepared to leave the subsistence sector of their society alone even for the sake of constitutional stability. They pride themselves on the creation of a 'modern' society[48] and resent the gap between themselves and the peasant. The 'statist' outlook of the Indian intelligentsia which Wittfogel has noted with concern and which is hidden under Western constitutional forms has its own

[48] This point is convincingly developed by P. T. Bauer, *Indian Economic Policy and Development*, London, 1961.

dangers.[44] Impatience with the traditional ways of the peasant and the anxiety to see the creation of a socialist society may increase the temptation among the younger generation of government officials to force the pace of administrative penetration into the village. The atomisation of the traditional village structure would then not be due to the forces of the market but to the government's deliberate policy of destroying the village from above, to make the peasant a 'useful' and 'full' member of his society. It is at this point that the danger of totalitarianism would become real.

[44] Wittfogel, *op. cit.*, 443 and ff.

PROF. MORRIS-JONES: I will begin with two stories. The first concerns a Siamese student who wrote for me an essay on local government in Siam. When I criticised it as too formal and giving no impression how the system actually worked, he replied: "Ah, but on the way it really works I can write a quite different essay". The other story is that, when I was in Delhi recently, I mentioned to a friend that I was preparing a new book on modern Indian politics. To my dismay he remarked: "Of course, there isn't a single honest book on that subject".

There is indeed in Asian countries a large gap between forms and realities, between profession and practice. This often suggests that the former—parliament, the constitution, etc.—is mere facade. I believe this is over-simple and profoundly mistaken and I am glad that in "Parliament in India" I attacked that view. But although these modern institutions are not facades but are real and substantial, they are not the only real things, and I recognise now that my argument did not go deep enough. In the last few years, social anthropologists have taught us a great deal about the realities of traditional politics in India. My paper attempts to take account of these discoveries.

I see Indian politics as in a state of balance or tension, not only between unitary and federal tendencies, between law and planning, between private and public sectors, but more fundamentally between styles or 'languages' of politics which I have tentatively labelled 'modern' (I prefer this to 'Western'), 'traditional' and 'saintly'. I have tried to describe the character of these languages and to point out some of the great areas of politics where they are in competition; in the legislatures, especially in the states; in the middle levels of the Congress Party itself; in the working of the Community Development Programme. At all these key points, rival ways of looking at and doing politics are meeting.

For this reason I agree with Professor Spann: it is somewhat pointless to ask whether a constitution is 'suited' to a country and its social structure when that very structure is in a state of flux and change. What is 'suited to the genius of a people' when that genius is undergoing transformation? That is why the attempt of Jaya

Prakash Narayan to devise a genuine 'Indian' polity would, if successful, only check and hamper the process of change and adjustment.

At the same time Narayan's views on Western institutions indicate a widespread real disillusionment. Indians when denied self-government came to have high and envious regard for parliamentary government. But the glamour has disappeared with the attempt to work these institutions. This has been helped by our 'exposures' of our own politics through studies of electoral behaviour, pressure groups and the like. No wonder many Indians feel they have been sold a shoddy article and that they ought to try to manufacture something genuine for themselves. This seems to take the form of replacing individuals by village communities, representative government by popular participation, political parties by consensus.

These are mainly the dreams of sick intellectuals, frustrated by limited opportunities (economic, social and political), living on idealised notions of ancient village republics, memories of the self-sacrificing, united freedom struggle and impossible standards of political rectitude. But these dreams have some influence on the tussle between modern and traditional styles of politics.

I have spoken of conflict, struggle between the languages of politics. This could be misleading. I do not mean that any one 'side' has to win; on the contrary, the process is one of profound interaction from which something new will come. Nor do I imply a necessarily explosive situation; for what might elsewhere be un-endurable tension may in India, in spite of the intellectuals, be lived with. Apart from the Congress umbrella, one must also count two blessings: the Indian mind's capacity to contain the irreconcilable and the peasant's stubborn scepticism which is sometimes called apathy.

MR. H. WOLFSOHN: In writing my paper, I asked the question, "What is constitutionalism?" and gave the answer: either the conscious or the instinctive obedience to traditional or constitutional procedures.

I was struck by the gap between the sophisticated attitude at the Centre and the attitudes of the traditional/agrarian community at the periphery. Where this gap exists, there cannot in my view be said to be a political community. It is true that, in nineteenth-century England, there was a 'gap'—Disraeli's Two Nations. But the lower nation shared the same political idiom, and there was agreement on the machinery to be used, for example, the suffrage. In India, the lower nation is inarticulate and also administratively incapable and unready to use Western political methods. The agrarian sector has not developed political activity—the villages are full of faction 'politics', but they are 'village politics', operating according to their own self-moving norms, and very largely traditional. They are no kind of political education for a modern community, and do not interact fruitfully with the politics going on at the centre. The villages have a basic hostility to, and fear of, government, which comes from outside with a syringe administering 'freedom lotion'. The attitude of the villagers has been an attitude of *retreat* from using the administration for their purposes. A claim is made that democracy abides in the Indian village; that the villagers have enjoyed democratic living for a long time. But the old village society, which Gandhi tried to revitalise, has been undermined by economic change and the market structure.

A constitution is a document which implies a customary advance. This is not so for India. There the constitution has been introduced either by imitation or by imposition, by an intelligentsia saturated by Western ideas of institutionalised individualism. Arguments regarding 'Rule of Law', are very dangerous. If the Rule of Law had been interpreted as working law, then India would have been blown sky-high long ago. If the Indian Constitution works smoothly, it does so because it does not work properly, but conservatively.

As regards forms of government, there seems to be a choice between the Stalinist totalitarian approach of enforced penetration of agrarian society, of extending the arm of government forcibly into areas where it is not welcome; and the Indian method of restrained 'puncturing' of society. To the villagers the difference between democracy and totalitarianism means nothing. Government is for them 'dysfunctional'. The more efficient it is, the more destructive.

PROF. R. RETZLAFF: The models to which Asian leaders have turned for guidance in their attempts to devise constitutional systems for their newly independent nations have been largely Western. More specifically, the British parliamentary system and the American presidential system have been viewed as the main alternatives open to them. This has had certain misleading consequences, for both of these models, in the countries of their origin, function in a fairly homogeneous social, economic, linguistic and cultural context. In the nations of South and Southeast Asia almost the reverse is true. Substantial religious, linguistic, ethnic and cultural minorities exist, and within national boundaries there are often strong regional feelings. The prevailing condition of economic backwardness, and the sharp competition for the limited rewards available, all too often engender feelings of distrust and suspicion between majority and minority communities. At the extremes one finds the majority fearing that minority protectionist demands are but the forerunner of stronger separatist tendencies; whereas the minority views gains made by members of the majority community as stemming from unfair discrimination against the minorities.

In some instances nationalist movements have been able to bridge this gap temporarily by appealing to the essentially negative symbols of anti-colonialism. The disappearance of the colonial power has, as a rule, led to the weakening of the sense of common cause between the majority and minority communities.

The task facing the constitution makers in these nations has been to secure a considerable degree of consensus on such fundamental matters as the structure and types of institutions to be adopted, as well as the procedures and practices upon which they would be based. But in the process of doing this they have been faced with the more basic problem of insuring that the constitutional document provides a viable basis for the consolidation of national unity.

India is an excellent example. The framers of the Indian Constitution were faced with the task of devising constitutional solutions to the indigenous problems of communalism, provincialism and linguism, which would substantially meet the expectations of all concerned and yet provide a firm basis for the consolidation and furtherance of national unity. The paper which I have presented shows how the makers of the Indian Constitution sought to resolve the problem of communal minorities. It was the problem. It was a stumbling block to constitutional advance in *the* pre-Independence period, and partition by no means removed the difficulties. The constitutional solution adopted by the Constituent Assembly was one which had the support of the majority community and segments of the various minority communities.

Unfortunately, substantial segments of two of the most important minority communities, the Sikhs and the Muslims, did not join in this approval. The last decade, and particularly the last year, has seen repeated attempts by Sikh leaders to secure additional safeguards and considerations beyond those recognised in the constitution. There have also been increasing indications that elements within the Muslim community might once again consider entering political life on a communal basis in order to press for the satisfaction of Muslim communal interests.

These tendencies in the field of communalism, as well as other events concerning provincialism and linguism, such as the intensity of feeling evoked by the States Reorganisation problem, underscore the importance of the actions taken by the framers of the Indian Constitution for the furtherance of Indian national unity. How far are the constitutional arrangements which they adopted based upon an accurate assessment of the underlying problems? The answer to this question will go a long way toward determining the extent to which the present government of India will be able to meet the fissiparous tendencies inherent in the Indian body politic and bring about the consolidation of national unity.

MR. CHARI: The papers under discussion refer to a very delicate area of Indian politics and they and the speeches are on the whole too polite. Take the case of untouchability. There are certain facades: there are scheduled caste ministers in the central cabinet; in Andhra the chief minister is a scheduled caste man. But on the whole it is not a question which we have dared to face.

However, outside observers may attach too much importance to the problem of caste in politics. For the Indian, the advantage now is not always in belonging to a higher caste, as it was before; it may be more profitable politically to belong to a backward caste which has its reserved seats. In the old days caste was cohesive; today the principle of cohesion is lost. In voting, caste has come in in a general sort of way, but I am not sure that it deserves the stress it has been given by some people.

MR. H. MAYER: Mr. Wolfsohn has argued that the limits of authority in countries such as India are not defined by legal structure. The main reason for this is the so-called 'gap' between rulers and ruled. Relevant questions seem to be: what sort of a gap? how big is it? and is anything happening to narrow or fill it?

Professor Morris-Jones thinks of the gap as being filled by political institutions, in which a two-way process of interaction is occurring. Western politics are not simply being imposed on traditional politics; they can also be *used* by traditional politics—it gives the latter a new way of influencing Western politics. Mr. Wolfsohn does not stress this point. Morris-Jones, unlike Wolfsohn, also allows for 'gap-closers', such as the State Parliaments. On the other hand, Wolfsohn stresses certain things that Morris-Jones seems to under-estimate, including the disruptive effect of social and economic processes. Morris-Jones stresses the stability of caste in face of 'Western' politics, Wolfsohn stresses the break-up of caste in the face of 'Western' economic changes.

Finally, if there is a gap, it is not necessarily fatal. As Dr. Johnson said: "There is a great deal of ruin within any society".

MR. BOSE: I detect in the papers the idea that Indians had a certain audacity in choosing for themselves a way that was truly Western. It is true that Indians are operating a system which was historically imposed on them from outside, by the British. I think it is fortunate that it was originally imposed; in any case it cannot now be reversed. What is there wrong and foolish in accepting something which has been accepted in all but the Iron Curtain countries? There is, incidentally, one important advantage in constitutional imitation. To use the language of existing constitutions, makes one the inheritor of the wealth of interpretation of other courts. Nor do I agree that the Rule of Law has been lost. Indians are a very litigious people, and value the processes of the court. Similarly, in politics, they feel that they have some power in using the vote.

PROF. MENON: The extent of the importance of caste has been exaggerated. It will decrease in the future; its main significance has been in the past. Caste is not a major force at the present. It does not dominate the parties, though parties may use and manipulate caste.

DR. D. A. LOW: The Morris-Jones view is now an old one so far as African studies are concerned. In studies by Barnes, Gluckman, Mitchell, Apter and Epstein (among others) the interaction of differing political idioms has been studied in several different African territories. In his book *Bantu Bureaucracy* (Cambridge, 1955) Professor Lloyd A. Fallers in particular has described a situation where the interaction is not between different groups representing different idioms, but between different idioms demanding the allegiance of one and the same person. The chiefs of Busoga in Uganda, whom he describes, feel simultaneously the legitimacy of the demands of their kin groups, of their client followers and of the norms of the civil service to which they belong. A working equilibrium does not, however, seem to be beyond their capacity for adjustment, delicate and difficult though this often is.

PROF. STONE: One of the features which struck me most in India was the amazing capacity for coexistence of wholly diverse moral, political and cultural orders, combined with slow organic changes in society. The agonising difficulty is not that this chaotic pluralism is not possible: it is possible. It is that there are the most pressing reasons for changing these orders, and yet if you press on at all fast with social change, you are likely to find it hard to maintain constitutional government simultaneously with radical disturbances of the pattern of tribal and kin relations, or changes in the level and distribution of literacy. Much patience and time are vital to any constitutional growth especially in such conditions. "It is not for thee to finish the task; it is not for thee to desist from it." Yet not only his own years but the world situation lead Nehru to lack patience, and to doubt whether he has time.

PROF. C. P. FITZGERALD: The wish for consensus which Morris-Jones found in India is an idea found throughout the East, especially in China. This partly explains the growth of single parties in India, Burma and Malaya. There is the idea that there is a great truth which everyone must appreciate. There is often little or no idea of the right of an opposition to compete for government and the spectacle of a unified party and of political consensus is not repellent.

PROF. RETZLAFF: I agree with Fitzgerald that an understanding of the notion of consensus is basic to an appreciation of Indian politics, particularly politics at the State and local level. It is an important aspect of the system of traditional politics at the village level and goes a long way toward explaining the opposition one encounters to formal elections on the basis of majority rule; an opposition found not only in the villages but also in certain official and intellectual circles. The need to secure consensus in the decision making process has been an important factor which has enabled the upper caste groups in rural India to frustrate rapid socio-economic change. By making their approval necessary, regardless of their numerical status, they have been able to insure that the decisions taken would not pose a threat to their positions of dominance. Unfortunately, relatively little has been said about the challenge to such consensus-based systems posed by the introduction of modern political institutions, based upon notions of majority rule and the secret ballot.

MR. WOLFSOHN: Consensus can only exist while the speed of development is not overdone. I do not deny that integration is possible.

PROF. MORRIS-JONES: Prof. Menon is going too far when he says simply that "parties use and manipulate caste". This is true, but there is a two-way process. They are also 'used by' caste. One might compare this with the introduction of courts in India which gave traditional forces a new platform for their quarrels, but these traditional forces were also changed in the process. The same is now happening with universal suffrage and political parties.

I agree with Mr. Wolfsohn that speed is an important factor especially with the apathetic Indian masses. From the point of view of social stability, the pace should not be too fast. There is pressure from the educated urban elite to increase the pace, and such pressure will erode the apathy.

There are various factors in India which assist the survival of a large 'government' party. For example, things are weighted so that governments win elections, as in eighteenth-century England. The majority of votes are won by those who are in a position to do things in return for favours. It is likely that a big party will survive, so long as it can maintain internal coherence.

Maung Maung

THE SEARCH FOR CONSTITUTIONALISM
IN BURMA

THIS IS an attempt to study the important features of the Constitution of Burma, the big events in its young career, the problems it has faced and the solutions it has found for them. The story of the constitution is neither spectacular nor sensational, but it has revealed a quiet faith and a steadfast hope that promise well for the future. There have been times when, owing either to the stress of difficult situations or the complacency of the party that was in predominant power, the constitution seemed to lie dormant; but it never died. There were times when great pressures were put on it; but it never broke down. The constitution has even survived a government led by a General; peculiarly, and perhaps uniquely, the General was voted into office by Parliament, and he abdicated power voluntarily after conducting the freest and fairest of elections so far.

In May, 1947, when the leaders of the nationalist struggle, leading the united front called the Anti-Fascist People's Freedom League (AFPFL) met, after the elections to the Constituent Assembly, to draft the constitution, their main concern was to get it over with, to close the negotiations with His Majesty's Government in Whitehall and make Burma's freedom a reality. The leaders were young: the foremost among them, Aung San, was 33, and he had commanded the national army that was forged during the war and employed in the resistance. The other leaders, 'fathers of the constitution', were also young, and they came from the same background of political agitation and student strikes in their aniversity days, of the 'Red Dragon' leftist bookclub where they translated Fabian essays or Marxist literature or Hitler or Mussolini indiscriminately, of the army and the resistance. Whatever label they chose to wear, Marxist, Socialist, or Fabian, they were nationalists, and they dreamed their dreams of freedom and a brave new world.

114

Some of the dreams got written down in the preamble of the constitution; some find a place in the chapter on fundamental rights, some are more cautiously consigned to the chapter on directive principles which are guides but not binding law. It was fortunate that these young leaders who looked upon themselves as revolutionaries were able to work in calm on the constitution; the transfer of power from His Majesty's Government was by friendly negotiation and agreement, and it was to the basic constitutional principles as evolved by British genius that the young revolutionaries looked for their guidance. The assistance of judges and lawyers trained in the British system was also taken in drafting the constitution, and the final draft was given its polish by Sir Benegal Rau of India who was then Constitutional Adviser to the Government of India.

The constitution was adopted by the Constituent Assembly on September 24, 1947, and it came into force on January 4, 1948, when the Union of Burma launched out as an independent state outside the Commonwealth of Nations. Already at that time the Communists in the country, expelled from the AFPFL for their subversion, were crying out that genuine independence could only be bought in blood, and that the AFPFL, in receiving the country's independence by treaty with His Majesty's Government was guilty of a sell-out. To give the lie to the Communists the AFPFL decided that Burma must leave the Commonwealth with independence. The other factor that probably weighed with the drafters of the constitution was their choice of the republican form of state, and their traditional thinking that that form would not conform with Commonwealth membership; if the decision had had to be made a few years later, after a formula had been devised to reconcile Commonwealth membership with the republican form of government, it might well have been a different story.

Parliament

Sovereignty, under the constitution, resides in the people, and they exercise it normally through general elections held every four years. Parliament is bicameral; the Chamber of Deputies has 250 seats distributed on a population basis throughout the country; the Chamber of Nationalities has 125 seats allocated to racial groups in such a way that members representing the minorities, should they combine, can outvote the members representing the majority race, the Burman, at any time. There is universal suffrage without any property or educational qualifications, the voting age is 18. Buddhist priests and members of a 'religious order' are disqualified from voting. Every citizen who has the right to vote and has attained the age of 21 can stand as a candidate. Both chambers enjoy equal power in regard to legislation except that 'money bills' must be initiated and passed by the Deputies; the Nationalities can delay a 'money bill' for not more than 21 days after it has been sent to them. The Deputies nominate the Prime Minister who then selects his own Cabinet of Ministers.

From 1947 to 1952, the Constituent Assembly acted, as allowed by the transitional provisions of the constitution, as the Provisional Parliament. Unrest in the country made it necessary for the general elections to be held on a staggered and regional basis between 1951 and 1952. In those elections the AFPFL won an overwhelming majority, and Parliament was a rather formal and complacent affair, going through the motions. The Opposition—what there was of it —could not muster the necessary votes to move a no-confidence motion, and the most spectacular gesture it could show was the sit-down strike or the walkout.

There were two sessions a year, once in August to vote the budget, and then in February to vote the revised estimates; each session would last four or five weeks, and the daily meetings were short and sweet, sometimes lasting five minutes. Prime Minister U Nu himself, as he later admitted, did not care to appear in the Chamber of Deputies where he belonged, and when he had major statements of policy to make he would make them at his press conferences or at ceremonial functions. Legislation was apt to be hasty when the Government could translate every bright new idea into law, drafted in a few days and pushed through the two Chambers. Within the AFPFL party itself strength bred arrogance. Since the party ticket was an essential for electoral victory, members of Parliament who dared to ask embarrassing questions in Parliament or at party meetings were sternly disciplined or expelled, and soon members were quiescent. This state of affairs was reflected too in the behaviour of the government where party influence was unduly strong, and whose attitude towards Parliament and the Judiciary was tinged with some superiority complex.

In Burma the people do not like dictators. This may sound paradoxical when, in her long history of independence, Burma had always had absolute monarchs. Yet, kings and governments have always been classed as 'enemies', to avoid when possible, to keep away from, and to offer bribes to in the event of unavoidable collision. By and large the kings lived in their palaces, collected their taxes, and the people lived their lives and developed their own democratic way of life in the villages. Thus the AFPFL party, with its predominance and the arrogance and smugness that usually go along with it, began to lose its popularity. By 1956, when the general elections were held again, this time simultaneously through the country, voters in many areas were ready to vote for anyone who chose to oppose the party. The AFPFL, as the party in power, used its vast resources, including influence, in an effort to wrest total victory. However, the National United Front, an alliance of the Burma Workers and Peasants Party and other splinter groups and the Justice Party led by one-time Supreme Court Justice Dr. E. Maung, won some 46 seats in the Chamber of Deputies. The number of votes polled by the NUF was more impressive than the number of seats won: according to NUF research the Front polled 1,139,206 votes against the AFPFL's 1,743,816, or 44·8 per cent of the total (also counting its allies) against the AFPFL's 47·9 per cent.

For those AFPFL leaders who cared to see, it was the writing on the wall, and U Nu took leave of absence from the premiership to clean up and reorganise the party. After a few frustrating months he resumed office, and he promised Parliament that he would be more respectful to it, participate in its work and report to it first on major policies. He also promised to give fair play to the NUF opposition which was now in a position to move no-confidence motions. One of the first things that U Nu did, to keep his promise of keeping Parliament informed of major policy formulations, was to deliver a four-hour long speech, as if to pay a debt with interest. Parliamentary sessions, however, were still too brief, and according to the research service maintained by the NUF there were only 141 days and 402 hours of effective sitting of Parliament from 1956 to December 1959.

Union Government

The Prime Minister, the kingpin of the government, is elected by the Chamber of Deputies. He chooses his own Ministers whose terms of office depend on his pleasure.

The Communist rebellion broke out 83 days after independence was proclaimed, and for many years the Union Government had its hands full dealing with the rebellion, and others which followed. Partly to outdo the Communists and thereby take the wind out of their sails and partly from sincere conviction, the government launched many 'socialist programmes' such as nationalisation of industries, the taking over of land belonging to absentee landlords and their redistribution to the landless, and welfare projects in health and education. These programmes made big demands on the slender manpower resources, and it took the Government some years to realise that first things must be done first.

A big problem of government was the encroachment of the party into the day-to-day work of the administration. Division between policy and execution was often lost sight of, leading to confusion or frustrations on the part of the permanent staff. Senior Secretaries of the government who, normally, would run the administration of their departments, were often reduced in practice to the status of office assistants who submitted their files to the Ministers for the smallest decision. This happened partly owing to the fear of the civil servants of displeasing the Minister—displeasure would often attract dismissals or transfers to less attractive posts or demotions—and partly, in course of time, because of the laziness of the staff and indisposition to make decisions. Gradually, the Secretariat began to slow down as cases travelled their slow and uncertain way from one table to another and collected, sometimes, before the Cabinet.

The Union Government started off with high socialist ideals and the Ministers took much reduced salaries—k. 1,700 a month—and expected the civil servants to be likewise noble-minded. In the first few years, when the senior staff retired rapidly, promotions were quick and often meteoric, and the reductions in salaries were not felt. Later, however, when the young Secretaries found themselves faced with years of service ahead on fixed maximum salaries of k. 1,600, they did not find the prospect cheerful. In the 'golden days' before the war, the government officer enjoyed social status, and young graduates would often rather serve as clerks in the government offices than teach or take up an independent profession. After the war, authority waned and the social standing of the government officer fell; in the district it was the Member of Parliament or the party leader who liked to give the orders. The cost of living shot up, and government servants who did not resort to corruption—and they remain the majority—had to live on the borderlands of bare subsistence. When government activities increased and expanded into business and industry the responsibilities of the staff increased, but not their rewards; it was the same Secretaries who had to serve as chairmen of several boards and corporations, and much of their time was consumed by meetings.

At the Cabinet level another problem was the need to provide jobs for the party leaders. Political office had its glamour and privileges, and no party leader of standing wanted to remain at the party to organise: the scramble was for a ministry. The result was that the Cabinet had to be enlarged gradually, and ten years after independence its size had just about trebled. The party in power worked only fitfully in-between elections; its leadership saddled itself with office and liked it; in the districts too the party lost touch with the people as the leaders either took jobs at the capital, or spent most of their time there hunting for privilege. Ministries were carved out of ministries, so that they became small departments, and many of the ministers, with time on their hands, dabbled in the day-to-day work which should have been left to the permanent staff. The Ministry of National Solidarity, for example, was created on brilliant inspiration, but the Minister and his Secretaries had no work to do, and the only solidarity that was achieved there was the marriage between the Minister, a sturdy and brilliant Kachin, and his Burman stenographer.

The Judiciary

The constitution provides for an independent Judiciary and the Supreme Court has the power to check the Executive and Parliament by writs. Judges of the High Court and the Supreme Court are appointed by the President after Parliament in joint session has approved the government's nominations. The framers of the constitution toyed with the idea of electing the Judges for a period of ten years each time, but this was abandoned on the persuasion of Judges who were trained in the British tradition. There is a permanent judicial service into which a young graduate of law can enter without any practice at the Bar, and he can gradually rise to the High Court or the Supreme Court. Members of the Bar— barristers called by one of the Inns of Court in England, and Advocates who have qualified in Burma—are also eligible for appointment to the higher ranks of the judicial service or the High Court or the Supreme Court. Appointments, postings and transfers in the judicial service are in the care of the High Court and the Supreme Court where Judges serve during good behaviour till they are 60, in the former, and 65 in the latter. A Judge of the High Court draws k. 2,500 a month, a Supreme Court Justice and the Chief Justice of the High Court draw k. 3,000. The Chief Justice of the Union draws k. 3,500 and ranks near the top in the Order of Precedence.

The Judiciary has, in the years of trouble, come under many pressures and so far resisted them stoutly. There is the Executive with its impatience and claim for priority in handling emergency situations; there is the party in power which tends to look upon whatever stands in its path as unpatriotic. The Executive was armed by Parliament with special powers, such as the power to take into preventive detention persons who were suspected of being engaged in 'prejudicial acts', and it was left to the Supreme Court to correct, by entry of the writ of *habeas corpus*, abuses and excesses of the powers. The Executive would normally take such corrections with grace, but sometimes it would get Parliament to amend the law and vest it with even larger powers which it could wield with only formal checks by the court. There was also a tendency among the leaders of the AFPFL, and the Prime Minister himself, to criticise the decisions of the courts in Parliament or in their public speeches, complaining that the courts were too careful about the letter of the law and the lawyers too sharp in finding the loopholes.

Another danger to the independence of the Judiciary came, paradoxically enough, from the respect shown to it by the Executive. Judges were looked up to and in great demand to chair the many special enquiry commissions which grew like mushrooms. Some of the commissions were concerned with political matters, e.g. enquiry into the desirability of statehood for certain clamorous minority groups, parliamentary election tribunals, enquiry into the state of certain boards and corporations of which political leaders were chairmen, enquiry into the honesty or otherwise of certain Ministers. The Judges did not relish their role on the commissions, but in the shortage of men of their eminence and stature they could not well refuse, and sometimes these roles exposed them to misunderstandings. Another practice which often had unexpectedly bad effects was that of some Ministers to consult the Judges informally on matters of public moment; both sides were well-meaning, but when the matters flared into public controversy and the ministers blurted out that they had had prior consultations with the Judges they innocently drew the Judiciary into the controversy.

The States

There were three autonomous units or States in the Union of Burma at the time the constitution came into force, and the Karen state was created, after much bloodshed, in 1951, after an amendment of the constitution. The Arakanese and Mon minorities have also been clamouring for their own States, and Prime Minister U Nu has pledged that if the majority of their peoples express their wish for statehood the new States will be created. There is also a special administrative division for the Chins, who did not ask for statehood; the division has its Chin Affairs Minister and the Chin Affairs Council, but otherwise it operates very much like any other administrative division.

A peculiar feature of the constitution is the dual role played by Members of Parliament elected from each state. They attend the Union Parliament like any other Member, and in their state they compose the State Council. The Prime Minister of the Union after consulting the State Council appoints a Minister for the State who then becomes the Head of the State and plays a dual role again. This arrangement, it was thought at the time of writing the constitution, made for economy in money and manpower, and also for closer relations between the units and the Union. There is no 'centre' or federal structure; it is only in the States that there are miniature parliaments and cabinets. The drafters of the constitution drew their inspiration for this arrangement from the British, rather than a pure federal system. The arrangement worked well enough when the

AFPFL enjoyed unchallenged majority throughout the Union; when it split, and the split reached out to the states also, some Heads of States found themselves in the minority in their Councils, and there was deadlock and confusion in the government of the States.

The President

The fathers of the constitution did not want to restore the old monarchy, nor did they want to have a President directly elected by the people and invested with full executive powers for a fixed term for fear that he might, during that term of office organise to perpetuate his reign. Nor did they want a President who had only ceremonial functions, an expensive ornament of state. Their search for a mean between the two does not seem to have been too successful, for in normal times the President of the Union has only ceremonial functions. All executive business is done in his name, and the constitution takes pains to provide that he must act only on the advice of the Union Government. He signs bills passed by Parliament, but should he fail or refuse to do so the bills are deemed to have received his signature seven days after reaching him.

In times of crisis, however, the President has an important role to play. If the Prime Minister were defeated in the Chamber of Deputies, for example, on a major issue of policy or a no-confidence motion, and he decided to recommend a dissolution, the President might or might not accept the recommendation. This, of course, is a prerogative of the Crown in the United Kingdom, but one which is of academic interest in the developed state of the party system and its employment would be guided by established conventions. In Burma, however, the party system is still young, and it is not inconceivable that a party which has enjoyed predominance might suddenly break up—as happened to the AFPFL—or the alliances shift for the sake of convenience or gain. At the time of the AFPFL split one big question which loomed over the entire desperate scene was whether, if the Prime Minister could be out-voted on the no-confidence motion, and if he did choose to ask for a dissolution, the President would comply. Fortunately, however, the Prime Minister survived the motion, and the question receded into the background unresolved.

There are also certain 'rights' and 'discretionary powers' belonging to the President. The right of pardon, for example, is an important one which has been used to proclaim general amnesty for insurgents by Presidential Order. Must the right be exercised only on the advice of the Union Government? The discretionary power to seek the advisory opinion of the Supreme Court on legal problems of national significance is also an important power which has been invoked by the President himself, by signing the letters of reference, on the request of the Union Government. Can a Minister or a Secretary pose the questions to the Supreme Court, signing the letter of reference in the name of the President as the rules of executive business allow for normal government transactions?

The President has the right to be informed, consulted, and to advise. He addresses Parliament in joint sessions, usually at the inaugural meeting, and he delivers the annual address on Independence Day in which the Union Government's policies are outlined.

The first President—the 'Provisional President' as he was called because the first Parliament had not yet been elected then—was a Shan chief who, after his term, served for several years as Speaker of the Chamber of Nationalities. The Chief Justice of the Union, a Burman, succeeded him, and a Karen leader, who for many years was a Minister, was elected in 1957 for the 5-year term. Parliament in joint session elects the President; if he is a Member of Parliament he gives up his seat on taking oath of office. U Win Maung, the President today, is a young man even by Burmese standards, being in his early forties and he has often complained that his office is more suitable for elderly men on the verge of their retirement from active life, than for young men of ambition. U Win Maung has, however, managed to reduce the ceremonial and ritual of his office and make it more popular; he has not hesitated to give his views on matters of public interest even if they happen to be controversial, and in his unique way he is helping the development of the role of the President.

The AFPFL Split

After ten years of holding the State together, the AFPFL broke up early in 1958. The party had served the country well and the only alternative to its rule during the period would have been chaos and anarchy or a communist dictatorship. Like people everywhere, the party's leaders had their weaknesses, but they were up against too many odds and it was to their credit that they kept the name and some of the essence of democracy alive in difficult times. The party broke too because the party system itself was still young and tender; its roots did not go very deep, and people voted for personalities rather than principles and programmes. And the men who had led the AFPFL, the young men who led the university strikes and the resistance, were growing weary of each other's company and getting on each other's nerves.

The break-up of the AFPFL was the biggest test for the constitution and the greatest opportunity. The two factions called each other names, and dug up the blackest deeds of their past. But they did not go 'underground' and take up arms as did the communists in 1948. They fought their wordy wars in the Press and the public places. The constitution, which had lain dormant and forgotten, was remembered and each faction swore by it and pledged itself to die guarding it. The smallest word in the constitution, a full-stop or a comma, took on new significance as different interpretations were advanced of some obscure powers and privileges. Parliament, for many years a formality, now took on great importance, and each individual Member, for many years a mere number or vote, now became a man to woo and win. Resort was had to many sharp practices to win the Members, from bribing them with money or promise of office, to kidnapping or nursing them in well-provided homes for the precious day of voting on the no-confidence motion. Those were not practices to be proud of, but they were fun, and the people enjoyed the fun, as did the newspapers whose sales soared. The main thing was that the constitution survived, and even grew stronger from the crisis. Politicians also began to look upon the Judiciary as a refuge, not a rival, and within a few months of the split in the party two references were made by the President on the constitution, as compared with three in the ten preceding years.

The Prime Minister threw out the no-confidence motion, but his majority was thin—only 8—and the National United Front, which the AFPFL used to treat with contempt and dub the 'aboveground Communist Party', had supported him. It was an impossible situation, and it became more and more obvious that general elections must be held early to remove the tensions and break the deadlock. The AFPFL was trained in the struggle for freedom and power, and for long years had been accustomed to the exercise of power; now one faction of it was the government, and another was in parliamentary opposition, and the roles were strange to both.

Thus the tensions mounted, and Prime Minister U Nu with his inimitable shrewdness and statesmanship decided that power must be handed over to a neutral person or body on a caretaker basis while the parties prepared to seek the people's mandate in the elections. There were few who were neutral in the country at the time, and it was once again to General Ne Win, Chief of Staff of the Defence Services, whom U Nu had appointed as Deputy Premier in 1949 at the height of the communist insurrection, that the Prime Minister looked. General Ne Win accepted the invitation to lead a caretaker government with modest reluctance and gave a written undertaking, signed by several of his young Colonels as well—to work for the restoration of law and order in the country, and the conduct of fair and free elections within a specified time. U Nu resigned from the Premiership at a special session of the Chamber of Deputies and moved that General Ne Win be elected to take over; the NUF growled and grumbled that there had been a *coup*, but the AFPFL faction which had been in the opposition rejoiced, for now they could take on U Nu on equal terms.

The Ne Win Interlude

General Ne Win appointed a small Cabinet of Ministers, choosing from among Judges and senior civil servants in order to uphold the political neutrality of his government, and went to his task with zeal and vigour. His time was limited and the task was huge; he set as his prior objectives the suppression of insurrections and lawlessness, the lowering of the cost of living, and the creation of conditions in which free elections could be held. He did not seek special powers from Parliament to accomplish his task, nor did he ask the President to give him any by way of Presidential Ordinance. Parliament met as usual in regular sessions, debated and passed the budget and the laws. The General and his Ministers, however, were in the unique position of being able to carry out their work without having to lobby in Parliament or with the parties for votes; they were under no obligations to voters or followers and they were not going to stand for elections. Work therefore progressed smoothly and rapidly yielded remarkable results. Young Colonels and officers were also lent to the civilian departments to inject new energy and confidence into staff who were rather demoralised and confused by the political upheavals, and there was more efficiency and less corruption. Rangoon which was a city fast falling under slums of refugees from the villages was cleaned up and the refugees resettled in the suburbs; that was a task which party governments had attempted several times but given up in the face of demonstrations and demands. For that kind of work it was an advantage for the government to have no elections to face in its near future.

Many of the methods used by the Ne Win Government were drastic. The very speed with which things moved was drastic where insurrections and inefficiency had weighed down on everything and reduced motion to a minimum. The stern discipline with which things were done, almost on the scale and certainly on the pattern of military operations, was irksome to the people who were accustomed to a free and happy life. In the midst of all the zealous cleaning up, however, General Ne Win had his sights firmly fixed on the main targets: the upholding of the constitution, the conduct of free elections. His government respected the independence of the Judiciary and tried to give added vigour to the principle of the Rule of Law. People acquired a new confidence in the courts and the government services, and came forth to file reports or give evidence, and the crime indexes fell sharply in a short time.

The armed forces in Burma are not yet what are commonly called 'professional' or 'mercenary'. They have grown out of the struggle for freedom, and many of the army leaders were with the political leaders in the struggle. They have their ideals, therefore, and tend to look upon their role as larger than that of mere soldiers in arms. They have good intentions, and energy, and for many years when the country has been torn by civil strife, they have had to take on tasks, such as administration, education and welfare, which do not normally fall on soldiers. As soon as the insurrections were put under control, the army had started to train and re-educate itself, and in its search for an unerring and eternal guide had found the constitution. Political parties might come and go, the soldiers decided, but the constitution must abide for all time with its ideals undimmed, and they would respect it and protect it, serving the people and all constitutional governments with loyalty. The constitution thus came to be taught in army schools, and the soldiers became constitution-conscious even before the parties did. That was fortunate for the country, for when General Ne Win became Premier there was never a doubt that he would do his duty under the constitution, hold the elections and give up political power in due time, and, what was equally important, that his officers and men would take his orders and serve within the constitution unquestioningly.

Prospects

General elections were held early in February 1960 and U Nu has returned to power with an overwhelming majority. His battlecry in the campaign was 'Democracy', and in the few months that he has been back at office he has been showing magnanimity to his opponents and patience and tolerance in all his dealings. He has said that he will devote the next four years of his office to laying firm foundations for democracy and the rule of law, and will not play with fanciful ideas such as welfare and *pyidawtha*, the happy land. First things must come first, and he has likened Burma to a patient for whom the doctors have almost given up hope, and the administrative machinery to a broken down jeep without tyres or even the essential parts of the engine: "I can't drive this affair at 160 miles an hour!"

Burma is still at school, learning what democracy is, trying to make democracy more than a sweet-sounding word, to make it part of the habit and instincts of the people in their daily life. Much has been learnt in the last eventful decade; much more needs to be learnt.

The political parties need to learn, for they had been schooled in agitation, in slogan-shouting, demonstrations and strikes. They now need to be more constructive. They now need to learn to govern as responsible rulers, or oppose as the responsible opposition. The importance of the Opposition in Parliament was recognised by General Ne Win who established by statute the office of the Opposition Leader on an equal footing with that of a Minister of the Cabinet. Prime Minister U Nu is setting a good example by consulting the Opposition on matters of national interest, and by keeping up friendly relations with its leaders. So unused are the people and the parties to the sight of Government leaders and Opposition leaders smiling together or dining together that every such coming together still gives rise to rumours of reconciliation or a coalition government. The time when such friendly exchanges are taken as normal will be when democracy has found its firm feet.

The civil service is being encouraged to serve the government not the party, and the people loyally. To give them the courage to be independent, the Prime Minister has turned over such matters as appointments, postings and transfers to special committees appointed from the services, and has promised further to improve the conditions of the civil servant.

The independence of the Judiciary is respected; the rule of law is a priority; the government has promised to repeal or amend emergency laws, withdraw special arbitrary powers, and submit justiciable issues to the courts and abide by the decisions.

The soldiers have returned to the barracks, submitting with grace to civilian authority. The Prime Minister himself has taken the Ministry of Defence and the transition has been smooth. The role of the armed forces in peace-time needs to be thought of and defined, so that the young, eager men, imbued with ideals, may be given the opportunity to serve better in the nation-building.

The people need to learn too that democracy is a two-way traffic, a matter of give-and-take, that they too must give to make it grow. Demonstrations and demands, agitation and strikes do not build the nation; quiet, sustained endeavour is required. The people, however, have their lovable traits. They are cheerful, and their Buddhist philosophy teaches them tolerance and patience; they have resilience to recover quickly from the many troubles that have come down on them in recent years. They have also discovered the magic of the secret ballot, and at elections they will always defy the bully and reject the pompous; like all peoples, they may be swept along on emotional waves and vote by the heart and not by the head, but they will vote as they wish.

The constitution has come through intact, but its search for its levels must continue. Some way must be found, for example, to make the delicate machinery of parliamentary government work; there has been an avalanche for U Nu and he has been able to gather massive majority for his government, but it is not improbable that parties will splinter and split and future governments come under the curse of multi-party parliaments: yet there is no way to develop the two-party system except by the slow process of weeding out the undesirables at elections by educating the voters. Values need to be adjusted and the perspectives set, giving to each his own place, the politician, the civil servant, the professional man, so that all can work and march forward together instead of scrambling for privilege and superiority. The future no doubt has its problems and perils for Burma, but with patience, tolerance and a free mind she should be able to go ahead and grow a democracy which is best suited to her soil.

PROF. MACMAHON BALL (Chairman): We may have to give a broader definition to constitutionalism in the setting of a country where the primary need is economic development. It will not necessarily be identified with any particular democratic form but with freedom from caprice and the arbitrary decisions of rulers, as 'authority' or 'authoritarianism' but without injustice and without terror.

MR. JUSTICE ELSE-MITCHELL: I should like to take issue with the Chairman. We all like the generality of such phrases as 'justice'. However, the essential point is who is to decide in the particular case when authority has overstepped the bounds. Ultimately in any system where you have power in the hands of any group, there must be some organism to determine the limits of that power. Parliaments play part of this role in relation to the executive. But in the final issue no better way has been found than by confiding this task to the courts.

MR. NISH: The first impression which one derives from reading Dr. Maung's paper and hearing his remarks, is that the Burmese constitution has had very little effect on the history of Burma in the last formative decade. "The constitution seemed to lie dormant; but it never died." "The constitution came through intact." The constitution has been a passive rather than an active force in Burma's political development. Up to 1958 Parliament held only brief sessions; and the Prime Minister made his policy statements at press conferences rather than in the Chamber. Yet the constitution has not been repudiated, even during the period of military rule.

Another impression left by Dr. Maung's paper is that he has not asked us to look at the Burmese constitution or its politics as those of a Buddhist state. This surprises me because I have always thought that there was something about Burmese politics which could not be explained in Western terms. When in 1956 U Nu retired from politics, he announced that he was entering a monastery. Here, we thought, was something which could only happen in a Buddhist State. At the same time in India, Pandit Nehru frequently announced his intention of going into retreat for a year, a type of abnegation which is quite alien to Western politicians. We would like to hear more from Dr. Maung about the part played in Burmese politics by Buddhism which has lately been so active in Ceylon.

Our interest is naturally focussed on the period of military rule from October 1958 until February 1960. The cause of the military take-over appears to have been the split of the AFPFL party. This raises the important general issue: the working of a single-party system with one large 'independence' party which has been a feature in Asian countries. Perhaps the situation is not dissimilar to that in India where the Congress Party probably still receives great support at elections because of its past record as an 'independence' party regardless of its present constructive policies.

Dr. Maung states two interesting propositions on this subject. First, when the single party—the AFPFL—was supreme, the constitution was dormant; when an opposition party came into being, the constitution became the battle-cry and parliamentary institutions began to matter. Second, as party politics increased, the efficiency of the administration declined. When power returned to U Nu after the elections of February 1960, there was a sharp decline from the efficient administration of the Ne Win regime.

From Dr. Maung's special knowledge, he is able to escort us behind the scenes of the military take-over. He reminds us that General Ne Win was voted into office by Parliament; and praises U Nu for his statesmanlike action in making over office to the military. U Nu can be applauded for his shrewd political manoeuvre but surely this was an act of desperation and can hardly be described as a statesmanlike solution. I had always suspected that what happened in Burma was a seizure of power by the army in the same way as within a matter of a few months Marshal Sarit took over in Thailand and General Ayub in Pakistan. But Dr. Maung tells us that "when General Ne Win became Premier there was never a doubt that he would do his duty under the constitution". Indeed the uniqueness of the Burmese military take-over was not in the army assuming power but in the army returning power to the civil government. Burma's experience is distinguished by the devotion of the military and the strange abnegation not just of General Ne Win but also of the 'young colonels'. This suggests an unexpected respect for the otherwise nominal constitutionalism in Burma about which I should like to hear more.

PROF. SAWER: On the question of the influence of Buddhism, I remember an experience when I sat in on meetings of the Ceylon committee on capital punishment. Professor Norval Morris attempted to find out the Buddhist attitude to capital punishment, but the Buddhist hierarchy refused to commit themselves. Eventually he managed to get three young Buddhist intellectuals to express a view, but they proved very slippery during questioning. It was clear that in principle Buddhists felt they could not have any attitude on this matter, nor indeed on any practical matters of state.

This is in some respects a good thing, since probably democracy works best in countries where powerful organised religious groups or churches interfere least in the ordinary day-to-day business of government. But it is also a great difficulty in any society if there is no general acceptance of a set of moral values and even acceptance of a common moral code, at least in general terms, and it is also very desirable that these values and this code should provide some guidance to the makers of constitutions and of laws, even on relatively mundane affairs. A legal system having no relationship to the moral system of the people concerned would be unworkable. If, however, the dominant organised religion of a country refuses on principle to supply any practical guidance at all to the legislator, then there is serious danger of the constitution and the law becoming disassociated from the people's moral code.

PROF. MORRIS-JONES: I sense in some of the non-lawyers here a certain sceptical impatience with complacent talk about constitutionalism in Asia. They are perhaps scared that if we listen only to the lawyers we shall be caught napping by the next military *coup d'etat*.

I want to defend the lawyers. They do well to dwell on procedures, for these are not 'mere' means; they are not neutral in effect, they are 'end-conditioning'. In countries like India where a constitutional system has been in steady operation for some time, people are moulded by it. Even those who follow procedures without understanding the point of them are nevertheless changed by doing so. The following of certain rules—in courts, in parliaments, even in electoral behaviour—points men towards certain values. One might add the further small point that legal ways of thought cannot be uninfluential in countries where so many politicians are lawyers.

Moreover, adherence to constitutionalism need not always be fragile just because men seem not to care enough about Liberty (with a capital L). After all, constitutionalism in Britain developed out of the protection of privileges, small-l liberties. It was also born of suspicion of government. In many Asian countries deep-seated distrust of government still plays a part in strengthening attachment to constitutional procedures.

DR. MAUNG: I would like to add to my paper some words about the period of army rule in Burma, as I think this has been widely misunderstood. The period of army rule was distinguished by the following features: First, Ne Win was *invited* by the Prime Minister U Nu to assume power for a limited period; secondly, the psychology of the army was interesting. The men concerned were not always very bright but were honest and courageous and hard-working. They came to work early in the morning and left late at night—not a common feature previously. They had respect for regulations and worked 'by the book'. If you could show them a law they would stick to it.

They respected the idea of democracy and wanted to work it. In fact, it was under the Ne Win Government that official recognition was first given to the post of Leader of the Opposition.

Javid Iqbal

THE ISLAMIC STATE IN PAKISTAN

IT HAS been declared time and again that Pakistan is an ideological
State, a State which is founded on the ideology of Islam. A question
may be asked: to what extent is the Pakistanis' claim to be the
inhabitants of an ideological state justified?

I

The Hindus and Muslims of the Indian sub-continent entered
modern history as two distinct and separate religious communities—
the former, a majority, and the latter, a large minority. Whereas the
infiltration of such new ideas as nationalism, radicalism, secularism
and constitutionalism from the West made the Hindus politically
conscious and forward-looking, it had the effect of making the Muslims look back to their glorious past, to the days when they were
the masters of India. Consequently Muslims clung to their medieval
social order, refused to accept modernity, and let Hindus take a lead
in modern education and economic development.

When the Hindus came under the spell of Indian nationalism and
demanded the introduction of representative institutions or dreamed
of establishing self-rule in India, the Muslims, for the first time in
their political history, became conscious of their educational, economic and numerical inferiority. A democratic government, they felt,
would mean the rule of the Hindu majority. Accordingly, to safeguard their interests, they insisted that if democratic institutions
were introduced in India, it should be on the basis of separate
electorates for Hindus and Muslims. The acceptance of this demand
in the Constitutional Reforms of 1909 facilitated the introduction of
democracy in India; at the same time it established the Muslims as a
distinct political entity.

For many years the Muslims were on the defensive. Their
political activity continued to be inspired by the anxiety that if India

attained independence there would hardly be any share for them in self-government at the Centre owing to their numerical inferiority. However, there were territories in the Indian sub-continent where they predominated. As the Muslims progressed politically, they came to lose interest in the Centre and gave their whole-hearted support to the idea of federal government in India with a large amount of provincial autonomy. From 1925 to 1935 their political struggle concentrated on the demand for the extension of the reformed constitution to the North West Frontier and Baluchistan, separation of Sind from Bombay Presidency and its establishment as a separate province, and the bringing of the Muslim majority into power in the Punjab and Bengal.

The Hindus opposed the Muslim demand for federalism with a large amount of provincial autonomy, because it meant the creation of a Muslim bloc in the North West of India. Muslims started to regard 'the vast continent of India' as 'a geographical misnomer' having no unity except 'the misleading unity of opposition'. The cleavage between Hindus and Muslims gradually made the Muslims conscious of themselves as a nation.

The extension of constitutional reforms to the North West Frontier, the separation of the predominantly Muslim Sind from Bombay Presidency and the Government of India Act, 1935, provided Muslim India with a new opportunity for self-organisation in the Muslim majority provinces. It is, however, interesting to note that Muslim national consciousness developed in the Hindu majority provinces before it came to the Muslim majority provinces; in the latter Islam was not on the defensive. It was the Muslims of the Hindu majority provinces who made the whole of Muslim India conscious that Islam was in danger.

Muslim leaders pointed out that ideologically India had always remained divided into Hindu India and Muslim India; and that history had failed, in the previous twelve hundred years, to bring about a genuine unity between the two. The unity of India was artificial and was maintained by the British bayonet. Quaid-i-Azam Muhammad Ali Jinnah advanced the Two Nation theory. Between 1935 and 1940 he finally organised the Muslims politically and made them a group which could count, alongside the Hindus and the British, in the political balance.

In March 1940 the Pakistan Resolution was passed at Lahore.

This laid down the principle of the secession of the Muslim majority areas from India. The Muslims thereafter maintained that the Indian problem would not be solved unless and until the major nations were allowed separate homelands by partitioning India into autonomous national states. It was on the basis of this Resolution that Pakistan was created.

There were working at the same time other forces which influenced the trend of Muslim political thought in the Indian sub-continent. Ever since the decline of Islam in India, Indian Muslims had looked with pride and hope towards the vast, independent, autocratic and medieval Ottoman Empire in the Middle East. To them the Ottoman Sultan-Caliph was a symbol of Pan-Islamic solidarity. From the establishment of Muslim rule in the Indian sub-continent (in 711) to the accession of the Mughal Emperor Babur (in 1526), Muslim India has remained constitutionally linked with the rest of the Muslim world through acknowledgement of the central Caliphate (first established at Medinah, then at Damascus, Baghdad and finally at Cairo). However, before the Mughals established themselves in India, the Caliphate was transferred to the Ottomans and its centre shifted from Cairo to Constantinople. The Mughals and the Ottomans had dynastic rivalries; so throughout the period of Mughal rule, Muslim India remained cut off from the Ottoman Empire. When the power of the Mughals declined and India fell into the hands of the British, the question how were the Muslims of India or those living outside the Ottoman Empire related to the Ottoman Caliphate, came to occupy the Muslim mind.

By the close of the eighteenth century, expanding European powers had penetrated into the Ottoman Empire. This penetration resulted in some cases, in the occupation, and in others, the economic exploitation of Muslim lands by Western colonial powers. It led to a 'puritanic' revival in Islam and a violent condemnation of the West. But within a generation or two, the ideological clash between medievalism and modernity broadened the 'puritanic' beginnings of the Muslim revival into what has been termed 'liberalism'; the work of 'Islamicising' Western ideas was taken up by Muslim reformers. Accordingly, Muslim reformers began to lay stress on the acquisition of the techniques of European progress and exhorted Muslims to grasp the secret of Western power.

As external European pressure continued, it led Muslims to aspire for a certain solidarity which has been termed 'Pan-Islamism'. This movement for 'Pan-Islamic' solidarity helped to make the Indian Muslims politically conscious. Shortly after the 1914-18 War, when the Ottoman Empire was dismembered, 'Pan-Islamism' further developed into 'Muslim nationalism'. A multiplicity of independent and semi-independent States emerged from the ruins of the medieval Ottoman Empire, most of them overwhelmingly Muslim. But 'nationalism' raised a problem in countries like India where the Muslims constituted a minority. Consequently, Muslim India was much less inclined to accept 'nationalism' in the Western sense, founded on some purely secular basis, whether racial, linguistic or territorial. It was the contribution of Muhammad Iqbal to make it clear that Islam rejects the principle according to which the unity of a people is founded on a purely racial, linguistic or territorial basis. He maintained that as a political ideal, 'nationalism' makes claims which are contrary to Islamic teachings.

Iqbal taught that the Muslims are bound together not by racial, linguistic or geographical ties, but by their communal brotherhood. Each Muslim receives his identity not because he belongs to a particular race, tribe, caste, colour, linguistic group or territory, but because he belongs to the Muslim community. He believed that Islam was neither 'nationalist' nor 'imperialist' but a 'commonwealth of nations' which accepts racial and linguistic diversity, and the ever-changing geographical demarcations of which exist only for facility of reference and not for limiting the social horizon of its members.

So, in Muslim India, 'Muslim nationalism' came to mean the political and cultural emancipation of numerous races, speaking different languages, but professing Islam and inhabiting those territories which comprise the world of Islam, without that emancipation coming into conflict with the general principles of equality, fraternity, and solidarity among Muslims as established by their religious usage and cultural coherence. In this sense, and in this sense only, 'nationalism' could be Islamicised.

Iqbal attacked 'secularism' as a concept completely alien to Islam. In his opinion, it led to the establishment in Europe of a set of mutually ill-adjusted States dominated by interests not human but national. Instead of achieving a unity in the light of Christ's teaching on human brotherhood, these states trampled or the moral and religious convictions of Christianity and dragged Europe into internecine wars.

But Iqbal was ready to Islamicise 'constitutionalism'. He approved of the growth of a republican spirit in Muslim countries, which he regarded as a return to the original purity of Islam. The establishment of legislative assemblies in the Muslim lands necessitated the revision of old Muslim legal institutions in the light of modern experience. Accordingly, he laid emphasis on the need for a reform in Muslim law as well as in Muslim legal instruction, and recommended the revival of *Ijtihad* (independent inquiry) to enable Islamic law to be re-interpreted in the light of modern experience and the altered conditions of modern life.

Iqbal furnished the Muslims also with an Islamic interpretation of 'socialism'. He argued that, from the standpoint of Islam, human society was founded on 'the equality of spirits' and not on 'the equality of stomachs'; private ownership was regarded as a trust, and capital should not be allowed to accumulate in such a way that it dominated the real producer of wealth. He believed that Islam could create a new world where the social rank of man would be determined not by his caste or colour, or by the amount of dividend he earned, but by the kind of life he lived.

Thus Pakistan came into being because the Muslims of the Indian sub-continent sought for a State in which to implement the social order of Islam, not because a State first came into being and then endeavoured to be Islamic. The racial and linguistic diversity within Pakistan and the geographical non-contiguity of Pakistan indicate that it must be an ideological rather than a 'national' State.

The Constitutional Discussions

In 1949, shortly after Pakistan came into being, the Constituent Assembly passed the Objectives Resolution according to which the future constitution of Pakistan was to be based on "the principles of democracy, freedom, equality, tolerance and social justice as enunciated by Islam". It was resolved that under the future constitution the Muslims of Pakistan should be enabled individually and collectively to order their lives in accordance with the teachings and requirements of Islam, and that adequate provision should be made for minorities freely to profess and practise their religion and to

ISLAMIC STATE IN PAKISTAN 139

develop their culture. The Assembly appointed a Basic Principles Committee to prepare a report on the main principles on which the future constitution could be framed. The Committee submitted its report to the Assembly in 1952.

The Committee recommended a democratic form of constitution based on a federation of the participating Units. It suggested the election of a Head of State, with a Council of Ministers headed by a Prime Minister to advise him. There should be a Federal Legislature consisting of two Houses, and elections should be held on the basis of adult franchise. For the Units, it recommended the appointment of a Head for each Unit by the Head of the State, the election of a Council of Ministers (headed by a Chief Minister) to advise the Head of each Unit, and the establishment of popularly elected Unit Legislatures. The Committee also made recommendations regarding the relations between the federation and the units, the constitution of the courts, and other matters.

The main features of the Committee's Report regarding the place of Islam in the future constitution were : that the Objectives Resolution 1949 should form the Preamble of the future constitution; that the Directive Principles of State Policy should be the preservation of democracy within the limits prescribed by the *Quran* and the *Sunnah*; that the State should take steps to bring the existing laws into conformity with Islamic principles; that no legislation be made which was repugnant to the *Quran* and the *Sunnah*; that the teaching of the *Quran* to Muslims should be made compulsory; that Islamic moral standards should be promoted and maintained, and so on.

To prevent the passing of legislation repugnant to the *Quran* and the *Sunnah*, the Committee recommended the appointment (by the Head of the State) of a Board consisting of not more than five persons well versed in Islamic law. This Board of *Ulema* should act in an advisory capacity and determine whether the laws that the Assembly passed were in conformity with or repugnant to Islam. The Committee also suggested that the Head of the State should be a Muslim; and that separate electorates should be maintained for Muslims and non-Muslims. Before the Report of the Basic Principles Committee was examined, the Constituent Assembly of Pakistan passed a bill of Fundamental Rights.

When the Committee's Report was considered by the Constituent Assembly, the Islamic character of the recommendations was severely criticised. There was not, however, much discussion on such matters as making the Objectives Resolution 1949, a part of the Preamble, or including the Directive Principles of State Policy in the future constitution. It was argued that these provisions were not legally enforcible and were merely 'pious hopes'. But the recommendations that the Head of the State should be a Muslim, that separate electorates should be maintained, and that a Board of *Ulema* should be appointed to supervise the legislative activity of the Assembly were very severely attacked in the Constituent Assembly debates.

Regarding the first of these, Sardar Shaukat Hyat Khan pointed out sarcastically: "They say that it will be an Islamic constitution because the Head of the State will be a Mussalman. Imagine the hypocrisy of this. Only a few months ago the Fundamental Rights were passed . . . (which said in one section) that every duly qualified citizen shall be eligible to appointment in the service of the State irrespective of religion, race, caste, sex, descent or place of birth . . . . (Now) they say that only a Mussalman will be the Head of the State. I am a Mussalman, and I am just as good a Mussalman as any one of them. But I am not a Mussalman who makes promises to the minorities . . . and just after a few months brings forward another thing which is quite opposite to what was agreed earlier. Now, Sir, is it a Report of the Basic Principles Committee or is it a report of hypocrisy? Sir, I imagine that the population of this country will be 85 per cent Muslim. If a Muslim cannot be returned as Head of the State with 85 per cent Muslim population and a Hindu is returned with a population of only 15 per cent that Hindu must be a saint . . . . So why put it hypocritically? Why try to say to the world that he will be a Muslim? Why put it that he should be a Muslim in a country where 85 per cent of Muslims live? Are they not competent to judge who is their representative? . . . Whom are you trying to please—the Muslims? Whom are you trying to displease —the minorities? The question is they are even doing things which must prick their conscience. They seem to be making a fun of our poor illiterate public opinion. They are trying to please the people by giving a little morsel here and a little morsel there which is absolutely meaningless. Now, Sir, this provision goes against the Fundamental Rights."[1]

[1] Official Report C. A. of Pakistan Debates, 13th October 1953, 127, 128.

In defence of this recommendation it was argued that it was a fundamental principle of an Islamic Constitution that a person who did not believe in 'Allah' could not be expected to rule over Muslims. Since Pakistan was an ideological State, the Head of State should be one who believed in the ideology on which Pakistan was founded. It was further argued that in the constitutions of Afghanistan, Argentina, Denmark, Greece, Iran, Norway, Paraguay, Saudi Arabia, Spain, Sweden, Syria, Thailand and England provisions were made regarding the religion of the Head of State.

As for the maintenance of separate electorates, Sardar Shaukat Hyat Khan said: "Sir, another hypocrisy, another great shame upon the so-called Muslims who are sitting there after the treaty with the minority community. They say they are protecting the rights of the Hindus by giving them separate electorates . . . (when the representatives of the Hindus) are asking for the joint electorates."[2]

On the recommendation regarding the appointment of the Board of *Ulema*, he commented: "Sir, they say here that no law will be made which is against the injunctions of the *Quran* or the *Sunnah* . . . . They say it will go back to certain people, who will pronounce upon it; after they have pronounced upon it then it will go back to the Assembly and then the Assembly can accept or reject it . . . . But what will happen is that these gentlemen . . . will be called Kafirs by all those who do not get a seat in that Board of advisors and who think they are fit enough to be there and who feel that they should sit on the advisory board . . . . Then if they do not declare certain laws to be un-Islamic they will be called Kafirs, in fact if the Assembly as a whole passes such a law it will be called Kafirs. Now why do you not trust the Members of the Assembly? If supposing an enactment comes here before the Assembly the Muslims will be in a majority and why do you not allow them to decide things according to their conscience and according to Islam? . . . It is all subterfuge, Sir, and it is trying to hoodwink the people. We are the people who are to be elected on the Muslim votes and we should come here and work and see what we decide is according to Islam and it cannot be against *Quran* and *Sunnah*, because none of us would have given up Islam when we get elected and come to the House as Members."[3]

[2] Debates, 13th October, 1953, 131.
[3] Debates, 13th October, 1953, 129–30.

It was argued that since the proposal of the appointment of the Board of *Ulema* had not received support from any section of the people, it should be dropped and the Supreme Court of Pakistan should be given the necessary jurisdiction to judge whether the laws passed by the Assembly were in conformity with or repugnant to the *Quran* and the *Sunnah*. This was agreed to by the First Constituent Assembly, but later dropped by the second.

The Constituent Assembly also discussed the proposal that Pakistan should be declared an Islamic Republic. In support of this, Sardar Abdur Rab Nishtar said: "It is necessary to give some indication about the nature of our republic. According to the Objectives Resolution the character of our constitution is to be based on principles of equality, democracy and tolerance as enunciated by Islam. Therefore, it is quite natural that this Republic should be described as an Islamic Republic. Take the name of the great country U.S.S.R. It is described as Socialist Republics. . . . Islamic Republic of Pakistan means that this republic would be run in accordance with the principles laid down by Islam."[4]

Consequently, in 1953 Pakistan was declared an Islamic Republic, in spite of the opposition of a few realistic Muslims and of many of the non-Muslim members of the Constituent Assembly. The Report of the Basic Principles Committee was eventually adopted by the Assembly in September 1954 with some amendments. The proposal for a Board of *Ulema* had been dropped; the question of separate or joint electorates was left to be determined by the Central and Provincial Assemblies formed under the Constitution. They adopted the principle of joint electorates.

The 1956 Constitution

By 1955, East Bengal was renamed as the province of East Pakistan, and West Punjab, North-West Frontier, Sind and Baluchistan were integrated into one unit called the province of West Pakistan. In the following year, the Constitution of the Islamic Republic of Pakistan was promulgated.

The 1956 Constitution was based on the amended recommendations of the Basic Principles Committee. The Objectives Resolution formed its Preamble, and the Directive Principles of State Policy

[4] Debates, 26th October, 1953, 461.

were specifically mentioned (though merely as 'pious hopes'). The Constitution contained a chapter on Fundamental Rights (which were legally enforcible), but no express attempt was made to show that they were based on Islamic principles.

The constitution was a mixture of the British and American constitutional patterns. It established a democracy based on a federation of the two participating provinces of East and West Pakistan. The members of the National Assembly were to be elected on the basis of adult franchise, and the representation in the National Assembly from the two wings of Pakistan was to be determined under the principle of parity. There were provisions for the election of the President by the combined votes of the National and Provincial Assemblies. There was also to be a Cabinet of Ministers headed by a Prime Minister.

As for the two provinces, the Constitution made provisions for the appointment of Governors by the President. These Governors were to act according to the advice of an elected Council of Ministers (headed by a Chief Minister in each province). The Provincial Assemblies were to be elected on the basis of adult franchise.

There were also provisions regarding the relations between the federation and the provinces,[5] for an independent Judiciary (composed of the Supreme, the High and the Subordinate Courts), Services and Public Service Commissions, etc.

As for the place which Islam occupied in the constitution, it has already been stated that the constitution was given the name of the Constitution of the Islamic Republic of Pakistan, its Preamble contained the Objectives Resolution, and it enumerated 'Directive Principles of State Policy', which were however devoid of force of law. These stated (*inter alia*) that the State "shall endeavour" to strengthen the bonds of unity among Muslim countries, to enable Pakistan Muslims to order their lives in accordance with the *Quran* and the *Sunnah*, to safeguard minority rights, to remove illiteracy, and to raise the standard of living.

Insofar as Islam was given any practical legal significance in the 1956 Constitution, it was in two ways. First, through Article 32(2)

---

[5] The Provinces had wider powers than the States have under the Indian Constitution. However, their independent sources of revenue were severely limited.

under which a person was not qualified for election as President unless he was a Muslim; and secondly, through Articles 197 and 198 (in Part XII, Chapter 1—Islamic Provisions). Under Article 197 the President was obliged to set up an organisation for Islamic research and instruction in advanced studies to assist in the reconstruction of Muslim society on a truly Islamic basis; and under Article 198 the President was expected to appoint (within one year of the promulgation of the Constitution) a Commission of Experts to make recommendations 'as to the measures for bringing existing laws into conformity with the Injunctions of Islam'. The Commission was to submit its report to the President within five years of its appointment. This report was to be placed before the National Assembly and the Assembly after considering the report was to enact laws in respect thereof.

As for the condition that no person could be eligible for election as President unless he was a Muslim, it did not in any way justify the claim of the 1956 Constitution to be Islamic. In almost all secular States the elected Head of State professes the religion (or belongs to the sect) the adherents of which constitute the majority in the country.

As to the obligation to set up an organisation for Islamic research and instruction in *advanced* studies, it was not carried out. Such organisations for Islamic research as were established were not affiliated with the universities. Consequently the students failed to derive any benefit from them, and the object of reconstructing the Muslim society on a truly Islamic basis through these organisations was not achieved. Article 198 was paradoxical. Although the Constituent Assembly was apparently able to determine the Islamic character of the Fundamental Law of Pakistan (the constitution) without the assistance of Experts, the ordinary laws of the Muslim community were left to be determined by such a body, but ratified again by non-Experts.

In short, the position which Islam occupied in the 1956 Constitution reflected the attitude of hypocrisy and vagueness of the Muslim framers of that constitution. Islam was presented in the constitution in the form of a legal fiction. On the eve of his retirement, Justice Muhammad Munir (former Chief Justice of Pakistan) summed up his opinion of the 1956 Constitution. In his farewell address to the West Pakistan High Court Bar Association, Lahore, he said: "Our

Constitution, though it purported to be a constitution for the Islamic Republic of Pakistan, had hardly anything Islamic except the repetition of the words Islam, Quran and Sunnah."[6]

The 1958 Revolution and the Islamic Ideal

If Quaid-i-Azam Muhammed Ali Jinnah had lived for a few years more, he would certainly have indicated the direction in which the Pakistanis were to move. Unfortunately he died soon after the establishment of Pakistan. After his death (and particularly after the assassination of Liaquat Ali Khan, the first Prime Minister of Pakistan), although the number of Pakistani political parties increased, they were unable to present to the people either a convincing programme or an inspiring leadership. Some of the political leaders who gained power during this period were more concerned to maintain themselves in power than to put into practice the ideology on which Pakistan was founded. Consequently the holding of general elections was postponed every year, and coalition governments came and went in rapid succession both at the Centre and in the Provinces. Sometimes a single person would manage to acquire power through his personal drive, skill or intrigue; at other times a group of individuals would manage to attain power and pull the strings from behind the curtain, or a small political party of alien ideology would become the decisive factor in the running of the governmental machinery.

In spite of progress in some fields, the state of the country's economy remained unchanged. The major problems of Pakistan, the settlement of refugees and evacuee property, the Kashmir issue, the distribution of canal waters, and the lack of basic necessities of life (such as food, clothing, housing, education and medical relief) remained unsolved. On the contrary, the system of permits, licences and price controls encouraged the growth of black-marketing, smuggling, corruption and maladministration. All this inevitably resulted in the spreading of a sense of frustration and despondency in the country. Even the Islamic State idea appeared to peter out and was neglected and frustrated, leading to a mood of disillusionment.

Political instability was not only affecting the prestige of Pakistan abroad, but making Pakistan internally weaker every day. It

[6] *Pakistan Times,* 23 April 1960.

came to be generally felt that even elections would not improve conditions but might lead to greater instability, confusion, disintegration and chaos in the country. On the morning of 8th October, 1958, the people of Pakistan woke up to find that a resolution had swept the country, the Constitution of the Islamic Republic of Pakistan had been abrogated and Martial Law had been imposed.

Ever since it gained power, the revolutionary government has endeavoured to check black-marketing, smuggling, corruption and maladministration. It is making strenuous efforts to solve the major problems of Pakistan. At the same time, it is trying to work out a democratic pattern of government which will suit the genius of the people. 'Basic democracies' have already been introduced in the form of local self-governing bodies, and a Constitution Commission has been appointed to submit proposals in the form of a report advising how best a democracy adaptable to changing circumstances can be secured.

As for the attitude of the revolutionary regime towards the Islamic ideal, a critical examination of its internal and external policy would reveal that it is not revolutionary in the sense that its object is to erase completely the past from the minds of the people and to start with a programme of reforms based on some wholly new and radical ideology. The regime aims at clearing up the political, social and economic mess which had resulted from the lack of vision at the top in the past ten years, and reviving the fundamental principles on which Pakistan was originally founded. Any form of turning back to the original principles which led to the establishment of Pakistan would automatically involve a revaluation of the Islamic ideology. The Pakistani revolution was entirely peaceful. It was a revolution without those elements of violence and ferocity which characterised the French, the Russian, the Chinese and the more recent Egyptian and Iraqi revolutions.

The Head of the present regime, Field-Marshal Muhammad Ayub Khan, is fully aware that the basis on which the Muslims struggled for and got Pakistan was Islam, and that the establishment of Pakistan was a magnificent achievement. He has frequently said that this achievement was wrongly considered by most Pakistanis as an end in itself. In reality it was, of course, only the beginning of the struggle, for the problem of building Pakistan and expressing Islam in a practicable way still lay before Muslims, and that was and is an infinitely greater and more difficult task.

Thus the terms of reference which the recently appointed Constitution Commission has to consider and to answer are worded as follows:

"To examine the progressive failure of parliamentary government in Pakistan leading to the abrogation of the Constitution of 1956 and to determine the causes and the nature of the failure;

To consider how best the said or like causes may be identified and their recurrence prevented;

And, having further taken account of the genius of the people, the general standard of education and of political judgment in the country, the present state of a sense of nationhood, the prime need for sustained development, and the effect of the constitutional and administrative changes brought into being in recent months, to submit constitutional proposals in the form of a report advising how best the following ends may be secured:

a democracy adaptable to changing circumstances and based on the Islamic principles of justice, equality and tolerance;

the consolidation of national unity; and a firm and stable system of government."

The Commission has issued and distributed among the people a questionnaire based on the above terms, and the replies have already started pouring into the office of the Commission. Recently a group of prominent *Ulema* of Pakistan sent a reply which has received a considerable amount of publicity in the Pakistani Press.

The *Ulema* submit that the future constitution of Pakistan should be based on the *Quran* and the *Sunnah*; that since the 1956 Constitution was never put to a test and general elections were never held under the old constitution, the question of defining the nature and enumerating the causes of the progressive failure of the parliamentary pattern of democratic government in Pakistan could not arise and need not be answered; that since the people of Pakistan were familiar with the parliamentary pattern, the introduction of the presidential form of government in Pakistan would lead to many new difficulties; that the political leaders should be told to fear God and to perform their duties sincerely and honestly;

and that the old constitution should be re-adopted after necessary amendments.

It is, however, premature to express any opinion on the replies which are being received by the Commission, or the form which the future constitution of Pakistan should eventually take. The present regime (revivalistic rather than revolutionary) has so far consistently shown caution about adopting any programme of social, economic, cultural or educational reforms which may involve radical changes in Pakistan. It is for this very reason that the Pakistani revolution, with all its zest and vigour, remains fundamentally middle class.

Whether this attitude of restraint and hesitation (or dependence on the advice of the older group which is basically reluctant to accept change) is wise and proper in the face of a paramount need for the implementation of radical changes in all the spheres of the country's life, is a question which bothers every young Muslim radical in Pakistan today. The adoption by a people of a 'conservative' attitude towards life as a whole may be justified for the purposes of self-preservation when a country is under foreign domination. But when an independent people are called upon to construct an independent country, it is always the energy, vigour and drive of the young independent minds that lead to the solution of problems. If the conservative logic of the complacent old were to continue to dominate, it would do so at its own peril, for there comes a time in the lives of nations when logic is thrown to the winds and life struggles relentlessly to determine its own direction.

II

Constitutional Theory

In the Western mind, the term Islamic State seems to conjure up, as Keith Callard has aptly put it, "vague (and usually unhistorical) visions of Muslim fanaticism, the holy war, the Mahdi, the conquest of empire by the sword, the forced conversion of the Infidel, and the destruction of temples and idols".[7] It will be discussed here first in the light of Islamic history and with due regard to the opinions held on this subject by the leading jurists of medieval Islam; and secondly, in the light of the teachings of contemporary Muslim

[7] *Pakistan—A Political Study*, 195.

reformers. Lastly, it may be worthwhile to consider the factors that hinder or impede the establishment of the Islamic State in Pakistan today.

The Prophet established no church or body of priests. When he died, the task of maintaining and interpreting his teachings was regarded as that of the whole Muslim community. It was recognised that some would be more expert and learned than others, but even the opinions of the latter had to secure acceptance by the people. Islam believes that religion and the rest of life cannot be separated. The ideal Islamic State would be a whole community living their lives in all respects according to Muslim ideals. It is thus quite wrong to speak of the Muslim ideal of the State as 'theocratic' in the sense of one ruled by a church, though any Muslim State must be religious in character.

Distinguishing the secular State from the Islamic State, Ibn Khaldun (1332–1406) points out that the secular State is based on the principles derived through human reasoning and therefore it promotes only material advancement; but since the Islamic State (Caliphate) is based on the Revealed Law, it promotes both the material and spiritual advancement of the people.[8]

The Muslim idea of a Head of State was a man of high personal qualities, to be elected or otherwise agreed upon by the Muslim community, who would lead them in all matters but also be answerable to them.

Up to the time of Al-Mawardi (991–1058) and even later, it was generally believed that the Head of the Islamic State should not only be a Muslim of upright character but must be from the tribe of Quraysh. (The Shia Muslims impose further restrictions, e.g. he must be a descendant of Ali). From at least the twelfth century onwards the conditions of Qurayshite lineage was discarded by many Muslim jurists (e.g., Abu Bakr Baqilani, Ibn Khaldun); but the condition of his being a Muslim was always accepted throughout the Muslim world.

The Head of the Islamic State could only be a Muslim for, apart from his secular duties, he was obliged to perform certain purely religious functions (the leading of the congregational prayers, the interpretation and promulgation of Islamic law, the propagation and defence of the religion of Islam and the suppression of the growth

[8] *Muqqaddima*, 190, 191.

of heresy). Secondly, by the time the Muslim jurists started form-
ulating Islamic constitutional theory, hereditary monarchies had
been firmly established and Muslim dynasties were ruling all over
the world of Islam. Although some of these Muslim monarchs
performed the religious duties which they were obliged to perform
under Islamic law, a large majority of them were merely secular
kings who ruled entirely on the basis of their military strength.

The Muslim claim that the original and ideal Islamic State is
republican in form, is based on the practice of the Orthodox
Caliphs (632–661), before the Caliph came to acquire kingly pre-
rogatives. Muslim jurists maintain that the basis of Government
according to Islam is 'General Consultation among the Muslims'
(Al-Shura). God says in the Quran: "And those who respond to
their Lord and keep up prayer, and their rule is take counsel among
themselves" (42; verse 38). Even the Prophet is urged by God to
consult the believers, for God says: "Therefore forgive and ask for
pardon for them, and consult them in the affairs" (3; verse 159). In
order to safeguard the state from disruption and chaos, the Quran
enjoins every Muslim to obey God, His Apostle and those members
of the Muslim community who command authority over the
Muslims (4; verse 59).

Although neither the Quran nor the Tradition suggested it, elec-
tion came to be regarded as the basis for the appointment of the
Head of the Islamic State (at least in the early stages) because it was
Arab tribal custom and was in conformity with the spirit of Islam.
Shortly after the death of the Prophet in 632, Abu Bakr was elected
Caliph at Medinah by a small assembly of Muslims. According to
Al-Mawardi there were five prominent Companions of the Prophet
who swore allegiance to him and then the rest of the community
followed. During the first phase election and nomination appeared
side by side as methods for constituting the Head of the Islamic
State. The First Four Caliphs were members of a single tribe (the
Quraysh), but no Caliph entertained the idea of getting his son,
brother, or father elected or nominated as Caliph. In other words,
the hereditary principle of succession was specifically excluded from
the early practice of Islam.

Although theoretically the Caliph was elected by the entire
Muslim community, in practice he was elected either by a single
eminent member of the community or by a restricted number of

eminent and influential men who had come to acquire 'the authority to bind and loose'. When the Caliph had been elected and the prominent members of the community had acknowledged him, only then the people of Medinah (the seat of the Caliphate) were called upon to take the oath of allegiance, and finally the people of the other important cities of Islam swore allegiance to the Caliph. The election of the Caliph was a matter that concerned Muslims exclusively and non-Muslims had no say. The term of office of the Caliph was not fixed. Theoretically he could be deposed under certain circumstances. But such a situation never arose during the first phase of the Caliphate.

The Head of the Islamic State was the successor of the Prophet (*Khalifah*), the interpreter and the promulgator of the law of Islam (*Imam*), the leader of the congregational prayers, the defender of the religion of Islam, the guardian of the Muslim community, the judge, the administrator and the supreme military commander (*Amir-al-Mominin*). Although the Caliph administered the State in consultation with the eminent Companions of the Prophet who composed an informal senate, he was not bound to accept their advice. He had wide powers, but he came under Islamic law and was answerable to the Muslim community for his actions. The duties of the citizens of the Islamic State were loyalty and allegiance to the Caliph and respect for the laws of Islam. The citizens were enjoined to co-operate with 'the leaders of the community' and to put them right in case they were led astray. The fundamental rights of citizens (Muslim or non-Muslim), as we understand them today, were fully secured during the first phase of the Caliphate.

Thus when Muslims refer back to the Orthodox Caliphate as the ideal Islamic State, they are referring not to any fixed mode of appointment of the Head of the State, nor to any fixed governmental structure, since each of the First Four Caliphs was appointed by a different mode and governed in a different way. The ideal which is to be derived from this period is that the Head of the State governed with the consent of the community, was completely open at all times to listen to and act upon criticism from any member of the community, and was subject to the law of Islam in the same way as any other citizen.

At the time of Abu Bakr's election, for example, another candidate was put forward by the people of Medinah; after discussion,

however, it was decided to make the election of Abu Bakr un-
animous because of his age, wisdom and moderation. As soon as
Abu Bakr assumed office as Head of the State he addressed the
people as follows:

"I have been put in this office to conduct your affairs, although I
am in no way superior to you. If I do right, help me; if I go
wrong, put me right."

The contest between Ali and Muawiyah for the Caliphate led to
the formation of three distinct religio-political parties. (The Shia,
the Khwaraj, and the Sunni). If the contest between Ali and
Muawiyah could have been resolved peaceably and without the
disaster of the battle of Siffin, (and the terrorist activities of the
Khwaraj which led to the assassination of Ali), it is quite possible
that the early republic of Islam might have developed its own
method of electing the Head of the State from among a number of
candidates put forward by different religio-political groups.

Muawiyah used unscrupulous methods to defeat Ali, and then
used his military strength to impose himself on the community as
Caliph without their consent or approval. He went on to establish
an hereditary Caliphate by nominating his son as his successor. He
justified this action on the grounds that to leave the matter of his
successor to the decision of the community would lead to civil war
and anarchy among the Muslims. The failure of the later revolts
against the hereditary Caliphs led to a spirit of disillusionment and
fatalism among devout Muslims. In Iqbal's words: "Thus arose, in
spite of open protests by Muslim divines, a morally degrading
Fatalism, and the constitutional theory known as the 'accomplished
fact' in order to support vested interests. This is not at all surprising.
In our own times philosophers have furnished a kind of intellectual
justification for the finality of the present capitalistic structure of
society."[9]

Legislative, Executive and Judicial Powers

The Caliph in consultation with the Companions exercised the
powers of legislation so long as he did not repeal, abrogate or set

[9] Muhammad Iqbal, *The Reconstruction of Religious Thought in Islam*
(London, 1934), 110–11.

aside the Law of God. However, he had the authority to extend or limit the application of a Quranic rule of law when such extension or limitation was sanctioned under a Shariah value. The Caliph also interpreted the Quranic rules of law in the light of the Tradition (*Hadith*), the Consensus of the Community (*Ijma*), and the use of Analogical Reasoning in legislation (*Qiyas*). There is reason to believe that the First Four Caliphs in consultation with the Companions interpreted as well as promulgated the law of Islam.

The Caliph was the supreme executive authority. He appointed or removed the Tax-Collectors (*Amils*), Governors (*Amirs*), Controllers (*Nazims*), and State officials, and supervised all the departments (*Diwans*) of the State. During the reign of the Abbasids, when the Caliphate came under the influence of Persian ideas of sovereignty and the office of Minister (*Wazir*) was created, the Caliph acquired the power to appoint or dismiss the Ministers (*Wazirs*). According to Al-Mawardi, the Caliph had the authority to appoint two kinds of State officials—officials with 'delegated' powers (*Tafwiz*) and officials with 'restricted' powers (*Tanfiz*). The State officials were responsible to the Caliph. But if a State official infringed the rights of a citizen, the citizen could seek redress in the courts of law.

One of the most important features of the Islamic State in the first phase of the Caliphate was that the Judiciary was made independent of the Executive. The Prophet is reported to have authorised his Companions to act as Judges (*Qazis*). Umar, the second Caliph, is reported to have issued instructions to *Qazi* Abu Musa al-Ash'ari; these instructions enumerated the qualifications and defined the jurisdiction of the one who held this office. The Caliph was the sole authority to appoint the judges. Once the judge had been appointed, he became entirely independent, so much so that even the Caliph could be tried in his court. The judge could be dismissed by the Caliph only if there was a valid reason.

The Department of 'Hisba'

The Department of *Hisba* (Religious Censorship), a peculiar feature of the Islamic State, came under the *Muhtasib* (Religious Censor) who enforced the moral discipline of Islam upon Muslim citizens. God says in the *Quran*: "And let there be (formed) of a you a community inviting to good, urging what is reputable and restraining from what is disreputable" (3; verse 104).

Under the law of Islam, the Caliph was expected to be *Muhtasib*. But if it was not possible for him to perform the duties assigned to this office, he was empowered to appoint the *Muhtasib*. The *Muhtasib* had a detachment of *Shurta* (police force) under his command, and he also acted as a magistrate of specific jurisdiction. The *Muhtasib's* duties were to detect, restrain or punish those who infringed the Rights of God, the Rights of Human Beings, and the Rights which were common to both God and Human Beings.

The Rights of God were public worship, the observance of fasts in the month of Ramazan, paying alms tax (*Zakat*) etc. It was the duty of the *Muhtasib* to see that the Muslims held Friday service in the mosque. He could punish those who were persistent in neglecting public worship, or were seen eating in public places during the month of Ramazan without any valid excuse. The *Muhtasib* made sure that the call for prayers (*Adhan*) was made at proper hours; he was responsible for the repair of mosques if they were left in a state of disrepair; he punished those who introduced heresies in Islam; or those who refused to pay the alms tax (*Zakat*) etc.; he checked women who went about without a veil; he checked men and women talking together in public places; he punished those who used instruments of music, or sold forbidden toys (such as dolls), or drank fermented liquors.

Wrongs that infringed the Rights of Human Beings were unlawful transactions, usury, false and defective scales, weights or measures, non-payment of debt, fraud in sale, coinage, etc. In this field the *Muhtasib* had jurisdiction over Muslim as well as non-Muslim citizens. It was the duty of the *Muhtasib* to stop anyone from building his house higher than that of his neighbour lest this interfered with the privacy of the neighbour, or implied disrespect of the quarters of the neighbour's womenfolk; or to order a man to cut the branches of his tree which spread into the courtyard of his neighbour. No wall or fence could be raised without the permission of the *Muhtasib*. Public thoroughfares could not be blocked. The *Muhtasib* punished those who treated their slaves or animals cruelly. He controlled teachers, shops, ferry-boats, buildings and in general exercised many of the minor functions of government often now associated with local authorities.

Wrongs that infringed the Rights common to both God and Human Beings were committed when, for instance, a divorced Muslim woman or a widow remarried without observing *Iddat* (a period of time to ascertain pregnancy); or when the *Imam* of the mosque (leader of public worship) lengthened the service unnecessarily so that the weak or old failed to stand it, or the people were hindered or delayed from performing other jobs; or when a *Qazi* made the people wait before opening his court. It was within the power of the *Muhtasib* to check these wrong-doers.

Religion and State

Islamic constitutional theory did not recognise the separation of Religion from the State. The Head of the Islamic State (Caliph) symbolised the unity of the spiritual and temporal in Islam. The Caliph was the supreme authority so far as the interpretation or promulgation of the law of Islam was concerned. He led the congregational prayers, and had the authority to delegate his powers to the persons appointed by him. Early practice in Islam was in conformity with a Tradition quoted in the *Mishkat* in which the Prophet is reported to have said that only the Head of the Islamic State (*Imam*) or the person or persons appointed by him are entitled to preach to the people.

Under the Ottomans, however (and also in Shia Iran, on the basis of the doctrine of the Major Occultation of the *Imam*), a functional division between the religious and the temporal was created for administrative convenience, and the office of *Sheikh-al-Islam* was established side by side with the offices of Ministers of State. The *Sheikh-al-Islam* was appointed by the Sultan-Caliph, and was delegated the powers to pronounce final Decisions (*Fatawa*) regarding the interpretation of the law of Islam, to administer the religious endowments (*Awqaf*), to manage the institutions of Islamic theological and legal instruction, to defend and to propagate Islam, to suppress the growth of heresy, to look after the mosques, to appoint the Imams of the mosque, mosque attendants, preachers and missionaries, and to pay them salaries from the State Treasury. The *Sheikh-al-Islam* held his office at the Sultan-Caliph's pleasure.

Attitudes towards Non-Muslims

The non-Muslim citizens of the Islamic State were called the *Dhimmis* (the protected people). Since Islam's attitude towards other religions is more than that of mere tolerance, freedom of religious belief and practice were guaranteed to non-Muslims during the early phase of the Caliphate, and none of the First Four Caliphs interfered with or declared any of the institutions and customs of the non-Muslims null and void.

God says in the *Quran*: "There is no compulsion in religion" (2; verse 256); and "And if thy Lord has pleased, all those who are in the earth would have believed, all of them. Wilt thou then force men till they are believers?" (10; verse 100). The Orthodox Caliphs, therefore, strictly followed the Quranic injunctions as well as the practice of the Prophet who never broke his treaties with the non-Muslims.

As for Jews and Christians, the *Quran* gave them the status of 'the People of the Book' (*Ahl-al-Kitab*) and allowed the Muslims to develop social connections with them. After the conquest of Persia, on the analogy of the status granted to Jews and Christians, Muslim jurists included the Magians and the Zoroastrians in the category of 'the People of the Book'. In Mughal India, under the influence of the Sufi orders, the Hindus also came to be regarded as 'the People of the Book', and the development of social connections between the Muslims and the Hindus was encouraged.

The *Quran* made it obligatory upon Muslims not only to show tolerance towards non-Muslims, but also to defend the places of worship of non-Muslims under their protection. God says in the *Quran*: "If God had not raised a group (i.e. the Muslims) to ward off the others from aggression, churches, synagogues, oratories and mosques where God is worshipped most, would have been destroyed" (22; verse 40). There are numerous examples in the history of Islam of Muslim tolerance and of Muslims defending the places of worship of non-Muslims.

The non-Muslim communities in the Islamic State were governed under their respective personal codes of law, and non-Muslim judges were also appointed to administer justice among them. The Head of the Islamic State was not empowered to declare any of the personal law of the non-Muslims null and void. On the other hand, although all the citizens (Muslims as well as non-Muslims) came under the Islamic criminal law, there was one major distinction; and that was that if a criminal offence had been committed by a non-Muslim, he was awarded half the penalty that the *Quran* had fixed for a Muslim offender. The non-Muslims, of course, did not come under the *Hisba* jurisdiction of the *Muhtasib*.

Non-Muslims were exempt from the compulsory military service, and for this exemption as well as for their protection and defence, the *Jizya* tax was imposed on them. There are, however, numerous instances when retreating Muslim armies returned the *Jizya* because of their failure to protect or defend non-Muslims. There is also no evidence to support the view that the *Jizya* was regularly enforced.

Under the Orthodox Caliphs, Christians and Jews held posts in the Accounts Department of the State. During the first phase of the Caliphate, the State accounts were kept in the Coptic language and usually Coptic Christians were employed to keep the State accounts. Under the Ummayads, however, Arabic was made the State language, the Arabic coinage was introduced for the first time, and Muslims were employed for keeping the State accounts. Non-Muslims held major posts under the Ummayads of Spain, the Fatimids of Egypt, the Ottomans of Turkey and the Mughals of India. Under the Mughals Hindus were appointed ministers as well as governors of various Mughal provinces, and Mughal armies were even officered by Hindu generals.

Thus in the Islamic Middle Ages non-Muslims were permitted to profess freely and practise their religion, they were employed in the State services, their legitimate rights and interests were safeguarded and they were allowed to develop their culture. The Islamic States provided security for everyone, so much so that whenever the Jews were persecuted in Christian Europe, they found refuge in Muslim Spain, Turkey, Egypt, etc. There is hardly any parallel in the history of other nations contemporary with the Muslim States to Islamic tolerance and zeal for protecting the rights and defending the places of worship of non-Muslims.

The Evolution of Islamic Law

From the establishment of the Caliphate (in 632) up to the sack of Baghdad by the Mongols (in 1258), the most important and significant feature of the Islamic State had been the growth, development and evolution of Islamic law. This evolution was made possible through *Ijtihad* (literal meaning, 'to exert'; in the terminology of Islamic law it means 'to exert oneself with a view to forming an independent judgment on a legal question').

Although there was no written law of Islam except the *Quran* in the first phase of the Caliphate, the Orthodox Caliphs exercised *Ijtihad* and assimilated freely what they found best in the surrounding cultures. Under the early Abbasids, there developed a ceaseless activity among Muslim legal thinkers to evolve and expand the scope of Islamic law in order to meet the needs and requirements of a growing civilisation. During this phase an elasticity of thought was encouraged in the field of interpretation of Islamic law and no fewer than nineteen schools of Islamic law and legal opinion developed. The outlook of the *Quran* came to be regarded as dynamic because the simple legal precepts laid down in the *Quran* were considered to possess great potentialities of expansion and development by interpretation. In the interpretation of Islamic law, although the legal thinkers of one generation would accuse one another of heresy on the slightest difference of opinion, the legal thinkers of the next generation would attempt to reconcile the differences of their predecessors.

Thus in the early phase of Islamic history, the Muslim legal thinkers, while remaining true to the original spirit of Islam, exercised *Ijtihad* creatively. They assisted the community in adjusting its religious outlook towards any new idea which infiltrated the world of Islam, and at the same time, they mitigated the apparent strictness of the Quranic laws by providing the community with broader interpretations.

However, certain other developments in Islamic culture brought an end to this creative phase. The development of Rationalism under the later Abbasids led to a misunderstanding among the conservative *Ulema* who thought that the inevitable result of a rational approach to the Revealed Law would be heresy and anarchy. On the other hand, the rise and growth of ascetic Sufiism tended increasingly to occupy the best Muslim minds and to turn them away from concern with the mundane world. Finally the sack of Baghdad by the Mongols gave such a severe blow to Islamic culture that it did not show signs of revival until recent times.

From this time onwards there is a marked tendency towards conservatism in all phases of Islamic life. The *Ulema* were afraid of the introduction of innovations in the Islamic law and being themselves uncreative, they slavishly followed the dictates of the past authorities. They attached finality to the established schools of Islamic law in spite of the fact that the original founders of these schools never claimed such finality for their systems. The right of independent inquiry was practically withdrawn. This eventually resulted in the closing of the gates of *Ijtihad* and consequent immobility, rigidity and stagnation in Islamic legal thinking.

III

Islamic Constitutional Theory and Modern Times

Now the question can be considered, how far is it possible to implement Islamic constitutional theory in modern times? A majority of modern Muslim thinkers agree with their predecessor, Ibn Khaldun, that from the standpoint of Islam the State must be founded on spiritual principles. Declaring Pakistan to be an 'Islamic Republic' or calling her capital by the name 'Islamabad' would serve no purpose unless these outward forms serve as a means for the attainment of the inner substance of Islam.

Is it necessary that the Head of a modern Islamic State should be a Muslim or is such a requirement a mere 'outward form'? It has already been pointed out that from the standpoint of Islam the Head of State must be a Muslim mainly because he is obliged to perform certain purely religious functions. If Pakistan had been inhabited by Muslims belonging to only one sect of Islam, or if she was governed by a hereditary monarch professing the religion or belonging to the majority sect, then there would have been no difficulty in maintaining that the Head of State in Pakistan should be a Muslim (belonging to this or that sect). But in the circumstances, when, besides non-Muslim minorities, Pakistan is inhabited by Muslims belonging to numerous different sects of Islam (although the Sunnis predominate in Pakistan, they have so far refrained from claiming that Sunni Islam be declared as the State religion), and the Head of the State is to be elected on the basis of adult franchise (the population of Pakistan being 85 per cent

Muslim), it may well be asked: what is the sense in emphasising this qualification?

If the Head of State has to be a Muslim because he is obliged to perform the religious functions enumerated above, then is he to perform these functions in accordance with the precepts of Sunni Islam or of Shia Islam? Anyway, if he is not obliged to perform the religious functions (so far the Heads of State in Pakistan have not performed any of these functions, although all of them were Muslims) then obviously an emphasis on this qualification would imply the retention of merely another outward form.

According to Islamic constitutional theory Absolute Sovereignty over the entire universe belongs to God; but since Man has been appointed God's Representative (*Khalifah*) on earth, earthly sovereignty vests in him as a sacred trust from God. (It is only in this sense that an Islamic State claims to be sovereign). A State which is established for the purposes of realising such ideals as 'equality, solidarity and freedom' in 'a definite human organisation'[10] cannot be other than democratic or republican, though it may assume the form of a parliamentary cabinet or presidential system. Similarly it is essential to incorporate Fundamental Rights in a modern Islamic constitution, not only because they are in conformity with the spirit of Islam, but because each of them could be directly traced from the *Quran* and the *Sunnah* (the practice of the Prophet).

Medieval Islam seems to have produced three distinct views on the Universal Caliphate (or Imamate). These are: that it is a Divine institution and therefore indispensable; that it is not obligatory but only recommended by God and therefore a matter of expediency; and that there is no need of such an institution, for the community can manage its affairs by itself (the last view was held by the Khawarjites).

Ever since the Turks abolished the Caliphate (in 1924), modern Islam has regarded the formation of legislative assemblies in Muslim countries as a return to the original purity of Islam and thus it seems to have adopted the Khawarjite view. Iqbal maintains that legislative assemblies in Muslim countries should perform the function of *Ijma* (the Consensus of the Community) and re-interpret the law of Islam in the light of contemporary experience and the altered conditions of modern life. He says: "The teaching of the

[10] *The Reconstruction of Religious Thought in Islam*, 154.

Quran that life is a process of progressive creation necessitates that each generation, guided but unhampered by the work of its predecessors, should be permitted to solve its own problems".[11]

Since Iqbal was aware that a present-day Muslim assembly would obviously consist of members who possessed little knowledge of the subtleties of Islamic law, he recommended that the *Ulema* should form a part of a Muslim legislative assembly and help and guide free discussions on questions relating to law. But Iqbal was, at the same time, conscious that such an arrangement was 'dangerous', therefore he suggested that if it was adopted at all, it should be only a temporary measure. "The only effective remedy," he said, "for possibilities of erroneous interpretations is to reform the present system of legal education in Mohammadan countries, to extend its sphere, and to combine it with an intelligent study of modern jurisprudence."[12]

It has already been noted that the Constituent Assembly of Pakistan rejected the proposal for the appointment of a Board of *Ulema* which should supervise the legislative activity of the National Assembly, and thus upheld the freedom of the National Assembly in making laws for the country. When it is generally accepted that in Islam the spiritual and temporal are not two separate domains; that the nature of an act, even if secular in import, is determined by the attitude of mind with which the agent does it; and that each generation is to solve its own problems, then there is indeed no reason why the power to interpret the law of Islam should not be given to the National Assembly.

However, the existing judicial structure could be incorporated in the modern Islamic Constitution of Pakistan with certain modifications. For example, those judges of the Supreme Court who have been specially trained in the knowledge of the principal sources and branches of Islamic jurisprudence and who have also been trained in the application of the rules derived from those sources to modern problems, could be given special powers to determine, after such hearing (of the *Ulema* as well as the Experts) as they think fit, whether the legislative activity of the National Assembly was in conformity with or repugnant to the injunctions of Islam. Any problem of Islamic law which requires a re-interpretation in the light of modern experience could be put to the judges by the

[11] *loc. cit.*   [12] *ibid.*, 176.

National Assembly through the President in the form of a Reference; and they could report their opinion on such matters to the President.

'Hisba' in Modern Times

Shortly after Pakistan came into being, some of the religious enthusiasts, impelled by their zeal for puritanism, attempted to assume the *Hisba* jurisdiction for themselves and went about the streets of the big cities of Pakistan imposing the 'religious discipline' of Islam on Muslim citizens. In Anarkali Bazaar, a business centre of Lahore, a religious enthusiast with a pair of scissors in his hands, attempted to clip the hair of Muslim women who had 'dared' to come out unveiled. In the walled city, a few Muslims who were seen eating in public during the month of Ramazan, had to pay heavily for their infringement of a 'Right of God'. Their faces were blackened, they were made to ride on donkeys and were taken around the city by a group of religious enthusiasts.

Although such incidents were few, and the law of the land soon managed to control and check this trend, it appeared in a more dangerous form in 1953 when a group of *Ulema* held an All-Pakistan Convention at Karachi and demanded that the Ahmadis (a sect regarded as heretical by most Muslims) be declared as non-Muslims and therefore a minority community, that the then Foreign Minister (who happened to be an Ahmadi) be dismissed and that Pakistan be made an Islamic State.

These demands, although outwardly of a 'religious' character (and perhaps in the opinion of these *Ulema* motivated by no other desire than to suppress the growth of heresy) were really the result of a conspiracy on the part of the Ahrar (a religio-political organisation which had, during the independence struggle, sided with the Hindu Congress and opposed the establishment of Pakistan) to regain their lost political prestige. Numerous religious organisations joined the Ahrar; meanwhile some of the members of the Provincial as well as the Central Cabinets supported the Ahrar demands, keeping in view their own political ends.

These *Ulema* passed a 'Direct Action' resolution and gave an ultimatum to the Government that if their demands were not conceded, they would launch an agitation. Khwaja Nazim-ud-Din, the then Prime Minister, tried his best to dissuade the *Ulema* from starting an unconstitutional campaign for the enforcement of their demands. He pointed out that such an agitation would lead to bloodshed. Furthermore, he argued that the Constituent Assembly had passed an Interim Report regarding the basic rights of all the citizens of Pakistan (on October 6, 1950) under which every qualified citizen of Pakistan was eligible for State service irrespective of religion, caste, race or country of birth, and every citizen was granted liberty of conscience and freedom to adhere to any religion. But the *Ulema* were not prepared to listen to the reasoning of the Prime Minister. As a result they were arrested and the agitation followed shortly after. The big towns of West Punjab became scenes of rioting and arson; complete lawlessness prevailed in Lahore until the troops were called in and martial law was proclaimed. The agitation was suppressed by rifle fire and hundreds lost their lives for a cause which, according to them, was 'religious'.

There are other spheres in which certain 'religious taboos' have been maintained in Pakistan. Although poetry and other forms of literature are now generally accepted as part of Pakistani culture, zeal for puritanism has hindered the development particularly of fine arts (painting, sculpture, music, singing, dancing and all varieties of dramatic arts) in spite of Government patronage. The laws preventing the consumption of alcoholic liquor, prostitution and gambling are also unusual and peculiar. Although these laws attempt to effect a balance between individual liberty and collective order, they fail to achieve their real object and tend to create a farcical situation.

The 'liberal' interpretation of Islam as put forth in the writings of Iqbal emphasises the development of free and creative individuals as the basis of a good society. He maintains that the realisation of the moral ideal presupposes the freedom of the human will. Hence the 'liberal' view of Islam will maintain that the younger generation should be educated to understand and appreciate the significance of Islamic moral standards; it also assumes that adult Muslims should be regarded as capable of regulating their personal moral conduct (including the freedom to adhere to any sect or to adopt any interpretation of Islam which they may choose) without external interference on the part of the State. In the past, although theoretically *Hisba* has been considered part of the Islamic State, there is no evidence that it has been regularly and strictly enforced. In the modern Islamic State there need be no *Hisba* as such, but positive steps should be taken by the State to guarantee adequate religious education for all Muslim citizens. The State must also encourage the development among the Muslim citizens of a more mature religious outlook so that their narrow and distrustful attitudes could be transformed into a broad tolerance and a genuine passion for righteousness.

It has already been shown that the spiritual and temporal are one in Islam. In Mughal India, the Sovereign appointed the judges (*Qazis*) who were empowered, besides administering criminal and civil justice, to preach, to lead the congregational prayers, to give sanction to the marriage tie, to look after the mosques and religious endowments (*Awqaf*). The British, however, abolished this institution in 1864. From that time onwards the above functions have been performed by unauthorised, self-appointed religious leaders (*Mullahs*). Although these religious leaders rendered great service in keeping the community together in the period of foreign domination, they are now an obstacle to progress since their influence tends to encourage a very narrow and confined interpretation of Islam. The modern Islamic State, therefore, has the responsibility of making provision for religious education, training, appointment and salary of preachers, missionaries and the leaders of public worship (the *Imams* of the mosque), and the maintenance of the mosques and religious endowments etc.

As has already been stated, Islam makes it obligatory upon the Muslims not only to tolerate non-Muslims but also to protect them and to defend their places of worship. Ideally speaking a sincere believer in one faith ought to respect the sincerity of the believer in any other faith. In Iqbal's terms, the Muslims should be aiming towards a much fuller and more complete expression of 'the hitherto partially revealed purpose of Islam'—that 'spiritual democracy', which Iqbal regards as 'the ultimate aim of Islam'. The modern Islamic State, therefore, should offer more security to believers in other faiths than a secular State.

The revival of *Ijtihad* is the major problem facing Muslims concerned to articulate a liberal and progressive interpretation of Islam. The essential prerequisite of such a revival is the establishment of centres for teaching and research in the law, history and theology of

Islam in the light of modern experience and the rapidly changing conditions of modern life. The modern Islamic State should establish such research centres, reform the institutions of legal and theological instruction, and encourage the holding of seminars which deal with the questions of relating traditional Islamic values and practices to contemporary problems.

IV

It has already been stated that contemporary Muslims differ in their views as to the nature of the Islamic State. These differences are caused mainly by differences in presuppositions and attitudes of mind. This is the basic reason for the present confusion on this issue. The following are some of the factors which lead to this confusion and impede the realisation of the Islamic State in Pakistan.

(1) *The Muslim Masses*

The essential concern of the masses is to obtain the basic necessities of life which are at present hard to come by. In religious matters, owing to illiteracy and credulousness, the common people in the rural areas are dominated either by the Pirs and Sufi orders or by the *Mullahs*. Hence their view of Islam is static, distorted and medieval. Change of any kind from the traditional beliefs, practices and customs is therefore unthinkable to them. In the towns the middle class Muslims tend to be smug and self-righteous. A majority of the Muslims who took part in the anti-Qadiani riots in West Punjab came from this class. Such Muslims are prompt to declare others unbelievers; their fervour thus takes a negative form, rather than the positive form of concern with making themselves good and virtuous Muslims. This negative attitude which is engendered by self-righteousness and smugness permeates all classes in all parts of the country and hinders the dissemination of a liberal and progressive understanding of Islam.

(2) *The Intelligentsia*

The term of intelligentsia is used in a broad and general sense to include the theologians (*Ulema*) and the Western-educated intellectuals. Both have been academically discussing the nature of the Islamic State for many years, but have approached the question with absolutely different attitude of mind.

Hardly any of the Muslim theologians in Pakistan have Western education. Therefore they have no clear understanding of contemporary problems. Most of them have been trained in the traditional way. They live in the past, retreat from the idea of change, reject history as a record of experimentation in applied ethics, and are unable to understand the necessity for a reconstruction of Muslim religious thought. They turn their backs on the future, shut their eyes to the demands of modernity, and live and breathe in a constricted medieval world. This attitude tends to make their approach to all problems idealistic and in a way romantic, but wholly impracticable. In the eyes of Iqbal, the Muslim theologians were intellectually stagnant.

The modern (Muslim) intellectual, a product of secular educational institutions, who has been brought up in a borrowed (Western) tradition of culture, takes great pride in applying 'scientific reason' to contemporary problems. Since he is fundamentally a rootless man, his approach to the problem of the Islamic State is curiously mischievous. He is thoroughly academic, and loves to define concepts in categorical terms. If the question of implementing the Islamic State is raised before him, he will innocently demand the definition of Islam. If he is told that Islam means belief in God's Unity and Muhammad's Prophethood, he will again ask, 'Would you be so kind as to prove the existence of God to me?' Now, here, he thinks, his triumph begins for it is obviously impossible to prove the existence of God in rational terms, whether the God of Islam or of any other religion. The intellectual therefore scornfully rejects everything that pertains to Islam and regards the Islamic State as synonymous with bigotry and fanaticism. His only contribution to positive thinking is usually his emphasis that the State should be founded on Pakistani nationalism. He fails to realise that once the principle of nationalism is conceded, it would automatically imply conceding the principle of regionalism. This would lead to the disintegration of Pakistan. The ideology of Islam on which Pakistan was founded is the only basis for unity and solidarity among the people of Pakistan who speak different languages, descend from different racial and cultural stocks and are geographically non-contiguous.

Hence the intellectual either looks towards the West for inspiration (without having any deep understanding of the real problems of the West) and is attracted by secularism, capitalism, atheistic socialism etc., or else he simply drifts as a nihilist, feeling frustrated by the emptiness and lack of sense of purpose in his life.

There is a liberal and moderate tradition of approaching theological and ideological problems which derives from the time of Syed Ahmad Khan[13] and comes down to Iqbal. These reformers influenced the minds of the people and directed their transition from medieval to modern ways of thinking. It is the tradition established by these reformers which eventually led to the political and cultural emancipation of the Muslims in the Indian sub-continent. Such men combined in their attitudes an awareness that the basic principles of Islam must be preserved, with a recognition of the value and importance of modern ways of thinking. Although the ideas of these liberal and moderate reformers have withstood the test of time, and the trend of history is moving in the direction which demands the fulfilment of their ideas, there is at present, unfortunately, no organised and coherent liberal movement in Pakistan. The liberalism which exists is confined mainly to the upper classes and tends to concern itself with matters of tolerance and personal morality rather than with a vigorous assertion of the need for social justice and reform.

(3) *Politicians*

Although there are no 'politicians' in power at the moment they have been very influential in the past in determining the form of the Islamic State, and will doubtless be influential again when they return in the future. Gibbon believed that to a historian all religions are false, to a philosopher all religions are true, but to a politician all religions are useful. The experience of the past ten years has clearly shown that most politicians have laid emphasis on the Islamic State in their speeches, statements etc. as a matter of policy, but so far as the problem of implementing the Islamic State is concerned, the people have been offered virtually nothing.

[13] Syed Ahmad Khan was one of the earliest 'modernisers' of Islam. His movement began after the British suppression of the rebellion of 1857, and was associated with the Muslim University at Aligarh.

The object of these politicians was to remain popular in the eyes of the people. They fully understood the psychology or the mental chemistry of the Muslim masses. They knew that the masses loved to be reminded of Islam, its glory in the past, and so on, but that they did not like to be told of their shortcomings and failings. And similarly they knew that the masses were too indolent and lazy to interest themselves in any change of religious outlook. Hence these politicians' emphasis on Islam was only verbal; they declaimed with passion on the virtues of religion because such was the popular mode of oratory.

(4) *The Press*

The vernacular press in Pakistan takes its origin from the Khilafat days when its circulation depended on raising the slogan, ' Islam is in danger'. The readers of the vernacular press belong to the Muslim middle class. (The upper classes read the English news-papers). A large portion of the vernacular press plays on the puritanism and self-righteousness of the middle class. Hence these papers are opposed to any liberal and progressive interpretation of Islam, and by exploiting the techniques of sensationalism and inciting the prejudices of the people, they make any attempt to disseminate liberalism immensely more difficult. Furthermore, it is against their vested interests to support liberalism because to adopt attitudes of tolerance and fair-mindedness would lead to a serious drop in their circulation.

(5) *Lack of Educational Facilities*

Although the recent Education Commission Report recommends the dissemination of a liberal and progressive interpretation of Islam and a revolution in the attitudes of the people, there do not yet exist adequate facilities to do the necessary research into the problems involved in relating Islamic values to contemporary problems. There is almost a complete dearth of adequate books on this subject. The dissemination of a liberal interpretation of Islam will require intensive efforts to train teachers and to implement effective methods of instruction. As the Education Commission Report says, a revolution in attitudes cannot be accomplished by fiat.

V

Much of the contemporary discussion about the Islamic State in Pakistan, whether conservative or nominally liberal, is in fact utopian. Its method is to define in abstract terms the characteristics of the ideal Islamic State and to say nothing practicable about the implementation of the ideal. Such discussion generally ignores entirely the essential question which is the poverty, degradation and suffering of the masses.

It is only too clear that conditions in Pakistan—the feudal landlords, the Westernised intellectuals, the professional holy men, the medieval religious leaders, and the alienated masses—resemble in many ways conditions in Russia before the Revolution. The static religion, and the ineffective liberalism of Russia disappeared in smoke before the organisation, discipline and coherent purpose of Lenin.

Iqbal contemplated the phenomenon of Lenin. In his poem, *Lenin before God*, the Muslim poet spoke of the destruction wrought by Lenin as a kind of necessary judgment on the sterile religion, blood-sucking capitalism and imperialism of the West. The Muslim poet also saw the possibility that if the Muslims continued to accept Islam in the form of a religion which teaches fatalism, keeps the poor oppressed, justifies social inequality, or rejects the idea of transforming conditions in the material world, then the explosive force of the alienated masses would swell up like a flood, break its confines and find its own direction.

The alternative to this possibility, in Iqbal's opinion, was an interpretation of Islam which emphasised, instead of a static utopian system, a view of history as a process. Muslims within history should always be moving towards a more perfect State and thus be always developing more adequate structures of social, economic and political justice. The adoption of the symbols of the Crescent and the Star on the national flag represents this very aspiration of the Muslim community—the State to achieve gradually (just as the Crescent moon passing through its numerous phases, eventually achieves) perfection under the guidance of God's Law (symbolised on the national flag as the Guiding Star).

DR. IQBAL: Muslims are not anti-nationalistic but they accept nationalism in a definite sense. They have an idealistic conception of Islamic solidarity, which I have illustrated historically in my paper. It is not incompatible with a high ideal of international friendship. Indeed, to Muslims, secular nationalism has come to be known as idolatrous nationalism and they believe that wars have sprung from the deification of this purely political ideal. The concepts of equality and social justice are basic in Islam.

The 1956 Constitution was hypocritical and vague in its framework. The group of politicians who followed Jinnah were disappointing compared to their predecessors and the masses of people were alienated from their leaders. As Ayub Khan had said: "We failed to define that ideology. . . . Also in our ignorance we began to regard the Islamic ideology as synonymous with bigotry and theocracy, and sub-consciously began to fight shy of it."

At present there is martial law, but there is a pre-constitutional arrangement for 'basic democracies', which brings an element of consent into the prevalent system. The constitution is in the making. Personally I feel that I have more liberty than under previous regimes—at least I feel more secure.

Beyond this I shall not add to my paper, which in any case is like the intestine of the Devil, it has no end.

PROF. L. C. WEBB: Many Asian countries are going through a second phase, in which we are feeling the ground-swell of traditional forces, and especially of religions. By concentrating on constitutions, it might seem that the religious factor was becoming less important. But is this so? In Ceylon, for example, there has been the Buddhist revival, which is making a mess of previous political calculations.

The religious atmosphere of Pakistan is complex. In West Pakistan, there is something of the climate of the Middle East, whereas in East Pakistan, there is the more sober atmosphere of a country like Malaya. This might be said to illustrate the dampening effect of humidity on religion. There is also a search going on for a form of Islam that will be compatible with modern institutions, with the unity of the State. Pakistan under Ayub Khan is from this point of view not unlike England under the Tudors. Islam has been handicapped by a set of fossilised political ideas.

There is an inherent tendency in all Islamic parties towards fission. This is understandable where the population is 80 per cent illiterate and the prestige of any literate man is great, however ill-informed. In Iqbal's book *Ideology of Pakistan and its Implementation*, he proposed that there should be a Ministry of Religious Affairs to take over the affairs of the mosques and religious foundations, to appoint and pay *Imams*, supervise religious education, and so on. This would probably reduce sectarianism.

All the same, it will be difficult to restore vitality to the Islamic ideal in the context of a modern State. Christendom has emerged with a structure of government within which the State tends to be regarded as of its nature secular and religion as a private affair. This is much harder for Islam, with its rejection of secondary causes. As Abul 'Ala Mawdudi, founder of one of Pakistan's most influential sects, put it: "The sun, the moon and the stars are . . . all Muslims", because they all obey God. Such Muslims bring the same style of thought into politics, and can only see an Islamic State as a theocracy, in which man's only duty is to obey the law.

PROF. MORRIS-JONES: I wish to compare the situation in Pakistan as described by Iqbal with that in India. One difference is that no Indian parties have been completely geared to religion. Secondly, the despair and distrust which Pakistanis feel towards the pre-1958 regime is apparent also in India. The difference is one of degree only. In Pakistan the disgust appears universal. Is there something about Islam which makes it less willing to tolerate a distinction between profession and practice, to accept and bear with incoherence and incapacity, which the Indians appear willing to do?

PROF. STONE: I would like to ask Dr. Iqbal, first, what is meant by 'idolatrous nationalism'? And what is the Islamic view of the national state, which has been summarised in terms of 'cultural emancipation' and 'territorial specification'? Do not these two add up to 'idolatrous nationalism'? My second main question is, how far would an Islamic republic of Pakistan be a theocratic state?

DR. IQBAL : Territorial nationalism is accepted by the Muslims only for the purpose of identification. Nationalist values must under no circumstances over-ride human values. This is how a Muslim feels. The Muslim concept of nationalism is, therefore, more idealistic than the Western concept. Secular (or idolatrous) nationalism brought forth Fascism in our times. Its narrowness and inhuman tendencies can be witnessed in the Union of South Africa and even in some parts of the United States.

Christians, dominated by a tradition of personal religion and Church organisations, tend to see the Islamic State as a theocracy. But to Muslims it never means a theocracy for there are no priests in Islam who may run the state. A modern Muslim state could conceivably exist even if its head was a Hindu for the Muslims are free to elect anyone as the head of their state. In Pakistan at the moment the Chief Justice of the Supreme Court, Mr. Justice Cornelius, is a Roman Catholic.

MR. D. SINGH : I am not clear how Dr. Iqbal's exalted view of an Islamic State can be reconciled with traditional Islamic law. Under the 1956 Constitution, it was provided that law would be linked with Islamic law as revealed in the *Quran*. If, for example, Pakistan were to introduce a new law of divorce, how would it be kept consistent with the *Quran*? How would the early Muslim texts be interpreted?

MR. JUSTICE ELSE-MITCHELL : Surely a system of judicial review such as Dr. Iqbal envisages must ultimately lead to divergence between the law authorised by the courts and the traditional law of the *Quran*.

MR. HINDLEY : I can attach no meaning to the idea of an 'Islamic State'. Two aspects of Islam have some applicability to politics. First, Islam is not democratic; second, it has no supreme interpreter like the Pope. I believe it is impossible to reach a definition of an 'Islamic State' that would be acceptable to more than a handful of Muslims. Anyone may define such a State as he wishes, and in the absence of a hierarchical 'Church' in Islam, there is no 'Muslim Pope' to lay down which definition is the correct one.

DR. IQBAL : I think that the whole approach to Islam has been medieval; the Muslim is always thought of as a man with a knife. There is no great difficulty about the interpretation of the *Quran* to develop a law suited to a modern State. Over three centuries there have been attempts to bring Muslim law into line with modern requirements. A Muslim State can be very tolerant. The old Moghul rulers did not interfere with the social system of India and impose ideas of Islamic law. Only if minorities are preserved, can the true ideal of the Islamic state be attained and Muslim ideals of respect for others be upheld.

Donald Hindley

A NOTE ON ISLAM AND POLITICS IN INDONESIA

ALTHOUGH ABOUT 90 per cent of Indonesia's 95 million inhabitants are classified as Muslim, Islam there has provided no guide for political action, nor has it welded together a political force of lasting national importance. In order to understand this failure, it is necessary to examine the history of the Islamisation of Indonesia, the nature of Islam itself, and the political situation in Indonesia since the transfer of sovereignty in December 1949.

The last Hindu kingdom in Java did not fall until 1478, while towards the end of the sixteenth and the beginning of the seventeenth centuries there arose in Central Java the nominally Muslim sultanate of Mataram which reasserted Javanese philosophy and ritual. The local agents of Muslim orthodoxy were purged because they competed for the loyalty of the population. The Dutch, too, were concerned to curb the influence of the Muslim leaders. Indonesian government officials were discouraged from a strict observation of religious duties, religious teachers were licensed, and severe restrictions were imposed on the import of religious literature in order to keep out political influences. In short, within Java two sub-communities were formed: that of the *santris*, the devout Muslims, and that of the *abangans*, those who were nominally Muslim but who maintained a basically animistic and Hinduistic set of beliefs and ritual. Furthermore, a majority of the Indonesian government officials, those whose children had the opportunity of higher education and who were to constitute an important part of the nationalist leadership, were not *santris*.

The dichotomy between the *santris* and the *abangans* was not marked until the present century when the Islamic reform movement reached Java. This movement was aimed primarily at purging the nominally orthodox Muslims of syncretic accretions. Indigenous, non-Islamic phenomena were rejected, such as traditional dancing and puppet plays, gambling, and even traditional clothing and music. Resentment and fear of the orthodox Muslims were heightened among the *abangans*. Today the *santris* and *abangans* are self-conscious, often antagonistic, sub-communities.

The 1955 general elections showed that the Muslim political parties received about 40 per cent of the votes in Java, and somewhat more in Indonesia as a whole. If the Muslims had been united, they would have formed, perhaps, the major political force in Indonesia. But they were not. The reason for their division lies in the nature of Islam itself. Islam has no 'Church', no supreme interpreter. Thus the devout Muslims in Indonesia are fragmented in their religious and political interpretation of Islam. In the political sphere, which concerns us at present, many of them are members of secular parties, even of the Communist Party, believing that by being so they are implementing what they consider to be the political message of Islam. Most devout Muslims, however, support one of the avowedly Muslim parties. The history of the Muslim political groups is one of recurrent squabbles and divisions. At the time of the 1955 elections, there were four Muslim parties worth noting: Masjumi (by and large the representative of the reformist groups) which received 21 per cent of the total votes; Nahdatul Ulama (representing the adherents of the four main schools of Islamic law) which received 18·4 per cent; PSII, which received 2·9 per cent; and Perti, a small Sumatran party, which received 1·3 per cent.

Although the Muslims are politically divided, one or each of the avowedly Muslim political groups might have used Islam in order to produce a concept of an Islamic state. This has not occurred. The ordinary party programmes of the Muslim parties are similar to those of the secular parties, and are based upon Western humanist traditions, while the bankruptcy of their religion as a guide for creating a modern State was clearly demonstrated in the Constituent Assembly debates from 1956 to 1959. Certainly they united in opposition to President Soekarno's Pantjasila, but on the other hand they were unable, separately or collectively, to formulate what they meant by an Islamic State. Beyond the desire for a stipulation that the President of Indonesia be a Muslim and that the State should be based on 'the teachings of Islam' (undefined), nothing concrete emerged. Their predicament was not unique, for what religion has been used successfully as the basis of a modern state?

A brief survey of the political situation since the transfer of sovereignty in December 1949, shows how the Muslim parties have been excluded from a major role in the government of Indonesia.

In 1950 it was widely believed that Masjumi (which until 1952 included Nahdatul Ulama) would win a clear majority in the event of general elections. Masjumi, with the adherence of the rural and urban *Ulamas*, was the only party at that time with a nation-wide and effective means of mobilising mass support. The principal Masjumi leaders also were inclined to be pro-Western and to consider the revolution as largely completed by the transfer of sovereignty. The other political forces closed their ranks through fear of a Masjumi victory and through their commonly-held belief that the revolution was a continuing social, economic and political struggle against the Western imperialists. The non-*santris'* fear of Muslim fanaticism was strengthened by the bloody revolts led in the name of Islam in West Java, Atjeh and South Sulawesi.

The Nahdatul Ulama broke away from Masjumi in 1952 and, like PSII and Perti, showed itself willing to co-operate with the anti-Masjumi forces. A loose alliance was formed of PNI (the nationalist party), the Communist Party, Soekarno, Nahdatul Ulama and PSII. Masjumi was first excluded from government office in the middle of 1953. By the time of the general elections in September 1955, the non-Muslim parties had developed their organisation to the extent that they could win 56·5 per cent of the votes. The end result of Masjumi's exclusion from a major role in government was the participation of several of its leaders in the PRRI-Permesta rebellion that broke out in February 1958. In August 1960, Soekarno ordered the dissolution of Masjumi.

Why could PNI, Soekarno and the communists use NU, PSII, and Perti in the process that led first to the isolation and then to the rebellion and destruction of Masjumi? They could because there was nothing to bind the so-called Muslim parties tightly together. Just as it failed to provide the Indonesian Muslims with a guide to a State constitution, Islam also failed to provide them with a guide for political tactics or government policy. If Islam could not provide unity on religious matters, how could it on political ones? In the absence of a hierarchical 'Church', there was no one with the authority to settle disputes or evict heretics. In short, the addition of the adjective 'Muslim' to a political party had little effect on its political behaviour.

NU, PSII and Perti leaders have declared, and they may believe genuinely, that their participation in any government, even an anti-Masjumi one dominated by non-Muslim forces, gives the Muslims some influence in government decision-making. In the event, this has not proved so. Because of their generally low level of formal education, their political weakness, and their lack of political expertise, the NU, PSII and Perti leaders have been given mainly menial cabinet posts. They have carried little if any weight in the formulation of government policy.

To summarise: Indonesia has the largest Muslim population of any country. Islamisation has been uneven in its intensity, leaving many nominal Muslims outside and often antipathetic to the influence of the Muslim religious leaders. And for the devout Muslims, Islam has provided neither the basis for a modern State nor the cohesion with which the avowedly Muslim groups could have become a major political force in the country.

J. A. C. Mackie

INDONESIAN CONSTITUTIONS, 1945–60

INDONESIA HAS been governed under three different constitutions since it proclaimed its independence in 1945. During the years of revolutionary struggle against the Dutch, 1945–9, the Republic based its authority on the 'Proclamation Constitution of 1945', drafted just before the Japanese surrender and promulgated on August 18. It served as a framework of government during the uncertain years of revolution and has again been in force since July 5, 1959. It is characterised by a powerful, almost unlimited executive, which cannot be overthrown by the legislature. (Hence, amongst other reasons, its restoration in 1959). The federal constitution of the shortlived Republic of the United States of Indonesia (R.U.S.I.), created by the Round Table Conference which ended the Dutch-Indonesian dispute in late 1949, lasted only until the transformation into a unitary state in August 1950. Its drafting shows strong Dutch influence, which also coloured the Provisional Constitution of 1950–59, since the latter differed from it only in minor respects, except on the one matter of rejecting the federal structure. (The constitutional framework of federalism was as vaguely defined as it was shortlived and it is not worth further elaboration here.)

The Provisional Constitution imposed a unicameral parliamentary system of responsible government, in which political parties played a dominant role. Among the reasons for the abandonment of 'liberal democracy' in 1959 was undoubtedly a widespread feeling that party politics within this framework were only leading to political deadlock. However, the 'rules of the game' were observed fairly scrupulously from 1950 until normal parliamentary politics began to go into eclipse in March 1957 as a result of promulgation of a State of Emergency, the political intervention of regional military commanders, the President's incursion into active politics and the unrestrained increase in budget deficits.

A Constituent Assembly had been foreshadowed in all three constitutions but could not be elected until December 1955, shortly after the first general elections for the House of Representatives. It met in November 1956, but by the end of 1957 it was clear that no agreement could be reached over the issue of an Islamic or *Pantja Sila* (i.e. secular) State. Although the two Islamic parties were vague about the precise structure of an Islamic state and the immediate point at issue was merely the preamble to the constitution, they were able to prevent the two-thirds majority required to settle it. A more substantial disagreement loomed in regard to the choice between a federal or unitary state and a bicameral or unicameral parliament, since the former was preferred by elements in the Masjumi Party which drew its support largely from regions outside Java. But before this issue came into the open, the Government in February 1959 proposed as an alternative course that the 1945 Constitution be restored: it coupled this recommendation to the Constituent Assembly with a compromise formula on the question of the Islamic State, designed to win over enough Muslim votes to obtain the two-thirds majority. However, at the last minute, one of the Muslim parties in the government, the Nahdatul Ulama, decided to oppose the government's proposal, which was defeated. The War Administrator under Martial Law then proclaimed a ban on political activities (since lifted, although not fully), the Constituent Assembly was wound up and on July 5 the 1945 Constitution was promulgated by Presidential Decree.

Legislative Power

(1) THE 1950 CONSTITUTION: Under the 1950 Constitution, legislative power was vested in 'the Government together with the House of Representatives' (Article 89). There was no second chamber. The government was "bound to ratify a bill which has been passed, unless the Government gives notice of having preponderant objections against this bill within one month after the bill has been submitted for ratification" (Article 94, *ii*). (This veto power was never used, nor, as far as I know, was the threat to use it employed against Parliament.) The House of Representatives had the right to submit or amend bills (Articles 90–91).

The government had a right to enact emergency laws on matters demanding immediate attention, but the regulations contained in such laws had to be submitted to the House of Representatives at the next session; otherwise they lapsed *ipso jure* (Articles 96–7). This power was used extensively in 1950–51, but less frequently in later years when Governments occupied a weaker position in the House and the use of the power met with some criticism. The Constitution also permitted the Government to issue regulations (ordinances) and to delegate authority to other organs of the State to issue further regulations for carrying out the laws and ordinances (Articles 98–100). The manner of promulgating laws and ordinances was to be determined by law, but the Constitution provided no machinery for review of ordinances, Ministerial regulations or rules of lower authorities and Parliament appears not to have attempted to establish any formal machinery of supervision, apart from its set of committees mentioned below.

There was no limitation on the legislative power of the central government, as had been implied (although in the vaguest terms) under the federal constitution of 1949, except in the implicit reservation of constitutional changes to another body (Article 140). "The laws are inviolable" (Article 95, *ii*), i.e. not subject to challenge in court. Article 1, *ii* of the Constitution bracketed 'the Government' together with the House of Representatives as the instrument of popular sovereignty. The House attempted to exercise supervision over the executive through a series of committees corresponding to the various ministries; but while these did weaken the authority of Ministers, their primary function seems to have been an educational one for members and they had nothing like the influence of French or American legislative committees. However the House of Representatives was not able to attain a primary position in the governmental system as the instrument of popular sovereignty. Its most serious weakness, derived from a practical problem of financial control; budgets were generally presented so late in the year to which they applied that the House had no real opportunity to exercise effective control over expenditure. Budget deficits became endemic, always exceeding the estimated figure, and the accounting process fell so far into arrears that only provisional estimates of expenditure in any year were published; accounting control was left very largely to the Auditor-General's Department.

The composition of the House of Representatives under the 1950 Constitution was initially determined by the agreement establishing the unitary Republic. The House included specified numbers of nominated members from former organs of the federal R.U.S.I. and the revolutionary Republican government, to an initial total of 236 members. The Constitution provided that it should consist of one representative to every 300,000 citizens and be chosen for 4 years by general election (Articles 56, 57, 59) on a basis of universal and equal suffrage exercised by secret ballot "or equivalent free voting procedure" (Article 35). The Electoral Law of 1953 provided for direct election through proportional representation; 16 electoral districts were designated and seats allotted according to population on a ratio of 1/300,000, with the stipulation that each district had a right to a minimum representation of 3 seats in the House of Representatives and 6 in the Constituent Assembly; 'remainder' votes were to be accumulated and distributed on a national basis. The franchise provided for universal suffrage (without literacy qualification) for all citizens over 18 and for married persons below 18.

(2) THE 1945 CONSTITUTION confines the House of Representatives to a purely legislative role. The sovereignty of the people is now exercised by a People's Consultative Assembly (Article 1, *ii*), which is to consist of "members of the House of Representatives, with the addition of representatives from the regions and groups, according to regulations to be determined by law" (Article 2, *i*). (The fact that this article can be interpreted to mean 'functional groups' contributes to its appeal to the President as a basis for Guided Democracy.) The People's Consultative Assembly is to meet at least once every five years; it is to elect the President (and Vice-President) and lay down the "general direction of State policy". An advisory Council of State, nominated by the President, has also been established (Article 16). A new electoral law amending that of 1953, which will make provision for representatives of 'functional groups' in the House of Representatives, has been foreshadowed but not yet (June 1961) published. The House of Representatives elected in 1955 continued to function under the new constitution from July 1959 to March 2, 1960, when it was dissolved by Presidential Decree: a new House was then nominated by the President, containing 130 members from political parties (several of which have not been represented), 35 from the Armed Forces and 118 from the 'functional groups'. The Provisional People's

Consultative Assembly was nominated by the President in August 1960, and met for its first session to lay down the " broad outlines of state policy " in November: it consists of 515 members.

The Constitution provides merely that the House of Representatives shall meet at least once a year; that its composition shall be laid down by law (Article 19); that laws require the approval of the House and, if rejected, may not be proposed again at the same session (Article 20); that members of the House have a right to propose bills—subject to the same limitation if the President refuses ratification (Article 21); and that the President has a right to issue ordinances in the place of laws, which must be submitted to the House of Representatives at the next session (Article 22). The President's frequent exercise of this quasi-legislative power (granted in Article 22, under the title 'Law-Substituting Ordinances') to avoid referring controversial bills to the House has further reduced the status of the latter.

Under the 1945 Constitution, legislative or quasi-legislative powers have been exercised in a variety of forms. At the top of the hierarchy come Presidential Decrees (*Penetapan Presiden*) under which the 1945 Constitution was proclaimed; a number of further Decrees have subsequently been issued, on the argument that they serve to *implement* the new constitution: they have embodied a wide range of basic decisions and have not been submitted to Parliament for approval. The decisions of the People's Consultative Assembly (*Ketetapan Madjelis Permusjawaratan Rakjat*) lay down the 'broad outlines of State policy' rather than legislative rules, but they are considered to embody principles which are binding on the Government and its agencies. Laws (*Undang-undang*) are still made by the House of Representatives in the usual way. The 1945 Constitution made no provision for Emergency Laws (*Undang-undang Darurat*) as did the 1950 Constitution, but it provided under Article 22 for 'Law-substituting Ordinances' (*Peraturan Pemerintah Pengganti Undang-undang*). At a level below legislation, government regulations (*Peraturan Pemerintah*), Ministerial orders (*Peraturan Menteri*) and Ministerial decision may be issued on the basis of a law. In addition, a new class of Presidential Regulations (*Peraturan Presiden*) is now used to implement Presidential Decrees.

During the period of revolutionary struggle from 1945–49, the status of the Central National Committee, which exercised the powers of the House of Representatives, was higher than the 1945 Constitution implied, despite (or perhaps because of) the fact that it was a nominated body whose numbers were augmented at several stages by the Government to reflect changes in political alignments. Cabinet responsibility to the Working Committee of the Central National Committee was virtually accepted from November 1945 to February 1948, when a 'Presidential' Cabinet under Dr. Hatta took office. It is unlikely, however, that the 1945 Constitution will again be modified in this way, since the primacy of party politics which gave rise to the demand for direct Cabinet responsibility to parliament in 1945-48 has now been disavowed.

Executive Power

(1) THE 1950 CONSTITUTION (*a*) *The Cabinet*: The 1950 Provisional Constitution followed the Dutch model in making the Government responsible to Parliament. It did not specifically debar a Cabinet from attempting to govern without the support of a majority in the House of Representatives, but none attempted to do so nor could have succeeded long in doing so. The executive powers of the Government were laid down by Article 82 of the constitution in very broad terms: "the Government is to promote the welfare of Indonesia and especially to take care that the Constitution, the laws and other regulations are executed". (The extensive powers vested in the executive authority under legislation of the colonial era were taken over without substantial change, as also was the colonial civil service, which constitutes a control mechanism reaching down to the village.) Ministers did not have to be members of the House of Representatives and, if they were, they were not permitted to exercise their parliamentary functions while in office (Article 61, *ii*); they could intimate their wish to address the House to the Chairman (Article 64) and were required to answer questions from it either orally or in writing.

Relations between the Ministers, the President and Parliament were not entirely clear. Article 83, *ii*; "The Ministers shall be responsible for the entire policy of the Government; jointly for the entire policy, and each Minister for his part in the Government". The President and Vice-President were 'inviolable'. The right to dissolve the House of Representatives was vested in the President

(Article 84) and no reference was made in the constitution to the Prime Minister's rights in the matter; the issue hardly arose, mainly because it would have been physically impossible to hold an immediate election before the one general election in 1955. The dissolution power was one of the obscure points in the Constitution's definition of the President's relationship with the Cabinet; it has been held to blame for the weak position of the latter and the unusual degree to which the President acted independently of the Cabinet. Article 83, *ii*, quoted above, implied a sole Ministerial responsibility for Government policy; this would seem to have confined the President strictly to the role of mouthpiece of the Cabinet, except in fields where specific functions were allotted to him. (But it has been suggested that the President shared *authority* for legislation, although not *responsibility* for it, with the Cabinet, since the term 'Government' clearly referred to both in Chapter II, section 1 and Chapter III, section 1.) The Constitution did not specifically prevent the President from vetoing or withholding approval for legislation and on several occasions he did so to the embarrassment of cabinets which were uncongenial to him. A further cause of friction between some Cabinets and the President was the latter's refusal to accept the usual limitations of a constitutional head of state in the matter of public speeches and official tours; in these fields, the extraordinary status of President and Vice-President as pre-eminent 'national leaders' was approved in a Ministerial statement in Parliament in 1951. The relative weakness of the Cabinet is to be sought, however, in political factors and the charismatic appeal of the President, rather than in a purely constitutional explanation.

(*b*) *The President*: The Provisional Constitution provided that the President (and Vice-President, whose functions were not specifically defined) would be elected according to rules to be laid down by law; no such law was passed, as President Soekarno was already installed in office when the Constitution came into effect, under the terms of the political agreement establishing it; the method of his election and the prescribed term of office were left for the Constituent Assembly to determine. The President's powers were specified as appointment of cabinet formateurs and appointment of Ministers in accordance with their recommendations (Articles 50–51), the right to dissolve the House of Representatives, to conclude diplomatic relations with other states, to award decorations, to grant pardons, the power to declare war and to declare a state of emergency (Articles 84, 87 and 120–129). He was also 'vested with supreme authority over the Armed Forces' (Article 127); in spite of strong arguments that this meant merely that the President exercised *nominal* authority above a Commander-in-Chief, his right to overrule the Minister of Defence in the making of appointments was invoked during the most celebrated political crisis of the 'fifties.

(2) THE 1945 CONSTITUTION: Under the terms of the 1945 Constitution, the President's executive powers are almost unlimited and Ministers of State, appointed and dismissed by him, are mentioned merely as assistants to him (Article 17). "The President of the R.I. shall be vested with executive power as laid down in the Constitution" (Article 4, *i*). He is also Commander-in-Chief of the Armed Forces. The constitution provides that he is to be assisted by a Vice-President, but none has been designated since July 1959. He is to be elected for 5 years by the People's Consultative Assembly by majority vote (Article 6, *ii*).

His authority is limited only by the stipulation that the concurrence of the House of Representatives is necessary for the enactment of legislation, for declaring war and terminating hostilities and for concluding treaties. (Articles 11 and 20, *i*). In circumstances of emergency, he is empowered under Article 22 to issue ordinances taking the place of laws, these ordinances being required to obtain approval by the House of Representatives in the following session, failing which they are to be struck out. If the President does not ratify a bill proposed by the House of Representatives (or if the House does not ratify a bill proposed by the President), that bill may not be proposed again during the same session (Articles 20–21).

Emergency Provisions

Since March 1957, Indonesia has been under Martial Law, initially under the provisions of a Dutch Ordinance of 1939 regarding the State of War and Siege, then under the Indonesian Law 74/1957, recently modified by Law-substituting Ordinance No. 23/1959. The earlier measures recognised two stages of 'siege' and 'war'; the latter establishes 3 stages of 'civil emergency', 'military emergency' and 'war emergency'. The Central War Administrator under the 1959 law is the President/Commander-in-Chief, assisted by a council consisting of the Prime Minister, Minister of Defence, Minister for Home Affairs, Minister of Foreign Affairs, Chiefs of Staff of the 3 armed services and Head of Police. (Until December 1959, each armed service head acted as Central War Administrator within the territory controlled by his service: in effect, the Army Chief of Staff was the principal authority.) In a state of 'war' and 'military emergency', the Regional War Administrator is the local military commander, in conjunction with a council consisting of the *Kepala Daerah* (see below under Regional Government), local chief of police and regional executive council; the difference between "war" and "military emergency" is merely one of powers. In a state of "civil emergency", the civil *Kepala Daerah* is the Regional War Administrator. Under the 1957 law, the State of Emergency was to last only 6 months and the State of War only 12 months; it could be extended by Parliament. The Government was obliged to submit a report on all actions performed under the special authority granted by the Act (Clause 5, *iii*). Neither provision is contained in the 1959 version of the law.

The Judiciary

The judiciary has played almost no part in Indonesian constitutional processes, except in conducting criminal cases with a political background. No cases involving interpretation of the Constitution have been dealt with by the courts, although the Chairman of the Supreme Court has been called upon to give advice to the President on the legality of procedures he has adopted. The 1945 Constitution states simply that "the Judicial Power shall be vested in the Supreme Court and such subordinate courts as may be established by law": the organisation, competence and conditions for appointment and discharge of judges are to be laid down by law (Articles 24–5). The 1950 Constitution added also that appointments were for life, subject to an age limit which could be laid down by law and that judges could be dismissed or relieved from office as the law prescribed (Articles 78–9).

The law of 1950 governing the Supreme Court provides that judges are to be appointed by the President from candidates (at least 2 to each vacancy) proposed by the House of Representatives. Judges may be honourably discharged from office by the President because of continued mental or physical illness or because of old age (60 is the prescribed retiring age unless the President gives a dispensation for reasons of State): otherwise they can only be discharged at their own request. They may also be dismissed if sentenced for committing a crime, if they become bankrupt, if they violate the provision against taking part in a case in which they have an interest or "because of improper or indecent behaviour or constant negligence in their duties". The two levels of lower courts for the Indonesian population have still the same general structure as in Dutch times, but the dualistic system of separate courts and legal codes for Dutch nationals has been abolished; the courts of first instance now exercise a wider jurisdiction also. *Adat* (customary) law is gradually being subordinated to the national code, whereas there was a tendency to preserve it in the later years of Dutch rule. On the other hand, religious courts still function, mainly in the sphere of family law, with a somewhat higher status than in colonial times.

Regional Government

The powers devolved by the central government to autonomous regional units, provinces and regencies (*kabupatens*) are not large and overlap those of the central government's hierarchy of local officials on inferior terms. This hierarchy, formerly the Dutch colonial service, extends down through 6 levels of authority to the village, each exercising control and supervision over the activities of lower organs on the basis of a mass of laws and ordinances accumulated over decades. 'Autonomous' institutions alongside the first and third level of this hierarchy (first established under the Dutch regime) are now based upon Law 1/1957, as modified by Presidential Decree No. 6/1959. Regional representative councils have been established at both levels, province and *kabupaten* or regency, and in theory are empowered to deal with all matters not specifically assigned to other authorities: in practice, there are few fields where the central government does not exercise prior authority, so that the principal powers exercised by the autonomous units are powers of *medebewind* ('sharing-in-government') in sharing administrative functions which the central government devolves to them. The central government's administrative hierarchy maintains a close degree of supervision to ensure that the decisions of regional authorities do not contravene or encroach on the legislation or regulations of higher units.

The key figures in the system of regional government are the *Kepala Daerah* ('regional head') at the provincial and regency level. Until 1957, the *governor* and *regent* (both members of the central government hierarchy) bore this additional title and authority, since they also acted as chairmen of the provisional regional councils. Law 1/1957 provided that the elected chairman of the council should be designated *Kepala Daerah*, although the governors and regents continued to exist alongside them as administrative figures, with ambiguous status *vis-a-vis* the *Kepala Daerah*, but continuing supervisory powers over lower units of government. To remedy the 'dualism' of this system, Presidential Decree No. 6/1959 has restored central authority over regional councils by fusing the two offices again and providing that the *Kepala Daerah* shall be a servant of the central government chosen by the central government from 4 nominees submitted by the regional councils; but an escape clause permits it to choose from beyond these nominees if necessary. The unitary character of the system has been strongly underlined.

Financial relations are now regulated by Law 32/1956 which assigns to the regions power to levy certain taxes (insignificant local ones) as designated by government regulation, in addition to varying proportions of the yield from other higher-yielding, centrally-collected taxes, as specified by the central government from year to year: part of the receipts from the main revenue-producers (import and export duties) is also to be devoted to the regions, but in very vague terms. No clearcut formula for allocating sufficient taxing powers to make regional councils fully independent or for allocating their respective shares of available central government revenue has yet been put into effect and central government grants to the regions appear to be made on an *ad hoc* basis: most provincial budgets have derived 90 per cent of their revenue from central grants, although the figure ranges much more widely (down to 40 per cent and less in a few cases) for regencies.

Fundamental Rights

The Provisional Constitution contained a substantial catalogue of fundamental human rights and freedoms (Articles 7–34), ranging from statements of legal rights guaranteeing equality before the law and just legal procedures to statements of aspirations such as the right to work, to education and to ownership of property. The legal status of these rights is indicated by Article 33; "limitations on the exercise of rights and freedoms described in this section can only be imposed by regulations as established by law, exclusively for the purpose of securing the indispensable recognition and respect for the rights and freedoms of others and to comply with the just requirements of public order, morality and welfare in a democratic community". An additional section of fundamental principles laid down that "the will of the people is the basis of public authority" and in broad terms prescribed freedom of religion and various welfare objectives. Article 38 i, which prescribed that "the national economy shall be organised on a cooperative basis", has given rise to much discussion as to its meaning.

The 1945 Constitution contains much shorter clauses of similar character, prescribing religious freedom, equality before the law, the right to work and to expect a reasonable standard of living, freedom of assembly, speech and Press and the right to strike, as provided by law (Articles 26–28). Legal rights are much less specifically spelled out than in the 1950 Constitution, being subsumed under the stipulation of equality before the law contained in the clause "All citizens shall have the same status in law and in the government . . ." (Article 27, i).

J. A. C. Mackie

ASPECTS OF POLITICAL POWER AND THE DEMISE OF PARLIAMENTARY DEMOCRACY IN INDONESIA

IN DISCUSSING a situation where constitutions are being made and altered and unmade, we are sooner or later led to reflect upon the relationship between the particular features of a constitution and the nature of the political forces it has to accommodate. Unless a constitution is in some sense tailored to the realities of political power within a community, there is likely to be deadlock or conflict. But we cannot briefly say much more than this about the relationship in general terms; our concepts are too vague, and political forces which can be contained within constitutional channels in one context might overflow them is a slightly different one. Yet if constitutions are to be worked out other than by chance in the turbulent polities of Asia, we need a more precise notion of which political forces matter, from this point of view. We also need to know more about the functional significance of constitutions. How far can they affect the way in which the more explosive forces within the community are going to work themselves out?

In Indonesia, the Provisional Constitution of 1950 was able to accommodate political activity for about 7 years according to 'the rules of the game'; then the rules began to be flouted and changed. Several years later, in July 1959, the government restored the revolutionary 1945 Constitution, because it was considered a more appropriate framework for political activity by the most influential elements in the country. The powers of the various instruments of government are now defined so broadly that one of the most basic functions of a modern constitution has been virtually abandoned— i.e. that of distributing and defining spheres of action so that some separation of powers is maintained and jurisdictional disputes between different bodies will not arise.

One of President Soekarno's purposes in rejecting 'liberal democracy' has been to create a concentration of authority that is not hedged round with constitutional limitations.[1] What purpose then does the constitution fulfil, if it does not act as a curb on types of political behaviour which are explicitly or implicitly condemned in 'liberal' constitutions? It is hard to conceive of any form of political organisation which would necessarily be ruled out by the wording of the 1945 Constitution itself; almost anything could be made compatible with it. (In fact, a parliamentary system embodying a principle of cabinet responsibility to parliament was welded on to it between 1945–47, although in broad outline a presidential system is clearly implied.) But the function of this constitution, or its usefulness to Soekarno, consists primarily in the fact that its general character (as the framework of a highly centralised regime) may be invoked as a justification for resisting tendencies of a 'liberal' or federal nature. The process of legitimising authority has always been peculiarly important in the Indonesian political tradition and it appears unthinkable to have *no* constitution at all, nothing that can be pointed to as a sheet anchor, even though an outsider may think that the anchor does not necessarily confine the ship of state in a very fixed position.[2] Thus the constitution has a certain legitimising or prestige-creating function, even though it does not significantly canalise or control the interplay of the most powerful political forces. Whether or not it will gradually develop this latter function is in the lap of the gods. One could only begin to approach a question of this kind after comparing the functional development of constitutional structures in similar polities.

It is not my aim in this chapter to explore questions of this kind analytically, but to reveal some of the forces that contributed to the

---

[1] It is revealing that the doctrine of separation of powers has been condemned as a 'liberal' institution by President Soekarno. (See his Independence Day address, 17 August 1960.) His emphasis on 'all pulling together towards one goal' derives from a desire to replace the 'oppositionism' of liberal democracy with a government that is strong enough to get things done.

[2] Indonesians use the word *pegangan* ('something to hang on to' from *pegang* —to hold) in various ways; it denotes something akin to the German *grundlage* —a philosophical basis from which one reasons. The *Dasar Negara* (philosophical basis of the State: in this case the *Pantja Sila*) may be thought of as a *pegangan*, equally the later ideological glosses of the President's 'Political Manifesto'. A constitution functions as a *pegangan* in the legal sphere, giving the justification or focus of reference needed for actions or laws.

collapse of parliamentary democracy in Indonesia and which would have to be taken into consideration in any attempt to constrain Indonesian political behaviour within a set of constitutional rules. My account of these forces will be expressed in terms of institutions which are entirely familiar to the Western political scientist. I do not mean to imply that these are the only relevant factors; the failure of parliamentary democracy certainly needs to be described to some extent in terms of the significance attached to exotic Western institutions in the very different socio-cultural environment. Writers with a sociological bent like Pye and Geertz have greatly enriched our understanding of what politics means in such circumstances, especially in regard to the crucial relationship between leaders and led.[3] But there is a danger that the political scientists may be seduced too far into these tantalising new pastures before we have finished dealing with our own field of enquiry. The strains of the Western political and administrative structures which Asian countries have inherited from the colonial powers are to a large extent explicable simply in terms of the changing circumstances in which they are now being required to operate. My purpose here is to direct attention back to a number of fairly straightforward questions about what these familiar institutions are expected to do and what they are able to do in the circumstances.

The Failure of Parliamentary Democracy

The crudest type of explanation for the failure of parliamentary government in Indonesia puts it all down to lack of tradition, to inexperience or to the shortcomings of the administrative apparatus —all measured against some unspecified standard. To this it may be answered that democratic institutions *have* survived in circumstances of less than Athenian perfection—which are rarely attributed, in any case, to the countries from which they originated. Why not here?

---

[3] Lucian W. Pye *The Policy Implications of Social Change in Non-Western Societies*. (Massachusetts Institute of Technology, Mimeographed. 1958.) The core of this work was published under the title "The Non-Western Political Process" in the *Journal of Politics*, Aug. 1958. Of the various writings by Clifford Geertz, the most stimulating contribution on political matters is his chapter on "The Javanese Village" in *Local, Ethnic and National Loyalties in Village Indonesia: A Symposium*, edited by G. W. Skinner. (Yale University, Cultural Report Series, Mimeographed, 1959.)

Going a stage further, we meet a different argument that Western political institutions may not fit the very different social and cultural environments of Asia: or that they must be tailored out of recognition to suit age-old traditions which have constituted the matrix of political activity until very recently. But again, there is no general rule to help us: in some Asian countries this adjustment has been made, in others not. We do not get very far by making debating points of this kind.

I believe we can throw more light on the matter if we approach the question from a different angle. Do the processes of political behaviour and the problems confronting governments in Asia appear to be compatible with the exercise of representative institutions, as bequeathed by the colonial rulers? To answer this, our attention must be directed first to the social and economic upheavals that have revolutionised Asian politics since the ferment of 'modernisation' began. It is not just a matter, in Indonesia, of the political instability and ineffectiveness of governments in the 'fifties. We must be able to go further back and explain why neither the cabinets nor the political parties of that period were able to remedy the ills which contributed to the ultimate demise of parliamentary democracy there. To do so requires that some attempt be made to analyse the forces which bear on that bafflingly elusive term, political power.

Summaries of the factors contributing to Indonesia's political instability by two of the foremost authorities on the country provide a useful introduction to the question at issue. Professor Kahin has written that: "Although there is a reasonable measure of agreement concerning the socio-economic role of the new state, there is no such consensus as to the proper nature of its political organisation . . . [parliamentary democracy's] waning attractiveness to Indonesians stems to some extent from unresolved conflicting ideologies and from their belief that its operation tends to exacerbate rather than bridge such differences. But the ineffectiveness of Indonesia's parliamentary system has been much more a consequence of irresponsible conduct by political parties having too little rapport with and responsibility toward the population. It has also stemmed from the failure to provide Soekarno with a clearly defined constitutional role approximately equivalent to his stature as a national leader, while nevertheless allowing him to exercise substantial power without responsibility. One source of these troubles has been Indonesia's vague and ambiguous constitution—one which could confuse and frustrate the best-intentioned men in the world. Clearly, however, the dismal record of Indonesia's quasi-parliamentary system derives to a major extent from the conditioning of a colonial order which did so little to prepare Indonesians for self-government, much less for the practice of parliamentary democracy".[4]

One would not want to deny that the factors mentioned here, particularly the last one, are all relevant to the collapse of democracy. But this passage, taken as it stands and out of context, puts a somewhat misleading emphasis on purely political arrangements. It seems to imply that more suitable constitutional provisions might have been able to reconcile the political tensions, perhaps even make parties more responsible. Kahin later suggests that perhaps if Indonesia is to develop in a democratic direction, the traditional *Mufakat* procedure of attaining consensus on community decisions may have to be adapted to the nation's representative institutions. This is certainly to be hoped for, although one cannot foresee just how such a procedure could be formally grafted on to a regime which must now, by the nature of things, have a strongly authoritarian (not necessarily a totalitarian) element. Despite the outward appearance of consensus on socio-economic questions referred to by Kahin, one basic reason why a democratic regime is unlikely to give Indonesia economic progress and political tranquillity stems from the fundamental cleavage of economic and social interests, which underlies the ideological conflict. At some point, a strong authority must decide how these cleavages are to be settled. Up till now, established authority has not been strong enough to do so.

The difficulty of attaining 'political consensus', in fact, is listed by Dr. Feith as the first of the causes of Indonesia's political instability. "It is a country with a multiplicity of diverse and conflicting social interests and a wide diffusion of political power. Thus its leaders' strong will to unity must contend with centrifugal tendencies derived from both history and economic structure. Desiring determined government, they are restricted because of the existence of a great number of small power centres, each in a position to veto some types of government action. These facts lie behind the splintered and fractionalised system of political parties which has contributed so

---

[4] G. McT. Kahin, " Indonesia " in G. McT. Kahin (ed.), *Major Governments of Asia* (Cornell University Press. 1958.) 573–4.

much to political instability".[5] From this underlying weakness stem most of the difficulties in solving the numerous problems confronting Indonesia's governments. These have been comprehensively listed by Dr. Feith and may be briefly summarised in four classes.

The first class consists of structural problems Indonesia inherited from colonial times—population growth outstripping the rate of expansion of agricultural production; a lopsided orientation of the economy towards raw material exports; and the government's dangerous dependence on revenue from this fluctuating source. All these problems had been aggravated, moreover, by the physical and social damage done during the Japanese occupation and the armed revolution. Second, problems of detraditionalisation and social convulsion; the revolution uprooted all classes and held out the promise of a stake in the new society, but there were too few opportunities to satisfy all the children of the revolution with its fruits. Thus the discontented form a turbulent displaced element, emancipated, literate, but with no stability created by an interest in the *status quo*. Third, inadequate government resources to control the political process—lack of funds and skilled personnel, inadequate constitutional powers, too little patronage to buy off discontent, diminished authority for the administrative services *vis-a-vis* mass organisations at the local level. (It is doubtful, however, whether any problems would be solved just by giving governments more of these powers.) A fourth category of weaknesses, the administrative and technical shortcomings of the governmental machine, has critically aggravated a situation which would in any case have been appallingly difficult to handle. It is these which spring to mind when we ask why governments, parliaments or parties were not able to take firm action to remedy some of the country's less intractable problems. Yet it is at this point that we find ourselves faced again with the apparently intrinsic weakness of governments in Indonesia, which requires analysis in another dimension, as it were.

This weakness is not just a matter of the faulty machinery of government—the overstaffing of lower administrative echelons side by side with gradual wastage of senior officials, the paralysis of initiative created by bureaucracy and the simultaneous insecurity of tenure created by political appointments, red-tape, bungling, inertia

[5] H. Feith, "Indonesia" in G. McT. Kahin (ed.), *Government and Politics of Southeast Asia* (Cornell University Press. 1959.) 207–10 and 219–20.

and frequent lack of technical knowledge. These faults are not peculiar to Indonesia, although nowhere else in Southeast Asia had the colonial government done so little to prepare for independence in the way of higher education or top-level administrative responsibility. The Dutch had left only one organisation; the *pamong pradja* (the regional civil service under the Minister of the Interior) in which Indonesians had been accustomed to considerable responsibility, and even there only up to the middle grades. It is still one of the most impressive pillars of the Indonesian administration, working efficiently along well-worn tracks, while experimenting to combine the old authoritarian system of local administration with the requirements of democratic local government. In fact, it is typical of Indonesia's experience in many fields that established institutions which can keep on running along familiar lines have often been reasonably successful. But complex problems requiring innovation and adjustment of government policies to radically new conditions have been less effectively handled. If Indonesia had not been faced with the urgent necessity of reorientating her economy and coping with the social problems thrown up by urbanisation and a cultural revolution, her machinery of government might have proved adequate. But there was no easy resolution to the tensions building up and only a strong government would have been able to introduce policies which might, in the long run, have eased them.

The chain of connection is all too clear. The administrative machinery inherited from the Dutch could only have coped with the stresses of a deep-seated revolution if the revolution had thrown up a strong government. The diffusion of power militates against strong government, as Dr. Feith has shown. Any political system would, of course, have been subject to the same weaknesses; it remains to be seen whether an authoritarian regime, such as we see there at present, will succeed in overcoming them. But Parliamentary democracy was additionally burdened with the handicap of relying on the consent of the governed in a very immediate sense. Governments were expected to deliver the goods—quickly and painlessly—before dissatisfaction set in. But party coalitions strong enough to do this were only possible if diverse interests could have been reconciled. Where basic conflicts of interest could not be settled by mutual agreement, the governments of the 'fifties were not strong enough to simply *impose* solutions. On the other hand, in the deteriorating atmosphere of suspicion between parties, regions and individuals, negotiated settlements would have had to be expressed in formulas that were virtually mechanical and proof against the wiles of other politicians. Solutions of this kind would have been almost impossible to achieve on several crucial issues, most notably the problem of decentralising powers and funds for economic development to local authorities, which underlay the *crise de regime* of 1957–8.

The Problem of Decentralisation

The arguments in favour of far greater decentralisation in Indonesia are commonly accepted, even in Indonesia. Kahin has epitomised a widely held view of this matter in his conclusion that, despite the opprobrium attaching to the name 'federalism' because of its association with Dutch divide-and-rule tactics in 1957–9, "Indonesia is a country peculiarly suited to a highly decentralised political system . . . . What may emerge is a system of government not called 'federal' by Indonesians, but having the essential properties of federalism".[6] This is certainly the desideratum. It would not even matter greatly if the principle merely found disguised expression behind a mass of seemingly incompatible regulations and institutions. But I am doubtful if the central government ever will or can distribute powers to the provincial authorities in a way that conforms to a strict interpretation of the federal principle. Federalism has been defined in several ways. Wheare's criterion that central and regional governments must be co-ordinate and independent may be impracticable in the modern world. But let us merely accept the much broader criterion that each is 'sovereign within its sphere', or draw a very loose analogy with the distribution of powers in Canada or India, where the functions of each government are specified and the centre has reserve powers which it may exercise or brandish, but generally prefers not to. Neither the political tradition nor the mechanics of power in Indonesia point towards a clearly defined relationship of this kind.

The traditional system of local government under the Ministry of the Interior and the distribution of functions between the various levels of government belong to Dr. Legge's province rather than mine. I will refer to it only to show how the structure inherited

[6] Kahin, *op. cit.*, 575.

from the Dutch will tend to prevent effective decentralisation.
Functions are not distributed exclusively between central and regional governments in unambiguous fashion, but are devolved either
by a process of *medebewind* ('sharing-in-government'—i.e. sharing
the administrative responsibility for the policies of a higher authority) or by allowing the lower unit to regulate in fields not
pre-empted by the higher authority, which retains a power of supervision over the lower unit.[7] The system sounds unwieldy and it
certainly stems from a centralised, authoritarian tradition which may
not be capable of effective devolution without being substantially
refashioned. But at least it is working—and extensive devolution
would entail the drastic dismantling of a complex network of laws
and ordinances. Meanwhile, under present conditions political forces
appear to be pulling in the direction of retention rather than modification of the structure. (It is, incidentally, hard to imagine the
Supreme Court taking over the task of interpreting a quasi-federal
division of powers in the Indonesian political and legal environment, in place of central government supervision. The Court has
previously tended to avoid constitutional issues and the judiciary has
generally been distinctly subordinate to political authority in the
past.) A precise delimitation of central and local government powers
of a quasi-federal nature that does not leave the centre a strong
discretionary right to interfere simply appears impracticable with
such machinery.

In regard to local government finance, the difficulty of eliminating an element of purely arbitrary decision by Djakarta is even
greater. The taxing powers of local authorities are woefully inadequate and, as long as the bulk of the nation's revenue comes
from indirect taxes on foreign trade, provincial and lower-level
autonomous governments will have to rely on the subsidies and
grants they receive from Djakarta, which alone can operate the main
revenue-earning taxes. Unless the allocation of revenue available for
distribution between the various regions[8] can be reduced to a purely

[7] The system of local government is most fully outlined by J. D. Legge in his
Problems of Regional Autonomy in Contemporary Indonesia (Cornell University,
Modern Indonesia Project, 1957. Mimeographed.) 34–38. *See* also his contribution to the present symposium.
[8] I use the term 'region' as a translation of the Indonesian word commonly
used in this context *daerah*. The precise denotation of *daerah* is 'district'; hence
it is strictly applicable to any subordinate unit of government. The two levels of

mechanical formula, as also the total amount of foreign exchange to be made available for distribution, the ultimate decisions must remain in the hands of the central government. Attempts have been made to compile a formula for distribution of available revenue to the regions in proportion to a number of weighted factors—population, area, length of roads, state of educational advancement etc.[9] Parliament did not get round to approving this and it would have been a miracle if the various regions could have reached agreement on the weight to be given to all the elements in the formula. The whole question has in any case been of merely academic importance in view of the severe financial situation since 1956, as also has a government bill of 1957 allotting certain tax revenues into the pool for distribution. But even here the central government retained the right to determine according to circumstances how great a portion of the major taxes it would transfer to the regions. It is hard to see how the central government can avoid retaining an ultimate discretionary authority in this field while the present pattern of taxation persists.

The unlimited discretion of the central government is bound to be augmented by a further peculiarity of the Indonesian economic structure which profoundly affects the problem of decentralisation. This is its control over the exchange rate—not usually thought of as a function that is relevant to the federal problem, but one which here touches on one of its most controversial aspects, redistribution of income from the wealthier regions to poorer ones. Some redistributive effect of federal taxing and expenditure policies is generally accepted as justifiable, although it is not usually of very substantial proportion. But in Indonesia the case is different because of the prevalence of multiple exchange rates. A country with a single

autonomous local government, to which it is most frequently applied, are *provinces* (of which there were 17 in 1957) or *kabupatens* ('regencies' in Dutch times, of which there were about 80 in Java alone). But the word has acquired a broader connotation since the dichotomy between *daerah* and *pusat* ('centre'— hence Central Government) has to some extent been identified with the political grievances of the regions outside Java. They are most deeply felt in areas remote from Djakarta. Yet even the regions closest to Djakarta may be very much aware of the dichotomy and sympathetic to the non-Javanese regions on some (but not all) issues.

[9] An admirable summary of this complex but important problem is given by Douglas S. Paauw: "The Role of Local Finance in Indonesian Economic Development", *Ekonomi dan Keuangan*, February 1955.

'equilibrium' exchange rate, or something near it, does not find itself artificially taxing its exporters and subsidising its importers as a country like Indonesia has been doing.

Indonesia's exchange rate has to deal with a unique problem because of a structural unbalance in her economy, which has its roots in colonial history and the changing patterns of development. Java, with nearly 70 per cent of the nation's population, produced less than 15 per cent of its foreign exchange earnings during the mid-'fifties. Sumatra produces roughly 70 per cent of the foreign exchange, with only 16 per cent of the population, and enjoys strikingly higher per capita incomes.[10] Sumatra holds out bright prospects for development in the future. Java has already experienced substantial development, but the crops which made it possible—coffee until 1870, sugar from 1870 to 1930—have collapsed beyond hope of recovery to their old levels. Until 1910, the wealth of the Dutch East Indies very largely arose from the development of Java: even twenty years later, when the rubber and oil of the Outer Islands were more valuable than the sugar, Java's exports exceeded her imports. But since the Javanese sugar industry collapsed in the Depression, nothing has been found to replace it. Industrialisation constitutes the only feasible prospect, but the capital must come from elsewhere—either the other islands or abroad. Meanwhile, the 'population explosion', which started in Java 150 years ago, continues to push beyond the 60 million mark. The island can meet the bulk of its food requirements. But its imports must, in effect, be subsidised.

Without going into the complexities of Indonesia's system of multiple exchange rates, it is sufficient to explain that the par value of the *Rupiah* has been overvalued ever since the war, but that a bewildering set of taxes and 'inducements' on imports and exports has created a variety of effective rates of exchange for different types of transactions. In this way, with the addition of a rigorous foreign exchange control, an overall balance of payments on current

[10] My estimate of Sumatra's contribution to Indonesia's foreign exchange earnings is based on the only figure currently accessible to me—her share of total exports from January-October, 1957. (See *Ekspor menurut djenis barang*. October 1957, Table 2. Biro Pusat Statistik. Djakarta.) It is not likely to be far from the average figure for the mid-'fifties. The population breakdown for 1956 is taken from the *Statistical Pocketbook of Indonesia, 1957* (Biro Pusat Statistik. Djakarta.) 12.

account has been maintained. There has been considerable capital flight through the black-market, however; the 'free' (black) market rate for foreign currency against *Rupiahs* has rarely been less than 250–300 per cent of the official par rate. This is not a true indication of what a 'real' or equilibrium rate would be if it could be struck, but the mechanics of the exchange rate are not generally understood. It is of little profit to go into the question of what a 'real' rate for the *Rupiah* might be, for there can be no single rate which will automatically bring supply and demand for foreign exchange into equilibrium through its effects on the cost structure, without further use of controls. (If one were to posit a hypothetical situation in which the different regions were able to strike individual equilibrium rates of exchange for their extraregional transactions, in relation to their resources and cost structures—as if each were an independent state—the Javanese *Rupiah* would inevitably be weaker than a Sumatran one. But not nearly as weak as a crude export-import balance suggests, since inter-island trade and the account for services modify the pattern greatly.) Even the I.M.F. has admitted that a system of multiple exchange rates is justifiable in Indonesia's circumstances.[11] The fact remains, however, that the system has generally worked as a subsidy on all but luxury imports and a disguised tax on exports. The burden on exporters has been spotlighted by the constant and wide disparity between their purchasing power when they smuggle their produce at a black-market rate and that received in *Rupiahs* at the official rates for exports and imports. But so long as there are foreign exchange controls, there will be a black-market of some sort, hence inducements to smuggle. And no matter what rate of exchange is set, there will always be some redistributive effect in circumstances like these.

Indonesia's problem of regional redistribution of income differs from that of a country like Australia in one striking respect, which underlines another political obstacle to a strictly federal solution. In Australia, the redistribution flows from the wealthy, populous States which are politically powerful to the economically and politically weaker. It is, in effect, an act of grace, grounded in a sense of moral obligation to equalise living standards. The same obligation would

---

[11] The problem of exchange rates is discussed in Benjamin Higgins, *Indonesia's Economic Stabilisation and Development* (I.P.R. 1957) 27–35.

be admitted in Indonesia by the richer areas, but there the wealthier regions are politically weaker. They are apt to feel that they are being exploited by a government dominated by the representatives of the populous consuming provinces—notably Java. The chances of reconciling this conflict of interests by consent, especially if it is inflamed by ethnic and ideological suspicions, as it has been in recent years, are definitely slim. This is, to my mind, the most intractable obstacle to achieving a system of government resting *directly* on the consent of the governed in Indonesia.

The Crisis of 1957–8

At this stage, an account of the political background to the decentralisation problem may illuminate the issues I have been discussing more clearly than an abstract analysis of them. What Kahin calls the "superimposition of ideological differences upon regional and cultural differences" (one might also add 'political') brought about a state of tension in Indonesia, which, by 1957, could only have been remedied by effective measures of decentralisation and a simultaneous political settlement restoring regional confidence in the Djakarta government. Yet the former could not have been instituted (for the administrative reasons described above) until the latter had been achieved, and *vice versa*. This vicious circle of cause and effect was not broken by various attempts to negotiate a settlement throughout 1957. Finally, armed conflict broke out in February 1958, as a result of which the side which stood for constitutional government on an orthodox Western pattern was crushingly defeated.

The ideological cleavage dates back to 1953, when the first cabinet of Ali Sastroamidjojo was formed. It was the first cabinet to exclude the large Masjumi party (Muslim, with 'modernist' leanings), which from this time on can be regarded as the nucleus of the 'opposition' to the President and the parties willing to support him, P.N.I. (Nationalist) and P.K.I. (Communist). Up-till this time, party alignments had not really crystallised. There were conservative and progressive wings in most parties, and to some extent the relative strength of either wing affected a party's position in the political spectrum from right to left. But there were few clearly defined differences in party programmes: all major parties accepted

'Socialist' doctrines to some extent, yet none (not even the Communist Party) was very specific about what these meant. The Masjumi and, later, the religiously conservative breakaway party, Nahdatul Ulama, drew their support from their appeal to the more fervent Moslems, but both were very hazy about their attitude towards making Indonesia an 'Islamic State'. The P.S.I. (Socialist Party) was until 1952 the most influential left-wing group; it had been the most 'progressive' of the 3 main parties, in the sense of being both overtly Marxist, although anti-Communist, and the most 'Westernised'—in the non-political sense—although its parliamentary representation was not great. The P.N.I. had a very amorphous programme and rather conservative leadership, so that it seemed to have no clearly defined basis of support among the people, except nationalist symbols he created. Yet after 1952, the willingness of the P.N.I. to co-operate tactically with the communists (for the sake of preventing the Masjumi winning a victory comparable to the Indian Congress Party's, when the long-delayed general elections were held) had the effect of determining party alignments thenceforward.[12]

During the period of the Sastroamidjojo cabinet (1953–5), two new developments began to unfold which presaged the later crisis. Both were intensified by the results of the general election in September 1955. Party attitudes to communism became a bitter subject of dissension, by 1957 perhaps the most bitter, since the President's overt entry into the political arena made it into a key issue in the struggle for power. Moreover, there was a great increase in regional discontent with policies for which Djakarta was responsible. Inflation, economic stagnation, proliferation of bureaucratic controls and reports of corruption were now becoming endemic. A reduction of imports in 1954–5 forced up prices and magnified the advantages of illegal 'barter trading', or smuggling, on the black-market rate of exchange which now rose from about 200 to 400 per cent of the official rate.[13] Inevitably, the islands outside Java, which

[12] The political parties and their programmes are described most fully by H. Feith in *The Wilopo Cabinet* (Cornell Modern Indonesian Project 1958. Mimeographed). On the crucial switch in P.N.I. policy in 1952, see *ibid.*, 121–3.

[13] The 'free market' rate of the *Rupiah* is given in Table F, 12 of *Statistik Konjunktur* (Biro Pusat Statistik. Monthly.)

earned over 80 per cent of the country's foreign exchange, began to feel that they were being exploited by the system, as well as neglected by the government.

The election results destroyed any immediate hope of improvement for the regions. Outside Java, the Masjumi proved to be by far the largest party—in fact, the only party that could claim to have substantial backing in all parts of the country. But it did surprisingly badly in Java and thus emerged as merely the second of the four big parties. More seriously, the other three major parties were revealed as essentially Java-based, with little backing outside.[14] Not that this was a bond between them. The second Sastroamidjojo cabinet of 1956 excluded the P.K.I. and contained the Masjumi. But it was clear that, with four big parties roughly evenly balanced, the Masjumi was in a permanently inferior bargaining position. The P.N.I. was prepared to co-operate with the N.U. in forming the nucleus of a cabinet. The P.K.I. was prepared to support any coalition that would keep out its arch-enemies, the Masjumi and P.S.I. The best the Masjumi could do was to accept a subordinate role in a coalition government so as to prevent the P.K.I. having a whip hand.

The elections had been awaited with quite unrealistically high hopes that they would prove a panacea solution to Indonesia's political ills.[15] Soon after the new government assumed office, these hopes began to turn sour. More seriously, the non-Javanese regions began to revert more openly to barter trading, with the connivance of local Army commanders. It was as if they now realised their inability to exercise an influence in Djakarta through their parliamentary representatives and decided to use direct action to put pressure on the central government. There was more to it than that, of course, particularly in the chain of incidents during 1956 which foreshadowed a challenge to civil authority by discontented Army officers. These created an atmosphere of increasing tension in which regional discontent suddenly boiled over to precipitate the crisis of 1957–8.

[14] Results of the general elections are tabulated in H. Feith, *The Indonesian Elections of 1955*, (Cornell Modern Indonesia Project. 1957. Mimeographed.) ch. 5.

[15] The panacea quality of the election was illustrated, *inter alia*, by the extraordinary atmosphere of expectancy and tension on polling day: *ibid.* 48–9.

Between December 1956 and March 1957, dissident movements erupted in four provinces, all demanding, *inter alia*, a change of government and a better deal for the regions outside Java. These movements marked the first serious challenge to normal constitutional processes, but the crumbling of parliamentary democracy was taken a stage further when President Soekarno decided to step down from his position as a constitutional figurehead and intervene personally in the political struggle with his own 'conception' of a solution to Indonesia's troubles. His 'conception' explicitly attacked the underlying assumptions of a 'liberal' parliamentary regime, although he did not initially propose any actual modification of the constitution. (This was hardly necessary, since a Constituent Assembly had just started to discuss a permanent constitution to replace that of 1950, which was only provisional.) But the development of the political crisis strained the spirit of the existing Constitution, if not its letter, in two respects. Martial Law was proclaimed in March 1957, when the Sastroamidjojo cabinet finally collapsed, so that the government was armed with emergency powers against its critics; these have, in fact, been maintained ever since. Secondly, the President took the unprecedented step of declaring himself cabinet formateur and then setting up an 'extra-parliamentary cabinet of experts', responsible to himself and not subject to overthrow by Parliament. (Both these steps were attacked as unconstitutional by his critics.) However, the cabinet, led by Dr. Djuanda, continued to treat Parliament with considerable deference and it began to address itself immediately to the grievances which had given rise to the regional dissident movements. Its two most important measures were the virtual devaluation of the *Rupiah* in June 1957 (which was intended to benefit the exporting areas) and an attempt to give substance immediately to a basic law on Local Government, passed by the Parliament just before the political crisis developed.[16] Since this law had been a triumph for the party politicians representing local interests over the policies advocated in the Ministry of the Interior, one must give the Djuanda cabinet credit for at least intending to concede greater powers to the

[16] On the significance of the Basic Law on Local Government, see Legge, *op. cit.*, pp. 50–8. The Djuanda cabinet's attitude to the application of this law is described by Dr. Legge in " Experiment in Local Government 1950–59 ", *The Australian Outlook*, Dec. 1959.

regions. But the mechanics of putting this law into practice were inevitably slow and in the meantime a political settlement was becoming more and more difficult to achieve.

In mid-1957, the political struggle had become concentrated on a straight-out tug-of-war between the two openly dissident provinces, Central Sumatra and North Sulawesi, and the Central Government —which, in effect, meant the President, his Cabinet and the Army leadership. The former were refusing to remit their foreign exchange earnings and trying to encourage other provinces to put pressure on Djakarta likewise. The Central Government appeared both reluctant and unable to enforce its orders against them—hence the widespread impression, which later turned out to be so misleading, that the regions would be in the stronger position if it came to a showdown. That they were of this opinion became clear at the one serious attempt to negotiate a compromise settlement, the so-called 'Musjawarah Nasional' of September 1957. On crucial issues of Army discipline and barter trading, the regions remained adamant. They would not accept any political compromise (except in terms of a last-minute, patched-up reconciliation between Soekarno and Hatta, which was an empty symbol, although a serious tactical error for the latter) and the Cabinet again revealed its inability to produce a formula that would break the deadlock.

The conflict was brought to a head by the unforeseen consequences of the anti-Dutch campaign of November-December 1957. "Power rolled into the streets", Trotsky once said of February 1917. Something similar seemed to happen in the first ten days of December 1957, as the 'take-over' of Dutch enterprises developed. Direct action by mass organisations created the opportunity for a dramatic increase in communist influence. For a short time the government seemed powerless to control the situation. At this juncture, three leaders of the Masjumi fled from Djakarta to Sumatra, where they joined the dissident provincial leaders. In February they presented the government with an ultimatum: unless it reversed the trend to the left and repudiated President Soekarno's deviations from the constitution, they would proclaim a rival Revolutionary Government (P.R.R.I.). The government refused and a week later bombed Padang.

The rebellion was a complete fiasco. It did not gather political support snowball-fashion from waverers and friendly neutrals, as it needed. Militarily, the rebels proved entirely unprepared for the expeditions launched against them. They were not able to force the government to its knees by choking it of foreign exchange. Evidently they never expected that the Central Government would call their bluff. Their apparently strong bargaining position of 1957 could only last so long as the issue was not forced to a trial of strength.

The consequence was a complete deflation of any remaining opposition to Soekarno's 'Guided Democracy'. The parties associated with the rebels were not formally banned until September 1960, but they were left at a hopeless disadvantage. Political parties in general were emasculated by the realisation that nothing could now prevent the creation of parliamentary representatives of Soekarno's 'functional groups'. At most they could argue about the details of such a change, to preserve the maximum of advantage for themselves. But the patience of the Army had to be considered too. Its dramatic success against the rebels had given rise to notions that it would be just as easy to clear up Djakarta's verbose politics. General Nasution was too wary to emulate the other Asian coups of 1958, however, though there were fears that he might. His 'middle way' merely consisted of giving Army officers a voice in political decision-making and a supervisory role over the new government estates and enterprises. They already had extensive martial law powers in the provinces as Regional War Administrators. They now assumed something of a role as the premier representatives of the 'functional groups' by virtue of their unrivalled services to the Revolution. The constitutional framework within which this new balance of power could most conveniently be expressed was achieved (despite surprising last-minute opposition from the two Muslim parties—united at last) by the return to the revolutionary 1945 Constitution.

Centrifugal and Centripetal Forces

The reasons for thinking that Indonesia would fly apart have attracted far more attention than the forces which have held her together. In 1957, it seemed undeniable that, if the government would not concede substantial decentralisation, the country must eventually disintegrate into military satrapies. There were two main reasons for believing that the centrifugal forces must prevail in the end. The strongest was the crude economic fact that most of Indonesia's export income, and much of her government revenue also, was produced in the thinly-populated outer islands, whereas over-crowded Java imported far more than she exported.[17] Open conflict seemed certain to upset this unbalanced state of affairs. The subsidiary reason was that the political conflict already brewing was partly rooted in the great diversity of the economic interests and social conditions of the different regions. Over-centralisation had been inflexible and inefficient. It was easy to imagine that a quasi-federal system could only be an improvement. It was also easy to oversimplify the equation of centrifugal political and economic forces, while neglecting the centripetal factors.

The most basic of these are very simple. Regional authorities, amongst whom the local military commanders have long been prominent, may feel a strong sense of identity with the people of their province and aspire to promote their interests rather than those of the Djakarta government. But their legal authority derives from Djakarta (except where they have specifically repudiated it, as the Sulawesi rebels did in proclaiming that their authority derived from their region) and the ultima ratio sustaining it is the Army. The Army has turned out to be one of the most strongly unified institutions in the country. It is not possible here to look into the numerous and inter-twined bonds of interest, organisation and sentiment which have made it so. It is enough simply to recall that when the show-down occurred in February-March 1958, the Army leadership was able to command the obedience of 'neutral' and wavering units; the rebels failed to split the Army seriously, although the circumstances were more favourable than they are ever likely to be again.

Next to arms, the key to power is finance. Here the central government has been in a much stronger position than is generally realised. It controls both the allocation of foreign exchange, which the export-producing regions would like to retain to themselves, and the disbursement of the lion's share of the Rupiah revenues needed by the autonomous regional governments, at both provincial and

[17] The belief in 1957 that the centrifugal tendencies of the Indonesian economy would shatter the political control of the Central Government was implied very strongly in an article by D. W. Fryer: "Economic Aspects of Indonesian Disunity" in Pacific Affairs, September 1957, 195–208.

kabupaten level. The latter are not in any position to seize back unto themselves the disposal of their export income and so cripple the central government financially while making themselves independent, for a number of reasons. The regions do not share a common interest *vis-a-vis* the Central Government on this issue and are unlikely to apply united pressure against it. The poorer provinces know perfectly well that if each had to live of its own, only the 3 or 4 richest provinces would really benefit. The rest gain from the redistributive effect of Central Government policies, although they may still be critical of the way they now operate. The richest of all is East Sumatra, which includes the wealthy Medan estate area, yet for peculiar reasons of local politics, the authorities of this province have all along been among the most loyal to the Central Government. Moreover, even at the height of regional 'barter trading' in 1957–8, there was a serious limitation on the extent to which a dissident region like South Sumatra could in fact channel its foreign exchange earnings into its own coffers, instead of paying them into the Bank Indonesia where they came under the central foreign exchange control. This limitation was that the oil companies and foreign estates did not dare to defy the Central Government openly by refusing to pay their foreign exchange earnings into the Bank Indonesia: they might co-operate to some extent with a dissident regional commander to take mutual advantage of opportunities to smuggle, but they could not afford to do so openly. Ultimate control over the purse-strings did not rest in the hands of the regional authorities, as many people had inferred from statistical charts which showed 80 per cent of export income originating outside Java. Much of that income came from producers who could not afford to repudiate the authority of Djakarta. Anomalously, among the strong centripetal forces holding Indonesia together as an economic unit (second only to the criss-crossing network of credit ties leading back to the Bank Indonesia) should have been counted the foreign estates and mining enterprises, which produced much of the country's export earnings. It might have been a very different story if the bulk of foreign exchange were earned by small-holders or indigenous enterprises, whose propensity to barter trading and scope for resisting taxation by Djakarta would be much greater.

These are the obvious factors that have made it possible for the Central Government to maintain its authority against manifestations of rebelliousness, which were too feeble to shake it seriously. A more recondite factor, that will tend to maintain a strong political advantage for the Central Government under any circumstances, arises from the peculiar situation concerning the exchange rate, already mentioned. Since there can be no automatic solution or obvious compromise in this field, the Central Government must be left with authority to make decisions which are unavoidably political. There is no alternative short of disintegration—and the cohesion of the Army is protection against that.

The Pull of Control Mechanisms

Nonetheless, having suggested that these are the most binding centripetal ties (the list is not exclusive; I have omitted the powerful sentiment of nationalism, since I am concerned only with institutional factors), I must now carry my argument a stage further. It may well be that these ties, which I have described in terms of the 1957–8 situation, are weakening as circumstances change. It is possible that recent economic and administrative changes have undermined some of the forces favouring the Central Government. As long-term, secular changes in the economic and administrative structures occur, some shift in political power seems bound to follow, and it may strengthen the hands of regional authorities in negotiating with Djakarta.

Stating the matter in somewhat extreme terms, I want to stress the paradoxical consequences of the shift to increasing reliance on direct government interference in economic life. This contrasts sharply with the widespread use of indirect controls in the 'liberal' period before 1958, as may be seen from the examples quoted below. I do not claim to be suggesting anything more than the direction and nature of change: to indicate how far it has gone would require far more evidence about current trends. But there is a kind of historical necessity about the process, which makes it plausible. And the forces at work seem relevant to any discussion of centrifugal and centripetal tendencies, even though there may still be a good deal more to be said about them.

The first of my examples of contrast is in the field of taxation. Throughout the 'fifties (and, indeed, even up till the present), *direct* taxes have contributed relatively little to the budget.[18] The bulk of government revenue came from import or export taxes, very little from land, company or personal income taxes. (Foreign estates, mines or trading enterprises provided the bulk of these in any case, since it was relatively easy to levy taxes on them and their products.) In particular, the fraction levied directly from Indonesian incomes was far lower than before the war and it was rather inadequately collected. Most of the revenue came from sources which were easily controlled by the central government; more rigorous collection or increased yields from land and personal income taxes would have been less easy to supervise. The taxable capacity that existed in these fields could only have been tapped if the government had either decentralised this source of revenue to the regions to assess and collect, or had a very efficient and dedicated taxation service, which it did not. But if revenue from trade taxes shows a secular tendency to decline, as seems likely, the yield from direct taxes will bulk larger in the scale; local authorities may then be driven to all sorts of expedients to raise revenue directly themselves, whereas previously they were able to rely on disbursements from the centre and Djakarta took a suspicious attitude towards local initiative. The consequence is bound to be a further diffusion of power, since the regions will become proportionately less dependent on the centre. It is a strange paradox that the tax structure Indonesia has inherited from the theoretically *laissez-faire* colonial economy should appear in this light as an essentially centralising force, while greater reliance on direct taxation, which will become essential if export trade declines, will have the effect of forcing the central authorities to devolve the taxing function to officials who will at least be subject to local pressures, even if they remain servants of the centre.

In the second place, the government is becoming directly involved in processes of production to a much greater extent than it was in

[18] *Bank Indonesia Annual Report*, 1958–9, table 13, gives the following breakdown of central government revenues.

(Figures in thousand million *Rupiahs*. Provisional estimates.)

	1956	1957	1958
Total receipts	15·7	16·9	19·7
Direct taxes	3·1	3·5	4·3
Receipts from indirect taxes and foreign exchange levies	10·5	11·8	13·4

the *laissez-faire* climate of the 'fifties. Until the takeover of Dutch enterprises in December 1957, only a minute sector of the economy was publicly owned. The Five Year Plan adopted by the government in 1956 had undertaken a substantial programme of developmental expenditure designed to raise productivity, but little of the new public investment would have either pioneered new fields of export production or expanded existing productive capacity. Implicitly, it was assumed that private enterprise would maintain its 1952–56 rate of investment, but no attempt was made to channel or guide it in order to shape the economy to pre-determined needs, as there has been (to a small extent) in the Indian plans. New investment was left, in effect, to be directed by market forces. Since the takeover of Dutch estates and commercial enterprises, which accounted for a large fraction of the private investment needed to sustain the economy even at 1952–56 levels of output, the State has become responsible for this large and vital segment of production and distribution, in fields where any breakdown or attribution will be felt very quickly throughout the entire economy. The political and social consequences of this cannot yet be anticipated with any precision, although the growth of a new elite with many similar interests (officers, senior bureaucrats, managers and technicians) could prove immensely important. But the financial consequences are obvious.

The estate enterprises are now under the direct control of one government agency (National Estates Central—or P.P.N.) and the commercial and industrial enterprises under several others. If the new organisation works efficiently, maintains the old level of foreign exchange earnings without requiring *Rupiah* subsidies and lays the basis for an expansion of export capacity, the Central Government will be able to manage, even if it received no nett contribution to the annual budget. If, however, the manifold pressures on a bureaucratic organisation reduce efficiency and create a drain on the budget, it will gradually weaken the government. There was a certain advantage to the government in leaving the responsibility for producing much of the nation's export income in the hands of foreigners, in that the costs of inefficiency did not fall upon the State budget; foreign enterprise was politically dependent on whatever conditions the state allowed it, provided only that the cost structure was reasonable enough to hold out a prospect of making some profit. Today, the state enterprises are only likely to prove profitable if rigorous economic discipline is maintained and stability achieved, so that inexperienced estate managers are not burdened with additional problems. Otherwise, the central supervisory mechanism is likely to crumble. Yet there is a danger that local pressures on estate managers will prove irresistible—including the temptation to connive at smuggling with the local military authorities.

A third major difference between the present and pre-1957 scene in Indonesia was the degree of direct local interference in economic life by local military commanders exercising powers under martial law. Where previously the distribution of goods had been left almost entirely to pressures of supply and demand, direct control over the price and distribution of essentials has now become widespread. A consequence has been that the authorities have had to intervene in the organisation and supply of essential goods, have taken action to prevent hoarding, to prohibit strikes and to fix wages. As military commanders have become responsible for the economic health of their territory, they appear to have taken over some of the functions of central control mechanisms. In at least one case, a local commander simply overrules central policies in order to maintain the flow of business in his territory. It seems inevitable that more and more power will accumulate in the hands of regional military commanders, since the Army has been vested with wide supervisory authority over the organisations administering former Dutch enterprises in addition to their authority as War Administrators under martial law. In their role as guardians of the Revolution against the follies and betrayals of politicians, Army leaders take an almost proprietary view of their regions. But, for the most part, other members of Indonesia's newly-emerging managerial elite seem prepared to acquiesce and cooperate with them.

The three examples I have given suggest that as the economic structure changes, power is more likely to be further diffused, rather than concentrated. The government is making efforts of various kinds to tighten up the political structure—by insisting on adherence to a national ideology, by indoctrination and by 're-tooling' members of the public service who are suspected of disloyalty. But it remains to be seen whether political measures of this kind will suffice to counteract the centrifugal trends whose roots are stubbornly institutional or economic. Every time the central authorities find it necessary to replace one of the indirect control mechanisms utilised during the 'fifties with some form of direct control, requiring a personal decision instead of mechanical application of a general rule, a new vested interest is created, a potential source of influence and corruption—which spells waste.

An example of this may be seen in the control of import licences: rights to obtain foreign exchange for imports were rationed out during most of the 'fifties by price differentials, modified by the complex structure of widely-ranging taxes on imports. Essentially, the system worked indirectly, with marginal resort to quantitative controls. Since 1959, the right to import most essential commodities, almost 80 per cent of total imports, has been restricted to nine big government import houses. Whatever the formal mechanics of the system since then, there is little doubt that, in circumstances of financial stringency, this most·important of economic controls will now be exercised directly. But it is not necessarily easier or more efficient to administer import controls in this way. Decisions between conflicting policy objectives may prove harder to make than before, since the vested interests concerned are now part of the machinery of government, with greater political influence.

If the government servants work efficiently and honestly, the built-in centripetal tendencies of bureaucracy might counteract the forces I have mentioned. If they do not, a host of pressures will compound them. Further diffusion of power would result and Indonesia would be so much further away from the strong central authority she undoubtedly needs.

J. D. Legge

INDIGENOUS AND IMPORTED INFLUENCES IN INDONESIAN LOCAL GOVERNMENT

IT IS obvious that Indonesia's constitutional forms since independence are based on Western models and informed by Western concepts of the State, sovereignty, and responsibility, and that the outlook of those who have operated these institutions is also, to a great extent, Western in character. Certainly during the first few years of independence political processes were dominated by an intellectual elite whose education had been obtained in Dutch institutions in the Indies or in Holland, and whose view of the task of creating a new independent State was moulded by the usual categories of Western political thought. It is equally obvious that Western models in the Indonesian environment acquire a different flavour, are worked in a different way and allow the operation of traditional procedures of decision-making. The kind of government resulting from this fusion of traditions might even be said to imply concepts of the state quite different from those which form the stock in trade of Western political theory.

These two propositions, stated in general terms, are commonplace. Difficulties arise when an attempt is made to stress one side or the other. The contrast between Western and 'indigenous' traits is, of course, itself a crude one, and the complexities of the effects of Indian, Chinese, Islamic and Dutch contacts over a long period of time render it impossible to sort them out precisely. Are the results of Hindu influence on Javanese society to be classified as 'indigenous' or not? Those who seek distinctively Indonesian procedures for the guidance of the country in the modern world do tend to emphasise features of Javanese social order which may well be derived from external contact. The same sort of point might be made concerning Indonesia's absorption of Islam, and it is worth noting van Nieuwenhuijze's general theme that Islam contains many elements which "go very well together with a closed community way of life

215

and thought".[1] It is not easy to separate them from the environment which absorbed them. (Would it be far-fetched, for example, to argue that the idea of *mufakat*—consensus—is related by analogy to the Islamic doctrine of ' the infallibility of the consensus'[2] as well as to so-called indigenous processes?)

But though it may be impossible to distinguish precisely the sources of current characteristics, the desire to make at least a broad, and no doubt crude, distinction between what is new and what is traditional, and to emphasise the latter, is common in Indonesia today. As might be expected the resulting interpretations of political life are often contrived and artificial, for the game of detecting influences can usually be played both ways. Because of the complexities of the case it is usually possible to point to two sorts of comparison—that which likens political institutions and procedures to Western, particularly Dutch, models and that which points to an earlier source. When President Soekarno, in 1957, claimed that Western liberal democracy had failed and that his proposed plan for a four-legged government and a national council based on functional representation would constitute a distinctively Indonesian solution it was possible to argue, without being too serious about it, that his blueprint had no traditional elements at all but was really based on the Western model with which he was most intimately familiar—the government of the Indies under Dutch rule. He cast himself for the role of Governor-General. His proposed Cabinet was the equivalent of the conference of department heads. The National Council was a substitute for the Council of the Indies. And Parliament, relegated in his plan to a comparatively impotent role, was the Volksraad. At the same time it is true that the principles of *musjawarah* and *mufakat*, deliberation and consensus, which Soekarno was attempting to clothe in new constitutional forms, were evocative principles in Indonesian political thinking.

It is not the purpose of this paper to advance any general view as to the relative importance of traditional and imported influences. It is proposed instead to notice the presence of both elements in the constitution and working of local government, and to draw attention to certain features of the Indonesian discussion of them. What is

[1] C.A.O. van Nieuwenhuijze, *Aspects of Islam in Post Colonial Indonesia* (The Hague, 1951), 17.
[2] Snouck Hurgronje, " Islam ", *Selected Works* (Leiden, 1957), 55.

important here is not so much the facts of the case—the actual degree of indigenous as against Western influence—as the growing and self-conscious determination to emphasise the traditional content of political forms, or to fashion new institutions which are held to be based on traditional procedures. This may be seen in the terms in which the debate on alternative constitutions of local government was conducted, just as clearly as it is illustrated in the discussions of guided democracy and the 'Indonesian identity' at the central level.

The Administrative Service and Local Government

The central problem in the whole debate on local government planning since 1950 has concerned the future role of the territorial administrative service, inherited from the Dutch, in a situation where it was intended to allow a considerable decentralisation of power to local councils. The territorial service—the *pamong pradja* —had survived into the period of independence and it remained the primary instrument of government—the means by which the centre, through its representatives in the sub-divisions of the country, provinces, residencies, regencies, districts and sub-districts, penetrated to the rural population. The Central Government was naturally reluctant to give up such an important means of centralised control. At the same time the very diversity of Indonesia has made it necessary to meet local feeling by conceding a reasonable measure of self-government to the regions. The result was a compromise which bore many close resemblances to the decentralisation experiments carried out by the Dutch during the 'twenties and 'thirties (and indeed to the local government system of Holland itself, since the decentralisation plans had naturally taken the Dutch system as the model for the Indies). As a result a foreign observer of Indonesian local government is likely, at first glance, to be struck by the direct carry-over from the colonial period of both the Central administrative system and the institutions of local autonomy.

Very briefly the independent republic, when it came to handle the problem of regional feeling, envisaged the reconstitution of provinces, regencies, and municipalities as areas of local government each with a representative and executive council. But the most controversial question concerned the character of, and the method of appointment to, the office of chairman of the executive or 'regional head'. Without going into the details of the several plans hotly debated during the 'fifties, the principal issue was whether the position should be filled, as formerly in the decentralisation experiments of the Dutch, by a member of the Central Government's administrative service, or whether it was to be purely political in character, filled by a person elected, directly or indirectly, by the region itself. The former solution was favoured by officials of the Ministry of Home Affairs since it enabled the centre to maintain a close supervision by its own officers over the work of local governments. The political parties which were responsible in parliament for the drafting of a local government law, however, resisted the idea of paternal control implicit in this arrangement. As a corollary to the debate on this question was the further problem : if local governments were to be supreme in their own sphere, and if the office of regional head was to be an elective one, was it open to the Centre to maintain its administrative hierarchy for its own separate purposes of 'general government'? The local government law which was eventually passed at the end of 1956 represented a victory on both counts for the political parties' point of view. The position of regional head was to be a purely elective office and, though the law was silent on the future role of the administrative service, subsequent legislation provided for the transfer to local governments of its functions and for the gradual disbandment of the service itself. Subsequently, however, a Presidential Edict reversed this trend and returned to the principle of appointment of regional heads. It thus made possible the continued close connection between local government and Central administration.

During the mid 'fifties the debate on these alternative solutions was conducted in a language familiar to the Western observer. The official view based itself on the special difficulties of the Indonesian environment: the ignorance and low rate of literacy of the rural population, and the strength of custom at the village level, made necessary a hierarchical administrative machinery; Indonesian society was not yet ready for a full exercise of democratic rights through an advanced form of council machinery at the local level; councils in regencies and provinces could meet the needs of the elite, but they were not really representative of the agriculturist. In a transition period, therefore, so ran the argument, paternal supervision

by the Central Government, exercised through the former colonial
service was a straightforward and necessary expedient. To the
political parties, however, the official plan represented a direct
return to the forms of colonial rule and as such was held to be
inconsistent with modern democracy. Even so the official view was
clearly a "Western" view and thus far the controversy over the
relation of the administrative system to local governments was
presented in terms of one Western model against another.

But as the 'fifties wore on, and as the President began to elaborate
his concept of guided democracy based on distinctively Indonesian
procedures, the local government argument began to clothe itself in
different forms. To the paternalistic argument of the official—the
argument that in Indonesia the operation of democratic councils
needed careful supervision by officials of a Central Government—
was added the further theme that the administrative service was
itself part of the Indonesian tradition. The service may have been
the main instrument of Dutch authority but the colonial forms were
based on earlier forms, and drew their strength from that fact.

There was some substance in this view. It would certainly be a
mistake to regard the administrative service as merely a survival
from the colonial regime. The lower ranks of the service were of
more ancient origin for they preserved the administrative forms of
the earlier Javanese kingdoms. The Dutch administration in its
various stages had merely imposed a higher apparatus at the top, in
the shape of governors and residents, but continued to use existing
forms below. Regents, *wedanas* and *tjamats* were thus absorbed into
the service of a centralised colonial government. And until the end
of the colonial period these lower ranks of the service continued to
be filled by persons of aristocratic origin (*prijaji*). These people had,
in effect, formed Indonesia's mandarinate. "Literati, gentry, pat-
ricians, brahmins, aristocrats—whatever you wish to call them—the
prijaji are the Javanese version of a social type, seemingly universal
in non-industrial civilisations: the men who are able to write."[3]
There was a mystical basis underlying the authority of this aristocracy. The ordered society of which it formed the higher levels was
seen as the earthly counterpart of a supernatural order. High rank
on earth, nearness to the king, was like nearness to god on the

[3] Clifford Geertz, "Religious Belief and Economic Behaviour in a Central
Javanese Town: Some Preliminary Considerations."

supernatural plane, and carried with it the same sort of mystical aura. It was partly for this reason that officials embodying the power of the Central Government were able to evoke a very special sort of respect, and this continued to be so even after the administrative service had ceased to be an aristocratic preserve. A modern member of the service, even if a commoner, would still carry more than a common authority.

The continued existence of such an administrative class was as vital for the Republic as it had been for the colonial administration of the Dutch. Indeed the problems of the two were not entirely dissimilar. Each had to explain its purposes and carry its power to a largely illiterate agrarian population whose immediate local loyalty was greater than that to a remote Central Government. And the most satisfactory channel to the village was through a territorial service whose lower levels fell within the village's traditional scheme of things. In the crisis of the 'fifties the service represented one unifying factor, and it became important for the Central Government to stress its distinctively Indonesian origins rather than its character as an arm of Dutch rule.

The fitting of the *pamong pradja* into this longer perspective was part of the refurbishing of the country's institutions which followed the return to the Constitution of 1945. On the face of it the 1945 Constitution itself might be described in 'Western' terms as providing for a strong presidential executive. Soekarno's own justification, however, was different: that the Constitution would enable formal expression to be given to traditional procedures. In particular he was concerned to stress the principles of deliberation and consensus—*musjawarah* and *mufakat*—operating under presidential guidance. The two concepts are not easy to translate precisely but they embody the notion of long discussion until an agreement emerges reconciling the various shades of opinion which have been expressed. It was Soekarno's claim that this was the procedure of deliberation and decision in the village assembly and his plan was to adapt the procedure by securing the representation of the various 'interests' of the country in appropriate policy-making machinery at all levels. In this way all important points of view to be found within the Republic would be expressed, and careful deliberation could thus eventually lead to conclusions about policy which would command the support of all groups. This was the role for which his

National Council of 1957 had been cast, and it was to be extended under the 1945 Constitution in the functional composition of the People's Deliberative Assembly, the Supreme Advisory Council, and even Parliament itself. The concept applied at the central level was applied with the same sort of rationale at the local level. At the local level the aim was to set aside the idea of an elected regional head and to place existing deliberative and executive bodies once more under the guidance of the administrative service. Hence the desire to insist that the service did have its roots in the Indonesian tradition. It is significant that the Presidential Edict of 1959 which extended this plan of 'guided democracy' to regional government, and which thus saved the *pamong pradja* from its threatened dissolution was based on such doctrinal considerations rather than on the considerations of straightforward expediency which had been advanced during the earlier stages of the debate.

Traditional Processes of Decision-making in Local Councils

The change in the arguments by which the administrative service was defended had its counterpart in the discussion of the local council system. Here too an early acceptance of councils because they were democratic bodies on a Western pattern was replaced by the later search for a distinctively Indonesian way of doing things. Emphasis was first placed on the way in which traditional procedures were expressing themselves within the framework of existing councils, and then on the need for constitutional changes to allow such procedures to operate in a more thorough-going fashion.

The local councils, which were first established in Indonesia under the provisional local government legislation, had followed the pattern of the Dutch decentralisation experiments in providing for an executive which included the main groups in the representative council. The permanent local government law of 1957 adopted the same principle. Instead of making the executive council the preserve of the majority party, or of a majority coalition, in the representative council, it was to be elected by proportional representation from the representative council, just as the representative council was itself elected by proportional representation by the electorate.

There were serious objections to this arrangement, the most important of which was the difficulty of securing strong government. A multi-party system was, in any case, likely to make it difficult for any one party to secure a majority of seats in the representative assembly. The fact that, even when one party did emerge with an absolute majority, it could not control the executive, further accentuated the tendency towards weak executives. It could be argued, of course, that at the local level government was essentially a business-like matter—the provision of services such as hospitals, water-supply or roads for the local population. For this purpose ordinary political party competition was less relevant and a multiparty executive might well be able to co-operate in a business-like way. However though such an argument might well apply to the lower levels of local government, the regency or the municipality, the government of provinces was a much more elaborate matter. Provinces resembled the constituent states of a federation rather than local governments proper, and at this level party divisions might be expected to follow more closely the national model.

In any case, whatever the defects of the system, its drafters were following one Western model rather than another. The reason for the adoption of the principle of proportional representation in the selection of executive councils was probably mere inertia. The republic was merely adopting a known system whose main outlines had been established thirty years before.

However as the desire to return to tradition began to assert itself there was a tendency to see, in the existing constitution of executive and legislative councils, the expression of a distinctively Indonesian idea. Multi-party representation on both councils was held to be well suited for the kind of deliberations which Soekarno desired at the central level.

It is certainly true that within the framework of democratically elected councils certain extra-constitutional conventions had been developed, and these might be held to express the principle of consensus. One may instance the desire of council representatives to avoid pushing any issue to a straightout vote. The tendency has been rather for prolonged discussion in an attempt to iron out differences before an actual decision is made. It is argued sometimes that the taking of a vote commits people to a position from which it is not easy for them thereafter to retreat. To leave the question open as long as possible enables an adjustment of differences without any loss of prestige. In any case it is difficult for the foreign observer to obtain any clear picture of regular 'divisions' of a representative assembly. He is likely to be informed that this is not the way that democratically elected councils operate in Indonesia. And he will notice the large number of decisions which are reached by 'acclamation' rather than by a vote in which a majority will carry the day over a minority. Something of the same determination to reconcile potentially opposing groups may be seen in the way important council offices are allocated. An examination of the way in which these offices are filled appears to reveal a tacit understanding between major parties such that, without any open conflict or friction, the various positions, regional head, chairman of the representative council, vice-chairman of the executive council and so on, are fairly distributed as between parties.

One may wonder, however, how distinctively Indonesian all of this is. One may even wonder whether the principle of consensus does operate at the village level quite in the way envisaged by Soekarno. Leaving that aside it must be recognised that other societies too have their methods of accommodation between competing groups without disturbing the formal constitutional framework. Just as individual parties may caucus outside the council rooms so quiet behind-the-scenes negotiations may enable the major differences between parties to be ironed out in advance of a debate. The important difference in the Indonesian situation is that these factors are formally elevated to the distinction of 'a concept', and this concept of consensus as a traditional political procedure has been allowed to condition the actual workings of local councils just as it has at the level of the national parliament itself. What may originally have proved not more than a by-product of a multi-party system and the use of proportional representation became an important element in the search for a traditionally Indonesian political system.

With the return to the Constitution of 1945, and the consequent attempt to extend the principles of guided democracy even to the field of local government, the President was less satisfied with the way in which existing councils, composed merely of party representatives, were able to express the idea of consensus. He therefore sought a modification of the system to bring it into line with changes he was making in the national parliament. The introduction of the principle of functional representation at the local level was introduced in 1960, and, as with the return to the principle of appointment of regional heads, the change was motivated by doctrine rather than by any consideration of convenience.

The Search for a Concept

The preceding discussion has been concerned only obliquely with the interaction of what Professor Morris-Jones has called the Western and the traditional idiom.[4] In his analysis the traditional idiom is something which an observer could notice—an element in the political scene which is there as a matter of fact. In Indonesia the question has been rather a matter of doctrine. That is to say that though the traditional idiom may be observed in Indonesia as in India, it has happened that discussion of its presence has been based less on detached political analysis of what happens, than on a determination to describe what happens as expressing the traditional idiom. In general, the institutions and practices of the new republic were at first taken as belonging essentially to a Western idiom, and discussed in those terms. Later it became the fashion to insist that these same institutions and practices were not Western, or only formally Western, and that the spirit was Indonesian. Finally it was argued that, with the introduction of certain changes in machinery, the use of the principle of functional representation in parliament and in local councils for example, the country's political system could be brought more closely into line with the 'Indonesian identity'.

There has been a self-consciousness in this discussion which is, in itself, on the way to becoming a marked feature of Indonesian political thinking. Connected with this characteristic is the significant fact that so many of the proposals which have been advanced for meeting the contemporary crisis are proposals concerning machinery—the establishment of deliberative bodies, the requirement that such bodies shall work in a particular way and be based on a particular kind of representation. These rather than proposals concerning the content of national policy have been the results of the President's intervention in politics.

A preoccupation with forms is perhaps natural during a period of experiment and construction, and this might have been expected particularly in the field of local government. It is suggested however

4 See above, 75–9.

that the reason goes deeper: that it is connected with what appears to be a distinctive Indonesian (or is it rather a Javanese?) characteristic—the desire to get things into the right conceptual terms. There is a tendency to an almost medieval exegetical approach to the study of political institutions, a determination to argue that forms do—or do not—express a general principle. In general it is never enough to devise workable machinery in response to a variety of pressures. The machinery must also be an expression of an idea, and there is the feeling that if the concept is right the machinery will be effective. Involved in the idea of the concept being right is the same Javanese idea of an approximation to a cosmic order on which temporal institutions should be modelled.

The intense concern with questions of form may be seen in discussions at many levels. An extreme example was provided by the attempt of the State Planning Council to organise its first report into seventeen chapters, eight parts, and one thousand nine hundred and forty-five paragraphs to symbolise the date of the country's proclamation of independence, August 17, 1945! A less extreme case, and one which illustrates the point more clearly, arose in the course of the local government controversy. It concerned the concept of 'dualism' and the desire to avoid a dualistic system of local government.

The Dutch system whereby a central official performed the combined duties of chairman of the executive and also supervisor of local government was said to be a dualistic system. The proposal contained in the provisional local government law for a regional head appointed from a list of candidates nominated by the regional representative council aimed at removing the dualism. The official response to the idea of election of the regional head—that if this system was to be adopted then there must be a clear division between the responsibilities of the Central Government and those of the regional government and that the *pamong pradja* must be retained to handle the former—was also said to involve a dualistic system. It would require the existence of two governments in a region—that of the centre and that of the region itself—and this was held to be undesirable. Such an objection, on the face of it, would seem to be making rather heavy weather of a comparatively simple point. Any society has a complex interaction between separate authorities, central and local, public and private. In this case, perhaps, there may have been more substance in the objection since the authority of the centre was represented in the person of a single individual at each level. In any case, the 1957 local government law appeared to dispose of the question by providing for election of the regional head and implying the dismantling of the centre's own special service. Hereafter, though central ministries might still have their local branches there would be no separate functionary to co-ordinate their work or to be responsible for 'general government'. In that respect the local government itself would represent the Centre.

When the President, in September 1959, suspended those provisions of the local government law relating to the election of the regional head and restored the principle of direct appointment to the office the question of dualism was again discussed. At first glance the effect of the Edict was apparently to restore a dualistic system. The Edict referred specifically to the two fields of responsibility—on the one hand there was the field of general government, which was the responsibility of the *pamong pradja*, and on the other there was the field of autonomy which was the responsibility of the local authorities. The Edict planned to place leadership of both these fields in the one pair of hands—those of the regional head. As an agent of the Centre he was to be responsible for the co-ordination of Central and local tasks. He was also to be the link in the *pamong pradja* chain— the officer to whom lower ranks were responsible and who was in turn responsible to the higher ranks in matters falling outside the sphere of autonomy. This arrangement would appear, in principle, to be a reversion to the practice of the colonial period and to that followed under the first, provisional, local government law. But the Presidential Edict did not confine itself to a change in the position of regional head. It went further and made an important change in the character of the Executive Council. Formerly the regional head (whether appointed or, under the later local government law, elected) had been simply the chairman of the Executive which was responsible to the representative council. Now the regional head was to be personally responsible for the execution of government in the region, and the executive council was to be responsible to him and not to the representative council. This arrangement represented the regional counterpart to the idea of a presidential cabinet at the Centre, no longer responsible to Parliament. The concentration of executive power, both regional and central, in the hands of the regional head involved, in effect, a fusion of the two sides, hitherto carefully distinguished. Though the Edict referred to the theoretical distinction it effectively obliterated any practical distinction between the two capacities of the regional head and thus, in the eyes of its defenders, removed the dualistic character of local government.

Even so the difference between the new arrangement and that formerly prevailing is not so great that it should have involved such abstract discussion. Many reasons of convenience might be advanced for and against the change, and it is hardly necessary that it should be defended at length on the ground that it removed a dualistic element which had formerly been present. The fact, however, is that it is so defended—in philosophical rather than in practical terms.

It is in the light of this more than platonic formalism that one must view the self-conscious preoccupation with tradition to which attention has been drawn. The search for appropriate institutions of government has gone hand in hand with the emphasis on the essentially Indonesian character of those institutions. Traditional forms, it would seem, are likely most fully to express cosmic principles. In particular the idea of consensus as the proper way of proceeding to decisions has an obvious consistency with the idea that there is one right answer to be found, so that the harmony of an agreed decision matches the harmony of the universe.

It is significant that this Javanese Platonism, as it might be called, is a recent growth. The course which political discussion has taken in recent years stands in sharp contrast to the character of the pre-war nationalist movement and to the frankly Western attitudes of the intellectual leadership of the first years of independence. The reason for the change may be related to the decline in the power and influence of the intellectual elite, to the challenges posed to the whole idea of Indonesian unity and to the critical position of the country's economy. Formalism may be merely a retreat from reality in a situation where there has been a shift in the internal balance of power and where there is a lack of sureness about policies for a time of crisis. The principle of consensus has grown in importance as its substance has receded.

MR. MACKIE: The point of my paper which I have hoped would come up for general discussion is the relation between the constitutional structure and the substance of political activity. A conference of this kind is bound to touch on the question of whether we can talk of any relationship between constitutions and political forces, especially the question of how different the processes of government are likely to become when constitutions either break down or cease to operate. It occurred to me yesterday that in some ways Indonesia's constitutional position might be only a few steps removed from the sort of forbidding situation that the people talking about India brought up: "When Nehru goes?" So far it has been possible to discuss Indian politics in terms of Western institutions. But people are apparently also asking what will happen if the floodbanks of a constitution break down.

However, I doubt the applicability to the Indonesian situation of some of the concepts used by Morris-Jones and Wolfsohn. I do not think that the collapse of the 1950 Constitution resulted primarily from the incompatibility of a Western idiom with a 'traditional' society. The trouble, as I see it, can be expressed fairly adequately in terms of Western institutions. Indonesian democratic institutions were simply unable to reconcile differences of interest amongst the various parties and groups involved in politics. They failed to satisfy Soekarno, who believed that they promoted oppositionism and thought he could use 'functional groups' to keep the electorate in order, as well as to express its aspirations. They also failed to satisfy the 'opposition', who indirectly backed the disobedience and revolt of 1956–58. (The 1955 election had shown up the Masjumi Party as regionally based, unable to win control in Java; so, although they took a stand on legality in respect of constitutional procedures, they were halfhearted about legality when revolt was brewing.) The proximate cause of the final collapse of the 1950 Constitution, however, was the proposal by Soekarno in 1959 to incorporate representatives of the functional groups in Parliament, to which the parties at first took only slight objection, but later rejected in the Constituent Assembly.

The argument that some different sort of constitution would have worked better leaves me unsatisfied. It is sometimes said that if it had been more 'federal' (or that if the party leaders had paid more attention to their policies and less to themselves) the problems would have been manageable. To me it seems that a constitutional division of powers between centre and regions is at present organically impossible in Indonesia. This is partly because of the peculiar economic conditions impinging on Indonesian politics, which I have explored in my paper.

At the same time there is no reason to suppose that because power is unusually dispersed, Indonesia will disintegrate; the economic stagnation of the country has perhaps given a false impression of its weakness. I agree with Legge's remarks about the toughness of Indonesian institutions. Moreover Indonesia's political structure is determined by its existing machinery of government, rather than by its formal constitution. Politics is worked out within a framework which imposes limitations on the participants; but they are not constitutional limitations, for the most part.

The basic argument behind my paper is that it is very hard to imagine how the peculiar forces operating in Indonesia could be made compatible with each other. What I feel is most interesting in this respect is the effect of administrative mechanisms, particularly forms of taxation, both in explaining the breakdown of political institutions and, I think, in throwing light on the questions which arise as soon as we arrive at the next step of the investigation. What patterns of political authority may we expect to see emerging? It seems to me that if we wish to look beyond the trends I depicted, we must simply wait to see what forms emerge under a constitution so broad that it virtually doesn't impose any limits. This question leads to the sort of subject I had originally hoped this conference might explore. How does the machinery of government crystallise in a society where a constitution is either very broad or non-existent?

DR. LEGGE : Sawer has spoken of Indonesia as a country without a constitution in a 'revolutionary' situation. But that can be very misleading. It certainly must not be taken to mean that there is no administrative system, and in my paper I have dealt with the local government system at provincial, residency and regional levels.

The battle between political parties and the administration produced the Local Government Act of 1956 which tried to abolish the old system of administration. The officials therefore lost the first round but Soekarno reversed the decision. Party politicians felt that the 'administration' was a relic of Dutch colonial rule; officers of the administration saw it as a specifically Indonesian solution—a thing quite in keeping with Javanese traditions. Though the forms may be Western in character, they are operated in a distinctively Indonesian way. The survival of Indonesian unity has depended a good deal on the fact that the administrative system she has maintained through this discussion of her system of government has both its traditional and imported aspects. The presence of the administrative core is, if anything is, Indonesia's Constitution.

DR. JOHNS: To my mind, Mackie and Legge have discussed the various mechanisms involved in the efficient functioning of Indonesian political institutions, and the reasons for their breakdown, but without analysing the nature of the problems that any system of government has to resolve before it can be accepted as a national, supra-regional authority. Put somewhat differently, we can say that the problem is for a constitution to gain legitimacy, and thus command loyalty. Every major area of Indonesia has its traditional pattern of local government and social organisation, usually referred to as *adat*. Ultimately, the sanctions of *adat* are magical, and if the magical pattern is broken, the group as a whole will suffer. In addition to these various *adat* systems, there are various systems of royalty, and in certain areas of Java, authority largely rests on the divine and cosmic function of the ruler. Although related, these systems of *adat* are by no means naturally sympathetic to each other. In some respects, they are incompatible.

Further, the dominantly Muslim tradition of the older generation in Sumatra distrusts the still too obviously living Hindu-Javanism of Central and East Java. Thus, the older generation, at least of the Minangkabau, tends to look on the Javanese as infidels. An additional problem lies in the difference between the type of loyalty given to the apparatus of government in a modern State, and that which ensures the stability of a traditional society. Allegiance to a modern state and acceptance of its authority rests largely on a rational basis; allegiance to a traditional way of life depends largely on its charismatic authority. Any Indonesian National Constitution then, has to be sufficiently broad in its formulation to accommodate the various groupings and tensions within Indonesian society, and likewise to invest itself with a suitable type of charisma, since the idea of a rational basis for submission to authority is meaningless to the mass of the Indonesian population.

It is against this background that Soekarno's constitutional experiments have to be understood. He is attempting to create a myth, a logical-meaningful pattern of integration in constitutional form, which can command the allegiance of the masses. In the last analysis, however, the success of any constitution will depend on the factor that has sanctified the traditional systems: time. Only the passing of the years will ensure the stability of an Indonesian constitution, and therefore the watchword for any Indonesian constitution that is to be functional in Indonesian society, must, in the first place, be: Endure!

PROF. SAWER: In defence of my position against Mr. Legge, I must point out that in classifying Indonesia as a country in a pre-constitutional position or one of continuing revolution, I was not implying any moral judgment nor any statement at all about the stability and values of Indonesian *society*. There have often been countries where in spite of persistent revolutions at the constitutional level, the basic life of the people goes on almost undisturbed; many South American countries supply examples of this. Indeed, there can actually be steady social progress at the grass-roots while the official governmental apparatus is in a state of constant upheaval. But such a system cannot be called a constitutional one; constitutionalism comes only when governmental power is defined in terms of rules that are reasonably well observed over a considerable time. Moreover, in the contemporary world there is obviously much greater danger in a perpetual revolutionary situation than there used to be, and much less chance of satisfactory social progress, because government and social development are today so much more consciously controlled and involve co-operation with constitutional states and participation in a world system beginning to look 'constitutional'.

From a historical point of view, my insistence on the observance of rules as a hall-mark of constitutionalism certainly needs qualifying. The Romans in spite of their elaborate legal system, tended in the Imperial period to think of government in terms of the personal power and authority of the Emperor, and in modern times revolutionary democracies have sometimes tended to endow elected assemblies with the same kind of power and 'charisma' as that of the Roman Emperor. Indeed, Austinian theories of sovereignty involve that sort of approach to the fundamentals of governmental power. The notion of government as being more a set of rules than a definition of power really grew up mainly in the U.S.A., but it is now widespread and even in England, the home of Austinian theories, there is a growing tendency to regard Parliament as a set of rules, not a group of powerful persons. Hence we can today talk intelligibly of person-oriented and rule-oriented societies. Malaya is a rule-oriented society and so is India; possibly Pakistan is too, but Indonesia is not. It should be noted, however, that these classifications do not solve the fundamental problem of why people obey governments at all; it is just as difficult to explain their adherence to a rule system as it is to explain their adherence to a system depending on personal charisma.

MRS. R. BRISSENDEN: I disagree with Mr. Mackie and think that the Wolfsohn and Morris-Jones approach and their notion of differing political idioms is of some relevance to Indonesia. I draw a distinction between the tradition-oriented forces and modern economy-oriented forces in Indonesian society. The difference between India and Indonesia is that the people who in India are the governors, in Indonesia are the governed. What we are seeing now in Indonesia is the victory of the traditional idiom in politics. The parties at the present time associated with government all in some way take their values from the traditional structure of Indonesian society.

So the P.N.I., the communists and the Orthodox Muslim Party all find their strength in Java and all draw their political style from the same framework. The P.N.I. on the one hand tends to depend on the traditional 'aristocratic' authorities, but also resorts to the personal charisma of President Soekarno where traditional values are lacking. The communists might seem hard to fit into this analysis—but they derive most of their success from providing a new set of values to fill the gap where the traditional values have broken down. All these parties may be said to orient themselves in relation to, and draw their loyalties from, the 'traditional situation'. They are the 'solidarity-makers', those who tend to talk about consensus.

In contrast, the 'administratively-minded', those who think in terms of a modern society and modern economic processes, are outside the government. They are represented in the Opposition Parties. It is true that the administrative structures which Soekarno has created include people who are 'administratively-minded', but the institutions are subjected mainly to the personal influence of Soekarno himself.

The problem of constitutional development in Indonesia is that there does not seem to be at present any prospect of the 'two-way traffic' between the traditional idiom and the modern idiom, which Morris-Jones spoke of as occurring in India.

MR. JUSTICE ELSE-MITCHELL: The real factors lie between the fields of law and sociology, in the absence of a sound administrative foundation for the Indonesian governmental system. The root of all notions of constitutionalism is some administrative basis for a form of government. For Indonesia there are two matters that are important. First, the Dutch had their own administrative system based upon their own free economy. The local inhabitants were not integrated into the administrative system of the Dutch. Secondly, the desire for a planned economy and the demand for economy-building that the revolution in Indonesia brought, as well as the weakening of the Dutch administrative system, necessarily involved a shortage of the necessary links which are required in any system. Whatever else may be said of it, the army represents an administrative system of an integrated, centralised kind.

PROF. STONE: I wish to address myself to those who have held that Indian constitutionalism is in some danger of disintegration. I agree with Professor Sawer that constitutionalism is related to a willingness to live according to rule. Willingness in living according to rule is a clue to the strength of the Indian Constitution. There are great tensions in Indian society; but there is also an enormous tolerance, an amazing capacity to sustain what look like unsustainable tensions. One could almost speak of a capacity of Indian society to live in controlled schizophrenia, a capacity to go its ways in face of the gravest internal incompatibilities.

To those, like Narayan, who want to found an Indian political system for the future on merely traditional institutions, rejecting Western admixtures, I would say simply that you can only start from where you are. This not only means that you cannot reach into another society and take from it an institution that works well there, and assume that it will work equally well with you. It also means that you cannot reach back into your own traditional heritage and pick out particular institutions which formerly worked, and assume that they will work again, if now revived; or invoke some concept like 'consensus' on the village level (which, in any case, often seems in practice to be dependent on a 'cabal' or clique, some individuals to whom power is left to decide on action after the meeting has adjourned, which may not represent anything that was really agreed).

DR. LEGGE: Among other points raised in the discussion was the contrasting attitude between the Indonesian and Indian elite. In India the elite represents a Western point of view and feels itself removed from the traditional idiom. In Indonesia the elite has been Western educated, but yet it is from this quarter that the appeal to tradition is made. Separated from the village and from customary law, the vestigial aristocracy of the country is still part of a traditional social order. However the emphasis on tradition has its elements of sham. It represents a self-conscious, not an unconscious, return to the past.

Discussion also referred to the role of the administrative service in offering in a way a substitute for a constitution, a means of institutionalising the otherwise arbitrary power of a Central Government. A constitution determines what individuals are to perform what functions. Over a great part of the Indonesian political system the distribution of responsibility has not been clearly elaborated. But below the Central Government and its central bureaucracy, the territorial administration is virtually all powerful. At least it embodies the authority of the centre and it operates in a paternal way. Its operations reflect a person-oriented not a rule-oriented system. The problem in Indonesia in the current crisis does not arise from the presence or absence of adequate 'constitutional' arrangements, but of a policy to be implemented through the machinery which does exist.

In this connection reference was made to Professor MacMahon Ball's view that, while one could not necessarily expect that Western democratic institutions would survive intact in Asia, one could hope that encroaching authoritarianism might still govern 'without injustice and without terror'. If the territorial administration represented the essence of Indonesia's system of government it could be said that it did offer a possibility of paternal justice, commanding consent by tradition.

MR. MACKIE: I am interested in the application to Indonesia of Sawer's distinction between rule-oriented and person-oriented societies. It will be intriguing to see whether in the latter, in politics where the rules have become vague, there is any hope of 'getting back to the rules'—a word which I prefer to 'laws' here. It is basic to emphasise the fact that you cannot solve Indonesia's problems by laying down clear-cut rules. Better administration would not solve the problem by itself. Someone has to sit at the top with pretty substantial discretionary powers. A lot of what Soekarno says about the need for getting away from alien institutions which have bred obstruction is undeniable. If the Masjumi party had got control, it would not have made any difference in this respect. A man like Djuanda is highly Westernised (like the Masjumi leaders) but he is an advocate of pushing on with the return to the 'traditional'. Indonesia cannot hope to achieve an economic take-off, until she has strong central government.

Brian Beddie

ISSUES AND PROBLEMS IN ASIAN
POLITICS AND GOVERNMENT

THREE PRELIMINARY considerations might be touched on before coming to the main substance of the Seminar.

(1) The subject of the Seminar was Constitutionalism in Asia. In fact with very minor exceptions discussion has been confined to the constitutions and politics of South Asia. In general, limiting the subject in this way has been necessary and valuable as the complexities and number of variables which have arisen in a discussion mainly confined to India, Pakistan, Burma and Indonesia, have been great. Nevertheless, it would be wise to remember that any generalisations that we might seem to have arrived at would still have to be tested in the light of Northern Asia's experience. Consider, for example, the statement that there is a strong tendency in Asia towards a single party system because of the traditional desire for consensus. While fundamentally true perhaps, this observation might still need qualification if we were to examine it in the light of Japanese or Filipino experience.

(2) At the beginning of the Seminar many participants probably began with the notion that constitutionalism is, as it were, a specific kind of thing: something that might fairly accurately be said to be either present or absent in a particular society. Professor Sawer provided such a definition in terms of the relation of lawyers to constitutions. Towards the end of the Seminar many were less certain as to whether constitutionalism was a 'specific thing' at all and were wondering if, like many of the other phenomena that fall into the hands of political scientists, it should not rather be regarded as a tendency—as something that can be more or less present in a society, present in some of its aspects and not in others and so on. The notion that constitutionalism should be regarded as a tendency gathered force because of the effective challenges that were made to the view that constitutionalism had broken down in Burma and

236

Pakistan. Some participants argued convincingly that the military regimes in those two countries represented a *restoration* of certain important aspects or ingredients of constitutionalism.

Of course regarding constitutionalism as a tendency (or set of tendencies) did not dispose of the question of definition. It was still asked "What kind of tendency is it"? Professor Morris-Jones raised an important issue in this connection. He questioned the extent to which constitutionalism was necessarily maintained by the conscious pursuit of liberty or of the other values connected with constitutionalism. He suggested that important supports of constitutionalism are simply the persistence of established procedures, established ways of doing things and established channels which enable private interests to bring their views to bear on governments. On this view constitutionalism would be something which, up to a point at least, happens automatically, something that lays hold of society and cannot always easily be shaken off.

This observation, if true, would be important because it would show that we should not be unduly pessimistic about popular criticisms of, or even revulsions against, constitutionalism in Asia. If the revulsions of opinion are temporary, constitutionalism may well survive them. Dr. Maung's remarks on the military regime in Burma have relevance here. He explained how, though the army leaders had no great attachment to the traditional values of constitutionalism, they were nevertheless much impressed by the procedures laid down in the 'Big Book' and were willing to follow these procedures (which did support constitutional liberties) to a considerable degree. Mr. Mackie too pointed out the great difference between those aspects of government in Indonesia where there are established procedures and those where the procedures have yet to be worked out. (He suggested that the establishment of full constitutionalism in Indonesia might have to await upon the working out of these new procedures.)

(3) It was fairly widely assumed that constitutionalism is something which is very firmly established in the West, which works well in the West and not only that, but something which in its Western application is pretty thoroughly understood. There was some incidental criticism of this view by Professor Morris-Jones (who referred to the new light being thrown on Western constitutionalism by electoral studies) and by Professor Stone who pointed to the

distinction between public and private law as one which presented a problem in any society. Professor Partridge suggested privately that in considering the relation of the Indian Constitution to the Indian village we should bear in mind the problems that would arise in considering the relation of the French Constitution to a French village.

It could be argued that Western constitutionalism presents more difficult problems than is generally admitted. This is because there is always a considerable element of myth or ideology surrounding constitutionalism everywhere. It is perhaps the essence of a constitution to set up a gap between aspiration and reality. Another typical feature of constitutionalism, at least in the British and American contexts, is that constitutional practice almost always runs ahead of constitutional theory. What Hegel said of philosophy seems to be certainly true of constitutional law. Rephrasing Hegel it could be said "constitutional theory appears only when actuality is there cut and dried after its process of formation has been completed".

This observation might be illustrated by referring to one of Professor Spann's suggested definitions of constitutional government. He suggested that the essence of modern constitutionalism is that it defines the structure and powers which the 'people' allows to the government, and which thereby limits the latter. While this definition has an undoubted element of truth it also has something of a nineteenth century ring. It might be said to neglect the extent to which in recent years the 'people' have relaxed their restraints on governments and urged them in the name of welfare and planning to assume greater responsibilities on their behalf; and it neglects the extent to which through the medium of the party (especially the governing party) 'people' have thus given themselves over to state control. One result of this process is perhaps that to a greater degree than we readily admit our present constitutional concerns have passed from 'people' and even parliament to the executive. In general, it might be said that relations within the executive or between parts of the executive have become constitutionally more important.

The Executive

Certainly in the early discussions during the Seminar by far the greatest concern was with constitutional relations within the executive, or with the non-parliamentary and non-electoral side of constitutions, and this despite Dr. Menon's introductory remarks which emphasised the importance of the electorate and of the parties. The reason why attention turned towards the executive is fairly clear. It is the demand in Asian countries that the executive should exercise very wide functions. Indeed, some participants have tended to suggest that executive action may have to be so great as to render any constitutional restriction impossible. This may be so, but if so, the danger is surely not confined to Asia.

Whatever the truth about the relation of strong executives and constitutionalism, the discussion did bring out the extensive functions claimed for executives in Asia. Summarising, it might be said that alongside the ideology of constitutionalism there are the stronger ideologies of nationalism and welfare. Nationalism implies a strong executive because of the need to check disintegrating forces (sub-nationalisms) that challenge unity in most Asian countries. The details of the federal structure—emergency provisions, the appointment of governors of States, the unified civil service, and so on—show the power which the central executive is given over constituent groups. Welfare, the set of social aspirations embodied in directive principles, also clearly requires large-scale and detailed State intervention in social and economic affairs. Mr. Chari's remark that in Asia law runs ahead of social practice, whereas the reverse has been true in Europe, points to the extent to which legislation is likely to have its source in the executive rather than in widely spread popular movements.

Hence it is not surprising that, at the beginning of the Seminar, the discussion on constitutionalism tended to be a discussion of constitutional arrangements within the executive, of relations between the prime minister, the president and the courts. It is a pity perhaps that this discussion was not accompanied by a more thorough investigation of precisely what it is that executives have to undertake in Asian societies. Had there been such an investigation it might have appeared important to extend consideration beyond relations between head of State, head of government and the courts to include relations with the civil service, public corporations, government commissions, etc. Japan is perhaps an example of the importance of inter-executive relations in a developing country. The 1890 Meiji Constitution provided for only very limited parliamentary control, but through its law and convention it provided for a complicated system of balancing relations among executive bodies —the cabinet, the Imperial Household, Privy Council, Genro and certain military and naval bodies. A kind of modified constitutionalism did continue in Japan at least until the nineteen-thirties.

Nothing in the above observations is meant to suggest that constitutionalism could be based purely on executive relationships; certainly unless popular pressures play on the various organs of the executive there will be no checking and balancing, there will simply be autocracy. Unfortunately, not a great deal of material was forthcoming on the functioning of the electoral and parliamentary side of Asian constitutions, though something was said on the surprising degree to which genuine and free elections can take place in Asian societies.

It was in the discussion of political parties that the real dilemma arose so far as popular control of the executive is concerned. The dilemma arose because of the difficulty of creating an effective opposition. Either it seems there is a single party system which makes the executive unduly powerful, or else a multi-party system which makes the executive so unstable as to create a demand for the superseding of constitutional government. Opinion differed on the issue of the single predominant party. None was willing to say that it was an entirely adequate vehicle of public opinion, and it was recognised that in Burma it seems at one time to have enabled the government to treat parliament very much as a rubber stamp. In India, on the other hand, Congress because of its range of membership and the difference in its membership at the union and state levels does constitute a more adequate check on the executive. Professor Morris-Jones, however, seemed to think that it failed to give adequate representation, particularly to middle class discontent in India, and that this could create a dangerous situation.

A point that clearly calls for more consideration is the apparent paradox that in Asian societies there is a strong tendency towards a single party (this perhaps being connected with Professor Fitz-Gerald's point about consensus) and at the same time a strong tendency towards factionalism. It would be interesting to explore how far the two apparently opposed tendencies spring from a single principle. Perhaps belief in, but the inability to find, the 'common good' accounts for both tendencies.

The Courts

The Seminar gave quite special attention to courts in India, Pakistan and Burma, and in the case of India had before it Mr. Chari's detailed and valuable documentation. While the general impression was that courts in the countries of Asia that came under British rule were a most important ingredient of constitutionalism, certain qualifications also emerged.

Courts in India as elsewhere have to be careful not to confuse rigidity (technical impartiality) with independence. They are likely to remain independent only so long as they adopt a liberal or broad interpretation, that is only so long as they are ready to look beyond the legal text to the balance of social forces in the community. It appears that in Burma at certain stages the courts may have been too strict. They apparently brought certain political pressures to bear on themselves, though for the most part their rulings were set aside by strictly constitutional methods.

Then there were certain problems concerned with the efficiency of the judicial system. Dr. Maung and other members of the Seminar raised the question of delays in granting justice in some Asian countries. The matter of delay is important because it raises the question: at what point does delay in granting justice amount to the denial of justice? Mr. Nish, while admitting the efficiency of courts at the highest level, questioned their efficiency at the lower levels. Professor Stone referred to the system of legal education established in India under the British and questioned whether it will be capable of turning out lawyers capable of sustaining the high standards which are maintained by present judges and advocates in India.

It would have been useful to discuss in detail a few specific cases which have been dealt with before Asian courts in recent years. Unfortunately, because time was limited and other matters diverted our attention, this was not possible. This is a pity because, especially in matters relating to human rights, the discussion of *crucial* or *test* cases is of great importance. It would be theoretically possible, I think, to have a situation where highly efficient and impartial courts might grant justice to a whole succession of individuals who came before them, but where the number of individuals were getting justice in that way would be outnumbered by those who were not. The crucial case is particularly important because it reverses a whole social tendency and renders it unnecessary for more people in the future to go to the courts.

I am not in any way suggesting that crucial cases of this kind are not being decided in Asia. I make the point simply because if we are to judge the social efficacy of courts anywhere we must go beyond the narrow criteria of their efficiency and impartiality.

Constitutionalism and Social Structure

In the last page of his paper Professor Spann asked how far we should expect Asian constitutions to conform to the social structure of Asian countries. There seems to have been general agreement that in an important sense Asian constitutions do not, and should not be expected to conform to social structure. There is, I suggest, a quite elementary sense in which Asian constitutions do *express* social structure and are to that extent unique. Read an Asian constitution and you find in it references to various parts of its society's social structure—to racial, caste and community differences, to the nature of the under-developed economy and so on. The constitutions do, therefore, express social structure.

Whether they *conform* to social structure is a different question. If we ask whether the Malayan Constitution conforms to the racial structure, as between Malays and Chinese, the Malays might say "yes" and the Chinese "no". In short, where there are different interests the question of conformity will always be controversial. Nevertheless the question of conformity to social conditions is closely connected with the question of consensus; if a constitution does not conform, in the sense that it does not reflect an element of consensus, it may not work or may only work through the exercise of non-constitutional pressures.

When Professor Spann raised the question of conformity of constitutions to social structure he had in mind a rather different question. He was asking: can a constitution be informed by the spirit of a society, or can the genius of the social structure be reflected in the constitution? This is an important question because it has come up explicitly in the case of Indonesia. Could there be an Indonesian constitution or polity which would be informed by the spirit of 'mutual assistance' and by other traditional Indonesian social values?

On the particular question of Indonesia Dr. Legge has probably given the answer. He suggests in his paper that in appealing to guided democracy, mutual assistance, and so on, Dr. Soekarno is doing little more than providing a traditional cloak to justify the return to the Dutch colonial system of government. In general, it would seem hard to understand how any modern society carrying on large-scale bureaucratic, commercial and industrial enterprises could possibly be administered through the governmental forms appropriate to a traditional Indonesian village. It is doubtful whether even the villages now find these forms appropriate.

But does this altogether dispose of the problem as to whether a constitution cannot be informed by a social structure or at any rate by certain parts of a social structure? It does seem to me to be sensible to say a good deal of nineteenth century constitution-making was informed by a 'bourgeoisie' concerned to write into constitutions its own rights and its desire for restraints against state action. And it seems to me that it is sensible to say that twentieth century constitutions have been informed in part by classes anxious to promote state intervention, anxious to establish rights and duties connected with the notion of welfare. In still other contexts both the Soviet Constitution, if it is a constitution, and the Meiji Japanese Constitution do seem to be informed each by a special ethos. If existing constitutions have been informed by an ethos in this way, on the face of it there would seem to be no reason why a constitution could not, for example, be informed by an Islamic ethos, as Dr. Iqbal suggests.

Whatever the precise points of agreement and disagreement on the problem of constitution and social structure, Professor Spann's association of the Asian middle classes with constitutionalism seemed to be widely accepted. It is perhaps an omission of the seminar that the middle classes were not discussed in any detail. We tended to talk first of government at the highest level, and then to turn to much lower regional or even village levels. A discussion of the middle classes—of their composition, solidarity or otherwise, their function in government and in business, the intermingling of modern and traditional values in their members, and so on, might have served in a valuable way to illustrate the concrete links between government and people. The difficulty with the study of village society is that it is likely to take political scientists deeper than they can really do. That considerations far removed from political science necessarily enter into the study of Asian society at this level was clearly brought out in Dr. Johns' remarks.

These observations are not, of course, meant to imply that the gap between the Westernised processes of modern government and traditional society can be neglected. Both Professor Morris-Jones and Mr. Wolfsohn showed that the existence of this gap goes to the heart of Asian politics and to the heart of constitutionalism in Asia. In the discussion of this gap, or more accurately of the dualism between modern Westernised processes and traditional indigenous processes, there did seem to emerge one point of general agreement. It was agreed that there is a two-way process of interaction between modernism and traditionalism. Mr. Wolfsohn was anxious to correct any impression that he believed that there was only a one-way process at work in the sense that only the modern forces were active, and that the traditional forces were passive.

This general agreement, however, still left open wide possibilities about which there could be and was disagreement. One view was that there could be and probably would be a fairly balanced process of mutual adjustment between modernism and traditionalism, that there would be a Westernising of the traditional going on alongside a traditionalising of the Western and in such a way as to allow fairly equal development. A second view admitted the incompatibility and even conflict between modern and traditional forces, but pointed out the degree to which such forces could and do *coexist* in Asia. They coexist not only in the sense that modern and traditional groups live side by side, but in the sense that modern and traditional forces coexist and without undue tension in the minds of the same individuals.

A third view, which might perhaps be attributed to Mr. Wolfsohn, might be put something like this: when the forces of modernism and traditionalism meet there is likely to be not co-existence but chemical change—an interaction as it were of two elements which produce a new substance—totalitarianism. In his paper Mr. Wolfsohn made passing references to Soviet Russia and it is possible that he, like other students, sees in communism this peculiar compounding of traditionalism and modernism to produce totalitarianism.

There seemed to be general agreement that the interaction between modernism and traditionalism and what would come out of it
were closely connected with the *speed* at which the governments of
Asian countries would attempt to develop their economies. The
question of speed is obviously highly important, but what was lacking was a discussion of the forces which would determine the speed.
Here again a discussion of the middle classes, particularly as they
exist at the national and state levels in India, would be of the
greatest importance.

INDEX

AMBEDKAR, DR., 67, 72–73, 98–99
Army and politics, 125–27, 207, 208
Ayub Khan, 146–47 ; quoted, 170

BHAVE, VINOBA, 79
Buddhism, 21, 130–31, 132
Burma, 114–29 ; A.F.P.F.L., 14, 114, 123–25, 131 ; cabinet, 119 ; civil service, 118–19, 128 ; courts, 52, 119–21, 128 ; parliament and elections, 115–18, 127 ; president, 14, 122–23 ; religion, 21, 130–31 ; rights, 18–19, 20 ; states, 17, 121–22
Business, control of. *See* Economic controls

CABINET GOVERNMENT, 13–15. *See also* under individual countries
Caste, 44, 72–73, 77–78, 110, 111
Ceylon, 20n., 22–23
Church and State, 21–22, 132, 155, 171. *See also* Buddhism, Hinduism, Islam
Civil service, 35, 47, 49, 65, 118–19, 128, 195–96, 219–20, 230
Congress Party, 23–24, 49, 67, 85–87, 113
Consensus, 22, 55, 82, 109, 112–13, 160, 194–95, 216, 222, 227, 233, 236, 240
Constitution and constitutionalism: defined, 3, 46–47, 107, 108, 132–33, 190, 231–32, 236–37, 238 ; differing notions of, 12–13, 191, 227 ; forms and realities, 11, 24, 106–07, 132–33 ; relation to social structure, 22–25, 50–51, 98, 193, 220, 237–38, 243–45
Courts: role of, 6–9, 241–42 ; in moulding law, 7–8 ; broad and

narrow views, 8, 51–52, 53–54, 241. *See also* under individual countries

DELEGATION, 42
Democracy, 4, 18, 22, 25, 36–37, 44, 46, 50, 63, 88–89, 97, 107–08, 127–29, 134, 147, 164, 172, 191–94, 216
Directive Principles, 18–19, 143, 189

ECONOMIC CONTROLS, 31–33, 36–40, 200–01, 211–14
Elections, 41, 62–64, 181
Emergency provisions, 14, 16, 34–35, 48, 122, 185–86
Executive, 238–39. *See also* President and under individual countries

FEDERALISM, 15–17. *See also* States
Finance, 16, 47, 188, 198–99
Freedom, Fundamental Rights. *See* Rights

GANDHI, 95–96

HINDUISM AND HINDU LAW, 7–8, 22, 28–29, 134

INDIA : CASTE, 44, 45 ; civil service, 47, 49 ; Constituent Assembly, 55–73 ; constitution, 11–12, 13–14 ; courts and law, 6–9, 26–45, 51–52, 52–53 ; delegated legislation, 42 ; economic controls, 31–33, 36–40 ; elections, 41 ; emergency provisions, 14, 16, 34–35 ;

247